New Regional Geopolitics in the Indo-Pacific

During the last twenty years, burgeoning transnational trade, investment and production linkages have transformed the area between the Indian and Pacific Oceans. The appearance of this area of interdependence and interaction and its potential impact on global order has captured the attention of political leaders, and the concept of the Indo-Pacific region is increasingly appearing in international political discourse.

This book explores the emergence of the Indo-Pacific concept in different national settings. Chapters engage with critical theories of international relations, regionalism, geopolitics and geoeconomics in reflecting on the domestic and international drivers and foreign policy debates around the Indo-Pacific concept in Australia, India, the United States, Indonesia and Japan. They evaluate the reasons why the concept of the Indo-Pacific has captured the imaginations of policy makers and policy analysts in these countries and assess the implications of competing interpretations of the Indo-Pacific for conflict and cooperation in the region.

A significant contribution to the analysis of the emerging geopolitics of the Indo-Pacific, this book will be of interest to researchers in the field of Asian Studies, International Relations Regionalism, Foreign Policy Analysis and Geopolitics.

Priya Chacko is a lecturer in international politics at the University of Adelaide, Australia. She is the author of *Indian Foreign Policy: The Politics of Postcolonial Identity from 1947 to 2004* (2012), also published by Routledge.

Routledge Contemporary Asia Series

For a full list of titles in this series, please visit www.routledge.com

49 Irregular Migration and Human Security in East Asia
Edited by Jiyoung Song and Alistair D. B. Cook

50 Renewable Energy in East Asia
Towards a new developmentalism
Christopher M. Dent

51 East Asian Development Model
Twenty-first century perspectives
Edited by Shiping Hua and Ruihua Hu

52 Land Grabs in Asia
What role for the law?
Edited by Connie Carter and Andrew Harding

53 Asia Struggles with Democracy
Evidence from Indonesia, Korea and Thailand
Giovanna Maria Dora Dore

54 China-Malaysia Relations and Foreign Policy
Razak Abdullah

55 Politics of the 'Other' in India and China
Western concepts in non-Western contexts
Edited by Lion König and Bidisha Chaudhuri

56 China–India Relations
Cooperation and conflict
Edited by Kanti Bajpai, Huang Jing and Kishore Mahbubani

57 New Regional Geopolitics in the Indo-Pacific
Drivers, dynamics and consequences
Edited by Priya Chacko

New Regional Geopolitics in the Indo-Pacific
Drivers, dynamics and consequences

Edited by Priya Chacko

LONDON AND NEW YORK

First published 2016
by Routledge

2 Park Square, Milton Park, Abingdon, Oxfordshire OX14 4RN
52 Vanderbilt Avenue, New York, NY 10017

Routledge is an imprint of the Taylor & Francis Group, an informa business

First issued in paperback 2019

Copyright © 2016 Priya Chacko

The right of the editor to be identified as the author of the editorial material, and of the authors for their individual chapters, has been asserted in accordance with sections 77 and 78 of the Copyright, Designs and Patents Act 1988.

All rights reserved. No part of this book may be reprinted or reproduced or utilised in any form or by any electronic, mechanical, or other means, now known or hereafter invented, including photocopying and recording, or in any information storage or retrieval system, without permission in writing from the publishers.

Notice:
Product or corporate names may be trademarks or registered trademarks, and are used only for identification and explanation without intent to infringe.

British Library Cataloguing in Publication Data
A catalogue record for this book is available from the British Library

Library of Congress Cataloging-in-Publication Data
Names: Chacko, Priya, editor.
Title: New regional geopolitics in the Indo-Pacific : drivers, dynamics and
    consequences / edited by Priya Chacko.
Description: New York, NY : Routledge, 2016. | Series: Routledge
    contemporary Asia series ; 57 | Includes bibliographical references
    and index.
Identifiers: LCCN 2015046317 | ISBN 9781138935495 (hardback) |
    ISBN 9781315677392 (ebook)
Subjects: LCSH: Geopolitics—Indo-Pacific Region. | Indo-Pacific
    Region—Strategic aspects. | Indo-Pacific Region—Foreign relations.
Classification: LCC DS341 .N48 2016 | DDC 327.5—dc23
LC record available at http://lccn.loc.gov/2015046317

ISBN: 978-1-138-93549-5 (hbk)
ISBN: 978-0-367-87402-5 (pbk)

Typeset in Times New Roman
by Apex CoVantage, LLC

Contents

Contributors vii
Acknowledgements viii

Introduction: the rise of the Indo-Pacific 1

PART 1
Understanding the rise of the Indo-Pacific 9

1 Australia's new strategic geography: making and sustaining an Indo-Pacific defence policy 11
 RORY MEDCALF

2 Japan and the Indo-Pacific 26
 PURNENDRA JAIN AND TAKENORI HORIMOTO

3 India and the Indo-Pacific from Singh to Modi: geopolitical and geoeconomic entanglements 43
 PRIYA CHACKO

4 Climate change as comprehensive security in the continuum: geostrategy and geoeconomics in the time and place of the Indo-Pacific 60
 TIMOTHY DOYLE

5 Indonesia's new geopolitics: Indo-Pacific or PACINDO? 74
 DAVID WILLIS

PART 2
Reflections on the rise of the Indo-Pacific 95

6 China anxieties in the geopolitical cartographies
  of the Indo-Pacific 97
  CHENGXIN PAN

7 Imagining the Indo-Pacific region 114
  MARIJN NIEUWENHUIS

Index 131

Contributors

Priya Chacko is a lecturer in international politics at the University of Adelaide and Associate Director of the Indo-Pacific Governance Research Centre.

Timothy Doyle is Professor of Politics and International Studies at the University of Adelaide in Australia, Distinguished Research Fellow at the Australia-Asia-Pacific Institute (AAPI), Curtin University, Western Australia, and Emeritus Professor, Politics and International Relations, Keele University, Staffordshire, United Kingdom.

Takenori Horimoto is Project Professor, Graduate School of Asian and African Area Studies, Kyoto University.

Purnendra Jain is Professor in Asian Studies at the University of Adelaide.

Rory Medcalf is Professor and Head of the National Security College at the Australian National University, a Nonresident Senior Fellow in Foreign Policy with the Brookings Institution, and a Nonresident Fellow with the Lowy Institute.

Marijn Nieuwenhuis is a lecturer in political geography and an Early Career Research Fellow at the University of Warwick.

Chengxin Pan is a senior lecturer in international relations at Deakin University.

David Willis is a PhD candidate at Flinders University.

Acknowledgements

This book had its origins in a workshop and policy round table discussion organised in 2012 by the Indo-Pacific Governance Research Centre (IPGRC) in the School of History and Politics at the University of Adelaide with support from the Australia-India Institute, Aus-CSCAP, the Asian Studies Association of Australia, the Confucius Institute and the School of Social Sciences and the School of Economics at the University of Adelaide. Many thanks to all who participated in, organised and funded these events. Thanks especially to the IPGRC's administrator, David Cannon, the administrative staff of the School of History and Politics and the Director of the IPGRC, Kanishka Jayasuriya. Little did either he or the IPGRC's founding Chair, Tim Doyle, know how much of a talking point their choice of name for the Centre would turn out to be!

Chapters 1, 3 and 6 by Rory Medcalf, Priya Chacko and Chengxin Pan, respectively, are revised versions of the articles 'In Defence of the Indo-Pacific: Australia's New Strategic Map', 'The Rise of the Indo-Pacific: Understanding Ideational Change and Continuity in India's Foreign Policy' and 'The "Indo-Pacific" and Geopolitical Anxieties about China's Rise in the Asian Regional Order', all of which appeared in Volume 68, Issue 4 of the *Australian Journal of International Affairs*, copyright © Australian Institute of International Affairs, reprinted by permission of Taylor & Francis Ltd.

Introduction
The rise of the Indo-Pacific

During the last twenty years, a process of proliferating transnational trade, investment and production linkages has emerged in the area between the Indian and Pacific Oceans. Intra-Asian trade has rapidly eclipsed East Asia's trade with North America across the Pacific and in 2010 amounted to $2,264 billion, trailing only the European Union at $3,998 billion and dwarfing North America's trade with Asia at $413 billion. At the same time, Africa's trade with Asia has also rapidly increased, and at $123 billion is only smaller than its trade with Europe at $184 billion (World Trade Organization 2010). This 'multi-faceted integrative socio-economic' process that Camroux (2007) terms 'regionalisation' has, in turn, been the product of processes of state transformation in Asian countries, in particular, which has resulted in high-growth economies, capitalist enmeshment into the global economy and shifting patterns of trade and investment. The emergence of this area of interdependence and interaction spanning the Indian and Pacific Oceans, and its potential impact on global order, has recently captured the attention of political leaders in five countries in particular. Japan's Prime Minister Shinzo Abe was the first political leader to raise the prospect of a 'broader Asia' fashioned out of the confluence of the Pacific and Indian Oceans in 2007. Australia's 2013 Defence White Paper adopted the term Indo-Pacific, defined as connecting the Indian and Pacific Oceans through Southeast Asia, in identifying Australia's strategic area of interest (Department of Defence 2013, 7). Similarly, the United States Department of Defense 2012 Strategic Guidance asserted that the United States' core economic and security interests lie in the arc extending from the Western Pacific and East Asia into the Indian Ocean region and South Asia (Government of the United States 2012). India does not have a tradition of releasing official defence or foreign policy strategic plans or white papers on a regular basis; however, since 2012 the Indo-Pacific concept has been used by many officials to define India's strategic, political, economic and cultural areas of interest (e.g. Singh 2013; Economic Times 2015). Furthermore, in 2013, Indonesia's former Foreign Minister Marty Natalegawa called for an 'Indo-Pacific wide treaty of friendship and cooperation'.

What has driven the emergence of the concept of the Indo-Pacific, what are the regional dynamics it is generating and what are the potential consequences for regional and global stability? More broadly, what does the emergence of the

Indo-Pacific concept tell us about regions and regionalisation, and these two key questions: 'What makes regions go around? Who determines their shape and role as building blocs of international order?' (Acharya 2007, 360). While the first wave of scholarly literature on regions, which emerged in the 1960s and early 1970s, focussed on defining and predicting regional integration based on 'objective' factors to do with geography and social, political and economic similarities between states, the burgeoning literature on regions that has emerged since the 1990s has highlighted the socially constructed nature of regions with greater emphasis on the role of domestic political projects in the making of regions (Breslin and Higgott 2000). The central issues and debates to emerge from this literature have concerned the roles of great powers and regional powers in the making of regions; the impact of local responses and resistance from weaker powers to power projection in the shaping of regional orders; the role of ideational factors, identities and norms in the construction of regions; and the role of material determinants and domestic structures (Buzan and Wæver 2003; Jayasuriya 2003; Katzenstein 2005; Acharya 2007). As the contributions to this volume show, the study of the emerging construction of the Indo-Pacific region has the potential to add significant insights to this literature. In particular, what they suggest is a need for a multilevel, multicausal approach to the study of regions and regional political projects, which considers the role of great powers and weaker powers, domestic and international actors, and material and ideational factors.

Drivers: the threats and opportunities of power transitions

Power transitions are times of uncertainty and anxiety for policy makers as established relationships between states and within states are revised or challenged. This is as true for those states that are seen to be in decline, such as the United States, as it is for those viewed as 'rising powers' like India and China, and those which may be labelled middle powers, like Australia, Japan and Indonesia. All the chapters in this volume make clear that the rise of China and India are the most important, if often implicit, drivers of the emergence of the Indo-Pacific construct. The United States' ability to shape international rules and norms and define regional space has been key to its global power and claims to global leadership. The Asia-Pacific concept emerged as an outcome of Cold War geopolitics and attempts by the United States to establish a bulwark against communism in Asia. The rise of new powers since the end of the Cold War poses a challenge to the role of the United States as the world's foremost rule-maker and military power. In the 1990s, as Wilson and Dirlik (1995, 3) put it,

> the rise of Tokyo, Hong Kong, Seoul, Taipei, and Singapore as resurgent powers on the Pacific Rim [and] the breakdown of the Cold War master narrative of bipolar superpowers that once legitimated the American military presence across the Pacific, has resulted in an ongoing de-centering of power beyond the hegemonic control and cartographic sublimations of the U.S. State Department.

Introduction 3

As a result, competing visions of the region, namely the more closed notion of East Asia, in which extra-regional powers like the United States are marginalised, began to gain strength (Camroux 2007). The continued growth of intra-Asian trade, the rise of India and growing inter-connections between Asia and Africa have the potential to further weaken the United States' global and regional role.

Doyle in his contribution to this volume shows that certain actors within the United States, particularly those associated with the Defense Department, are trying to reassert American military predominance by conceiving of the Indo-Pacific as a 'liquid continuum' requiring various forms of intervention to combat amorphous threats such as climate change. Other bureaucratic actors in the United States, namely the State Department, have adopted a different approach to the maintenance of an American-dominated world order, which involves seeking to design a new regional regulatory and security architecture. This is reflected in statements by State Department officials, like former Secretary of State Hillary Clinton, on the emergence of the Indo-Pacific, which is said to raise questions such as:

> Will this region adopt basic rules of the road or rules of the sea to mobilize strategic and economic cooperation and manage disagreements? Will it build the regional architecture of institutions and arrangements to enforce international norms on security, trade, rule of law, human rights, and accountable governance?
>
> (Clinton 2011)

The fact that Clinton raised these questions in a speech in the Indian city of Chennai was no accident. As the chapters in this volume make clear, India is a particularly important part of the American conceptualisation of the Indo-Pacific, given that it is the state most likely to have the potential to match China's economic growth and could therefore serve as a democratic counterweight.

The emergence of the Indo-Pacific concept, however, is not simply driven by the threat posed by China, since China's rise also presents an opportunity for states to reshape regional and international order and assert their roles within it. This is evident in the chapters on Australia, Japan, India and Indonesia. Periods of power transition are particularly difficult for self-identified middle powers like Australia which build their identities by being 'followers' of great powers but also attempt to influence them, and the global order more generally, by carving a leadership role for themselves in multilateral settings (Cooper, Higgott and Nossal 1993). Australia has long been preoccupied by the apparent disjuncture between its geographical positioning in Asia and its historical links with the West. The idea of locating Australia's strategic interests in an Asia-Pacific region became dominant in the Cold War and post–Cold War periods as Australia consolidated a 'special' relationship with the United States and cultivated an identity as a middle power, with initiatives focussed on trade liberalisation and human rights which aimed at positioning Australia as a mediator or bridge between the East and West and the North and South (Ungerer 2007). These international initiatives reflected a domestic agenda of economic reform, social inclusion and multiculturalism, and they helped to consolidate a post–World War II global constitutional settlement that sought to ameliorate Cold War conflicts and a US-dominated post–Cold War environment in which there was greater scope for multilateralism. Yet, the Asia-Pacific concept was not very successful in resolving the tensions between geography and history and debates over Australia's 'Asian' identity. In the past decade, the implications of continuing a close alliance with the United States, while growing increasingly economically enmeshed with Asia, and particularly a rising China, has become a prominent foreign policy issue. Underlying this debate, however, are broader concerns about Australia's place in a transforming world order in which the continued relevance of post-war institutions, rules and norms is unclear. The economic and political rise of China and other countries like India, Brazil and Indonesia, their challenge to post-war multilateral institutions and the relative decline of the United States leaves Australia in an especially uncertain position. Hence, as for Australian policy makers, adopting the Indo-Pacific concept has several benefits. Positioning Australia in the Indo-Pacific, which is perceived to be a geographical construct, rather than in the Asia-Pacific, which is seen as both a geographical and sociocultural concept, seemingly overcomes the debates over Australia's cultural and geopolitical identity because the issue of culture does not arise. Moreover, shaping the way in which the Indo-Pacific construct evolves gives Australia the opportunity to consolidate its middle-power identity. This view is reflected in Medcalf's contribution to this volume, and particularly, in the role that he advocates for Australia in the Indo-Pacific. For Medcalf, who has been a prominent promoter of the Indo-Pacific construct in Australia, the concept places Australia at the centre of global geopolitics and geoeconomics and at the forefront of efforts to build a new security and economic architecture.

As Jain and Horimoto make clear in their chapter, a similar mixture of threat and opportunity has driven Japan's promotion of a concept of 'broader Asia' that links together the Pacific and Indian Oceans and therefore extends Japan's strategic outlook beyond its traditional focus on the Asia-Pacific. The rise of China, with which Japan has long had tense relations, and the relative decline of Japan's key ally, the United States, poses a challenge to the strategic environment that facilitated Japan's economic growth and regional influence. Concurrently, however, this changing strategic environment has been used by conservative nationalists like Japan's Prime Minister Shinzo Abe to further their goal of making Japan a 'normal' state that can project military power beyond its immediate neighbourhood, taking advantage of the rise of India, and India's potential to become a strategic partner in broader Asia to do so.

Whether or not India will work with Japan, Australia and the United States within what Jain and Harimoto call a dense alliance-type grouping in order to balance China's growing clout remains to be seen. Chacko argues in her chapter that the Indo-Pacific concept was initially promoted in India by strategic analysts associated with various New Delhi–based think tanks that were concerned about China's rise. These analysts advocated a closer relationship with the United States and its allies within an Indo-Pacific regional framework, thereby abandoning India's long-standing policy of strategic autonomy through nonalignment. Government officials in the Congress Party–led United Progressive Alliance (UPA) government embraced the Indo-Pacific construct because of its parallels with India's existing 'extended neighbourhood' regional conception. However, they did so in a way that retained a focus on the maintenance of India's strategic autonomy through multiple partnerships and the establishment of a new 'plural, inclusive and open security architecture' to facilitate regional stability and India's economic enmeshment with the leading economies of the region, including that of China. The UPA's successor, the Bharatiya Janata Party–led National Democratic Alliance (NDA), has persisted with this overarching aim of strategic autonomy through multiple partnerships; however, its stated intention of pursuing a more proactive foreign policy and China's more active assertion of its claims in the South China Sea have resulted in the reinvigoration of historical narratives that position China as a threat to India's autonomy and territorial integrity. This has added a new dimension to India's discourse on the Indo-Pacific wherein the rise of China is not just viewed as an opportunity to advance a new regional architecture but a potential threat that needs to be countered.

In the case of Indonesia, as Willis shows, China's recent actions in the South China Sea are a concern to Indonesia given its potential impact on regional stability. For this reason, Willis argues that Indonesian strategic thinkers appreciate an expanded Indo-Pacific regional conception which includes India as a potential regional balancer. At the same time, Indonesia also has qualms about the implications of the American 'pivot to Asia' for its potential to destabilise the region. Moreover, China is key to Indonesia's developmental goals and Indonesia lacks the 'geopolitical anxieties' about China's rise that affect other states in the region, given that it is not tied to the American alliance system and does not have a serious territorial dispute with China. Indonesia also has a strong history of foreign policy independence and has claims towards middle-power leadership as a mediator in regional disputes. As Indonesia's traditional avenue for exercising its regional leadership, the Association of Southeast Asian Nations (ASEAN), begins to fracture under the weight of the South China Sea disputes, the emergence of the Indo-Pacific regional construct with its potential for new avenues for leadership has been welcomed.

Dynamics: operationalising the Indo-Pacific

The Indo-Pacific concept has evolved from being a discursive construct debated by analysts and occasionally mentioned in speeches by policy makers. Hence, another purpose of this volume is to detail the emerging Indo-Pacific security architecture. In the Indian Ocean region, much effort is being placed on revamping the existing organisations for regional cooperation and maritime diplomacy, the Indian Ocean Rim Association (IORA) and the Indian Ocean Naval Symposium (IONS), by India and Australia (as several of the chapters document) and increasingly Indonesia (as the chapter by Willis shows). Japan, the United States and China have become dialogue partners of IORA and China is an observer nation in IONS. Australia, Japan, the United States and India have initiated a number of trilateral maritime dialogues and military exercises in various incarnations such as the US-Japan-India 2015 Malabar naval exercises and the India-Japan-Australia trilateral dialogue. China and India also collaborate on smaller-scale anti-piracy and antiterrorism naval exercises. These new formations are characterised by Doyle in his chapter as 'promiscuous' and 'transient' forms of security cooperation which, given their multiple forms with ever-changing, ambiguous goals, are reminiscent of the strategies of new social movements. Doyle's focus, in particular, is on the American military's securitisation of climate change which legitimises extensive involvement in the Indo-Pacific.

Genuinely pan-Indo-Pacific institutions, however, are yet to materialise. ASEAN remains the acknowledged focal point of regional architecture in the Asia-Pacific, which continues to be treated by most states as a distinct space to the Indian Ocean region. Despite the announcement by the United States and India of a Joint Strategic Vision for the Asia-Pacific and Indian Ocean region, precisely what type of architecture this will give rise to remains unclear. As Medcalf notes, although Australia has institutionalised the Indo-Pacific construct in its foreign policy and defence bureaucracies, it is yet to go much beyond rhetoric in operationalising its Indo-Pacific 'pivot'. Ironically, it is the country that Pan describes as the 'odd man out' of most Indo-Pacific conceptions, China, that has articulated the clearest vision to link the Indian Ocean region with the Asia-Pacific through its One Belt, One Road (OBOR) initiative. China has not adopted the terminology of the Indo-Pacific, but the chapter by Nieuwenhuis argues that OBOR effectively constitutes an alternative Indo-Pacific territorialisation project. Hence, whether the terminology of the Indo-Pacific gains more widespread usage or not, the idea that the Asia-Pacific and Indian Ocean region should and can be viewed as an interlinked economic, political and strategic space is seemingly here to stay. The OBOR initiative consists of a 'belt' of rail and highway networks, oil and gas pipelines and other connectivity infrastructure from Xian in Central China, through Russia, Central Asia and connecting to Europe, as well as a 'Maritime Silk Road' of maritime infrastructure stretching from China's east to Southeast Asia, South Asia, the Middle East, East Africa, the Mediterranean and Europe. The project has various objectives including increased policy coordination in Asia, trade liberalisation and financial integration. These objectives are also linked to other recent Chinese-led initiatives, like the Asian Infrastructure and Investment Bank (AIIB), the New Development Bank (NDB) and a proposed new Shanghai Cooperation Organisation Financing Institution (Government of China 2015). As the chapters by Willis, Chacko and Pan indicate, the reactions to OBOR have been mixed. The Maritime Silk Road initiative was announced by President Xi Jinping in Indonesia, which has welcomed the project. Despite American pressure on Australia to reject membership in the AIIB, Australia has decided to join the initiative. Given that the OBOR project effectively seeks to create an alternative regulatory architecture, however, it could be conceived as a direct competitor to the American-led Trans-Pacific Partnership (TPP), of which Australia and Japan are members. India has been ambivalent about the OBOR project as a result of its lingering geopolitical anxieties about China, even though it is a member of the AIIB, the NDB and the Shanghai Cooperation Organisation, as well as a part of the Bangladesh-China-India-Myanmar (BCIM) economic corridor which China envisages as a part of the OBOR project.

Conclusion: consequences

While the first five chapters of the book are detailed case studies of five key Indo-Pacific states, the final two chapters undertake broader views of the emergence of the Indo-Pacific construct and reflect on its possible consequences. If the OBOR project proceeds as planned, China may well become, as Medcalf calls it, the 'quintessential Indo-Pacific power'. However, China's rise, as Pan details in his chapter, has clearly also fuelled a range of geopolitical anxieties which, he argues, underpins many Indo-Pacific discourses. Given that geopolitical anxieties are dealt with through practices of spatial security such as war, alliances and arms races, the deployment of the Indo-Pacific discourses, Pan suggests, risks exacerbating security dilemmas and rivalries. The proliferation of trilateral military exercises and dialogues between the United States, India, Australia and Japan suggests that this may already be occurring. Nieuwenhuis reflects more broadly on what the emergence of the Indo-Pacific tells us about the politics of geographical imagination. The rise of the Indo-Pacific, Nieuwenhuis argues, exemplifies Stuart Elden's dictum that 'space is political'. Hence, the Indo-Pacific has not just reflected a process of regionalisation, it is giving rise to the creation and re-creation of regional imaginations by states. The Indo-Pacific region is shown by Nieuwenhuis to be a 'performative spatial-political' category that produces new geographic identities, cartographies and 'counter-cartographies' as demonstrated in China's OBOR project.

Hence, this volume demonstrates that the study of the Indo-Pacific presents a dynamic new area of research for political geographers as well as for scholars of regions and power transitions in international relations. What the chapters show is that while we can identify a common set of drivers in the emergence of the Indo-Pacific concept in Australia, the United States, Indonesia, Japan and India – namely the rise of China and India and domestic processes of state transformation – we are still far from seeing the rise of a common Indo-Pacific regional identity or 'governance project' on which there is agreement about who is included and excluded from membership of the region, what the region's spatial delimitations are, and importantly, what the dominant governance structures will be (Jayasuriya 1994, 2003; Katzenstein 2000). Rather, the chapters in this volume indicate that the Indo-Pacific regional construction remains highly contested, both within and between states. This reflects its emerging role as a key 'building bloc' of rapidly transforming global order.

References

Acharya, Amitav. 2007. 'The Emerging Regional Architecture of World Politics', *World Politics* 59:4, 629–652.
Breslin, Shaun, and Richard Higgott. 2000. 'Studying Regions: Learning from the Old, Constructing the New', *New Political Economy* 5:4, 333–352.
Buzan, Barry, and Ole Wæver. 2003. *Regions and Powers: The Structure of International Security*, Cambridge: Cambridge University Press.
Camroux, David. 2007. 'Asia . . . Whose Asia? A "Return to the Future" of a Sino-Indic Asian Community', *Pacific Review* 20:4, 551–575.
Clinton, Hillary. 2011. 'Secretary of State Hillary Rodham Clinton on "India and the United States: A Vision for the 21st Century"', 20 July 2011, IIP Digital, http://iipdigital.usembassy.gov/st/english/texttrans/2011/07/20110720165044su0.7134014.html#ixzz1UxWVNLPL (accessed 18 March 2015).
Cooper, Andrew F., Richard A. Higgott, and Kim Richard Nossal. 1993. *Relocating Middle Powers: Australia and Canada in a Changing World Order*, Vancouver: University of British Columbia Press.
Department of Defence. 2013. *Defence White Paper 2013*, Canberra: Commonwealth of Australia.
Economic Times. 2015, 'If American "Trumpet" Was More Certain in Asia-Pacific, It's Helpful: India', *Economic Times*, 16 March, http://articles.economictimes.indiatimes.com/2015-03-16/news/60174859_1_south-china-sea-asia-pacific-region-asia-pacific (accessed 15 June 2015).
Government of China. 2015. 'Vision and Actions on Jointly Building Silk Road Economic Belt and 21st-Century Maritime Silk Road', National Development and Reform Commission, 28 March, http://en.ndrc.gov.cn/newsrelease/201503/t20150330_669367.html (accessed 23 June 2015).
Government of the United States. 2012. *Sustaining US Global Leadership: Priorities for 21st Century Defense*. Washington, DC: Department of Defense.
Jayasuriya, Kanishka. 1994. 'Singapore: The Politics of Regional Definition', *Pacific Review* 7:4, 411–420.
Jayasuriya, Kanishka. 2003. 'Embedded Mercantilism and Open Regionalism: The Crisis of a Regional Political Project', *Third World Quarterly* 24:3, 339–355.
Katzenstein, Peter J. 2000. 'Regionalism and Asia', *New Political Economy* 5:3, 353–368.
Katzenstein, Peter J. 2005. *A World of Regions: Asia and Europe in the American Imperium*, Ithaca, NY: Cornell University Press.
Singh, Manmohan. 2013. 'PM's Address to Japan-India Association, Japan-India Parliamentary Friendship League and International Friendship Exchange Council', 28 May, Ministry of External Affairs, http://pmindia.nic.in/speech-details.php?nodeid=1319 (accessed 20 June 2013).
Ungerer, Carl. 2007. 'The "Middle Power" Concept in Australian Foreign Policy', *Australian Journal of Politics and History* 53:4, 538–551.
Wilson, Rob, and Arif Dirlik. 1995. 'Introduction: Asia/Pacific as Space of Cultural Production', in *Asia/Pacific as Space of Cultural Production*, edited by R. Wilson and A. Dirlik. Durham, NC: Duke University Press, pp. 1–16.
World Trade Organization. 2010. 'World Trade Developments', World Trade Organization, http://www.wto.org/english/res_e/statis_e/its2011_e/its11_highlights1_e.pdf (accessed 18 March 2011).

Part 1
Understanding the rise of the Indo-Pacific

1 Australia's new strategic geography
Making and sustaining an Indo-Pacific defence policy

Rory Medcalf[1]

The Australian Defence White Paper released by the Labor Government of Julia Gillard in May 2013 included a notable departure from previous such policy documents: a categorical shift towards identifying Australia's region of strategic interest as something called the Indo-Pacific. The concept is referred to dozens of times within its pages. The document asserts that a new 'Indo Pacific strategic arc' is beginning to emerge, 'connecting the Indian and Pacific Oceans through Southeast Asia' (Commonwealth of Australia 2013, 7). Strikingly, the concept has since been endorsed by the conservative coalition governments of Tony Abbott and Malcolm Turnbull, with Defence Minister Kevin Andrews signalling that the 2015 Defence White Paper would 'underline the importance of the Indo-Pacific region to Australia's national security and economic prosperity' (Andrews 2015). This Australian policy tilt was to some degree foreshadowed by the 2009 Defence White Paper released by the earlier Rudd Labor government, with its references to a 'wider Asia-Pacific region' (Commonwealth 2009, 52). Such perspectives have shifted far from the white paper of the Howard government in 2000, which took little note of the Indian Ocean.

The 2013 White Paper (Commonwealth of Australia 2013, 7) explained the Indo-Pacific construct as being forged by multiple factors including India's emergence as an important strategic diplomatic and economic actor to that country's east, and 'growing trade, investment and energy flows across this broader region' which in turn strengthened 'economic and security interdependencies' and brought increased focus to the Indian Ocean. Although Indo-Pacific terminology has become increasingly common in government speeches in a range of countries, the 2013 Defence White Paper marked the first time any government in Asia or beyond had defined its region officially as the Indo-Pacific. Strikingly, this formulation, introduced under the Labor government of Prime Minister Julia Gillard, has continued under the conservative Liberal/National coalition governments of Tony Abbott and Malcolm Turnbull (Bishop 2014a, 2014b; Johnston 2014; Andrews 2015). The Indo-Pacific framework is becoming bipartisan defence and foreign policy orthodoxy. It is officially Australia's new map.

This development warrants examination from several angles. First, what is meant by the Indo-Pacific and does it make sense as a coherent region or strategic system? Second, where does the Indo-Pacific idea come from? Third, where does the Australian policy community's embrace of the Indo-Pacific idea fit with developments in the wider region? Finally, how seriously should we take Australia's Indo-Pacific tilt, and what are the implications for Australia's defence and wider foreign policy settings?

Defining the Indo-Pacific

What precisely is the Indo-Pacific? At its simplest, the Indo-Pacific means recognising that the accelerating economic and security connections between the Western Pacific and the Indian Ocean region are creating a single strategic system. At its heart, a strategic system can be understood as a set of geopolitical power relationships among nations where major changes in one part of the system affect what happens in the other parts. Historically, distance has often had a bearing on these relationships of security interdependence: thus Barry Buzan has described Asian regional security complexes and subcomplexes during the Cold War and beyond (Buzan 2003). Even then, Buzan's work to some extent foreshadowed the Indo-Pacific in his idea of an 'Asian supercomplex', although his assessment was based more on security interactions than the growth of economic connections that has so driven the emergence of the Indo-Pacific over the past decade.

The Indo-Pacific system is defined in part by the geographically expanding interests and reach of China and India, and the continued strategic role and presence of the United States in both the Pacific and Indian Oceans. This recognises the arc of trade routes, energy flows, diplomatic bonds and strategic connections between the two oceans. These links in turn emerge especially from the rise of China and India as outward-looking economic and military powers, the expansion of their economic interests and their strategic and diplomatic imperatives into what each might once have considered its primary maritime zone of interest (Mohan 2012). In particular, the concept underscores the fact that the Indian Ocean has replaced the Atlantic as the globe's busiest and most strategically significant trade corridor, carrying two-thirds of the world's oil shipments and a third of the world's bulk cargo (Commonwealth of Australia 2012, 74). Taken together, these developments are making the Indo-Pacific the world's economic and strategic centre of gravity.

The Indo-Pacific is not simply a new name for the Asia-Pacific, nor is it a radically redefined regional concept that downplays the centrality of Asia. This is a region with Asia at its core, and might most accurately be termed Indo-Pacific Asia (Medcalf 2013). Indeed, the 2013 Defence White Paper rightly defines Southeast Asia as the 'geographic centre' and the key part of the Indo-Pacific for Australia's defence force to be engaged in (Commonwealth of Australia 2013, 8). Nor is it accurate to suggest that the Indo-Pacific somehow excludes China from the regional order. Quite the contrary: it is the expansion of China's interests, diplomacy and strategic reach into the Indian Ocean that most of all defines the Indo-Pacific. With 80 percent of its oil imports being transported across the Indian Ocean, with a million of its citizens now said to be living or working in Africa (Kushner 2013) – where it is also a principal foreign investor – and with signs of an ongoing naval presence in the Gulf of Aden and the Indian Ocean, it is China, not India, that is the quintessential Indo-Pacific power.

From an Australian perspective, the term has distinct merits. Indo-Pacific is an objective description of Australia's two-ocean geography as well as the region in which China is rising. Given that China, India and Japan – as well as other nations in Asia – are becoming so acutely dependent on energy imports across the Indian Ocean from the Middle East and Africa, and given that Australia in turn relies so heavily on seaborne commerce with those powers, it is difficult to find another simple formulation that so satisfactorily describes Australia's region. This is especially the case as Australia's economic, security and societal links with India continue to grow, a relatively new phenomenon. Another virtue of the Indo-Pacific concept is that it breaks down the artificial idea of East Asia and South Asia as separate strategic settings. Although a late twentieth-century generation of Australian policy makers and diplomats was reared on this notion, it was in reality a brief interruption to a long-term pattern of economic, strategic and cultural connections between the Asian subregions. Finally, the Indo-Pacific idea recognises that Australia is an integral part of its region, not peripheral to it. At last, here is a definition of Asia that automatically includes Australia.

For all of that, does the Indo-Pacific make sense as a coherent region or strategic system? Of course, the Indo-Pacific concept can easily be criticised on the grounds that it refers to an exceptionally big region. Much of what happens in one part of the region will not necessarily be of critical importance to other parts. Moreover, when it comes to solving security problems, the scale of the region would seem to preclude a cohesive institution. These are fair, if obvious, points, but neither of them need be disproved in order to uphold the validity of the Indo-Pacific concept.

The Indo-Pacific is best understood as a super-region with hard-to-define outer limits and distinct subregions yet with an unquestionably Asian core. Admittedly, its outer geographic boundaries are fluid: are East African littoral states, for instance, strictly Indo-Pacific? More important than lines on a map, however, are the clear organising principles that are beginning to knit this region together, most notably the economic and strategic interactions of great and rising powers. Thus geographically peripheral countries, from Madagascar to the Marshall Islands, may count as Indo-Pacific players to the extent that they feature in the intersecting interests of the key Indo-Pacific powers: China, India and the United States.

Of course the idea that the entire Indo-Pacific is becoming one connected region has its limits. The subregions remain home to Asia's hottest near-term security challenges. Thus the tensions on the Korean Peninsula are principally a North Asian concern, as is China-Japan strife in the East China Sea, not to mention the China-Taiwan problem, while rivalry between India-Pakistan is principally a South Asia concern. What needs to be grasped, however, is that this is a multilayered and complex Asian system where subregional contests exist alongside wider regional and global dynamics. If Asia is becoming the global centre of economic gravity, then any conflict here involving a major power will have world impact. In any case, tensions can no longer be quarantined in neat neighbourhoods.

The United States and China will almost certainly be crucial to the path and management of any future India-Pakistan crisis. Tensions and territorial disputes in the South China Sea are not narrowly a matter for East Asia, let alone China. They are being watched as a series of test cases for how a powerful China may behave; trading nations have stakes in its shipping lanes; and the United States, India, Australia and others have a deep interest in what it means for a stable, rules-based order. Indeed, Australia has interests at stake in any major security crisis involving one or more of its key Indo-Pacific trading partners: China, Japan, India, South Korea and the United States. Above all, the nations projected to be the weightiest global powers in this century – China and India alongside the United States – are the big Indo-Pacific three. A major disruption anywhere in the region will have large repercussions for their interests, and the future of the Indo-Pacific will be shaped or shaken by whether their relations are principally cooperative, competitive or confrontational.

Lost and found: the provenance of the Indo-Pacific idea

One reason we can be confident the Indo-Pacific is no mere flavour of the moment is that it is not new. It has been a far more enduring way of understanding the map of Asia than the late twentieth-century separation of East Asia and South Asia. Economic and cultural interactions between Asia's subregions go back millennia, as the spread of Buddhism from India to East Asia attests. At a more material level, the idea that the Indian Ocean mattered to East Asia had a false start in the early fifteenth century when a Chinese emperor grounded the treasure fleet of his eunuch admiral Zheng He after seeing little merit in his seven voyages west. European adventurers, on the other hand, soon came to see merit aplenty. In colonial times, European maps titled 'Asia' encompassed a swathe from the Indian Ocean rim, through Southeast Asia to China, Korea and Japan. They might as well have been labelled Indo-Pacific. By the nineteenth century, this breadth was reflected in British imperial practice: the trade arteries and military sinews of that Indian empire reached China and Australia via Singapore, and went west to Africa and Suez, as Indian strategist Raja Mohan (2012) has shown. He also points to precursors of the Indo-Pacific in the geopolitics of a century ago, arguing that American sea power theorist Alfred Thayer Mahan and British geographer Halford Mackinder, each in his way, saw Asia as an integrated region (Mohan 2012).

Indo-Pacific definitions of Asia came to further prominence, but also took a wrong turn: the writings of another early twentieth-century advocate, German geographer Karl Haushofer, later provided a rationale for Axis aggression in World War II (Rumley, Doyle and Chaturvedi 2012, 10–11). Inspired by Mackinder, Haushofer drew on his travels in Japan, China, Korea and India to come up with his own geographical determinism. In 1924 he envisaged a world of four 'pan-regions', claiming that each warranted a dominant power (Haushofer 1924). The Indo-Pacific was becoming an accepted term in ethnography and marine science. Applying it to geopolitics, Haushofer saw the strategic and economic unity of this pan-region as making it the preserve of Japan, to be shared perhaps with

Russia. Today's Indo-Pacific conceptions are precisely the opposite of Haushofer's. They are about finding ways to manage the intersection of multiple powers' interests in a vast common domain, rather than some imperial carve-up or life-and-death struggle.

Ideas about the Indo-Pacific retained a quiet currency even as the Pacific and Indian Ocean regions became estranged in the late 1940s, not least due to early Cold War dynamics and the economic inwardness of newly independent India and communist China. In 1945 K.M. Panikkar (1945) reflected on the war just ending to conclude that events in the Pacific would be crucial to his country's long-term quest for security and power. Australian defence documents still assessed the nation's security outlook in terms of risks and challenges across the 'Indo-Pacific Basin' well into the 1960s (Defence Studies Project 1965, 1966). And at least one Southeast Asian country was pursuing Indo-Pacific diplomacy from its very creation, even if it did not use the words. It can be argued that much of India's post-1993 'Look East' policy had its origins in Lee Kuan Yew's earlier efforts to enmesh a then reluctant India as a security partner for Singapore, to offset other influences (Datta-Ray 2009).

Still, from the late 1960s until recently, another grand design came to dominate conceptions of Asia. That was the Asia-Pacific, and much of the aim, encouraged by Japan and Australia, was to reflect the United States' crucial strategic and economic role across the water. By the late 1980s, with the establishment of the Asia-Pacific Economic Cooperation (APEC) process, the Asia-Pacific idea seemed here to stay. And just as well, as it helped allay concerns about US retrenchment at the end of the Cold War. By the time China began engaging with Asian multilateralism in the 1990s, the game was distinctly Asia-Pacific: not only APEC, but the Association of Southeast Asian Nations (ASEAN), and its wider security dialogue, the ASEAN Regional Forum (ARF).

Yet the limits of the Asia-Pacific enterprise were already becoming clear. The ARF soon came to include India and other South Asian players. And at its crowning moment – the establishment of the East Asia Summit in 2005 – the process of Asian institution-building took a decisive turn. The Southeast Asians accepted India, Australia and New Zealand as members of that regional leaders' forum meeting from the outset – against China's lobbying – and so the contemporary Indo-Pacific era began, even if few noticed it at the time. Indeed, one of the first documented twenty-first-century usages of the term Indo-Pacific in a geopolitical context comes from a prescient analysis by veteran Australian Asian-watcher and journalist Michael Richardson, when he anticipated that the East Asia Summit would become the crowning institution of an Indo-Pacific region. (Richardson 2005). This assessment has been borne out by former Indonesian Foreign Minister Marty Natalegawa who claims, however retrospectively, that the shaping of the East Asia Summit was a conscious act of Indo-Pacific diplomacy by Southeast Asian countries (Natalegawa 2013). In any event, by 2011, when the United States and Russia took their seats at the summit in Bali, any notion that East Asia's strategic future could be managed in isolation from the wider region was strictly for the history books.

Sailing the Indo-Pacific in company

It would be inaccurate to portray Australia as the only country whose leaders or senior officials have articulated the Indo-Pacific idea in recent years. The United States, India, Japan and Indonesia have also begun making use of it. After some debate within India about whether to adopt Indo-Pacific terminology (Chacko 2012), Indian Prime Minister Manmohan Singh began doing so in late 2012 and into 2013, notably as a way of defining his country's relations with ASEAN and Japan (Singh 2013). An Indo-Pacific world view was clearly adopted and articulated by the next Indian prime minister, Narendra Modi, from 2014 onwards. His avowed 'Act East' policy of deepened strategic and economic engagement with East Asia is very much in the Indo-Pacific spirit, and his historic speech to the Australian Parliament in November 2014 was categorical in the importance it placed on a pan-regional vision and the role of Australia-India relations therein: 'Today, the world sees Australia to be at the heart of the Asia Pacific and Indian Ocean region. This dynamic region holds the key to this world's future; and Australia is at its cross-currents' (Modi 2014).

Japanese Prime Minister Shinzo Abe has long spoken of Japan's interests across the 'confluence of two seas' (Abe 2013) and has more recently begun putting this into explicitly Indo-Pacific terminology, again including in his 2014 speech to the Australian Parliament:

> Let us join together all the more in order to make the vast seas from the Pacific Ocean to the Indian and those skies open and free . . . I believe strongly that when Japan and Australia, sharing the common values, join hands, these natural rules will become the norm for the seas of prosperity that stretch from the Pacific Ocean to the Indian.
>
> (Abe 2014)

In May 2013, Indonesian Foreign Minister Marty Natalegawa began an initiative for an 'Indo-Pacific treaty' to safeguard the regional 'engine of global growth' (Natalegawa 2013), and Indonesia's advocacy of the Indo-Pacific idea was taken further by then President Yudhoyono as well as his vice president and minister for defence (Jakarta Post 2014). The subsequent rhetoric of President Joko Widodo has defined Indonesia as a global maritime nexus and its archipelagic geography as a strategic advantage (Neary 2014).

The Indo-Pacific appears to have entered the official American foreign policy lexicon in 2010, when then Secretary of State Hillary Clinton and Assistant Secretary of State Kurt Campbell started deploying it in speeches leading up to the US 'pivot' or rebalance to Asia, notably in the way they defined US strategic relations with India and Australia (Clinton 2010, 2011). In early 2013, Secretary of State John Kerry picked up their characterisation of the new Burma as part of an 'Indo-Pacific economic corridor'; such language is becoming a staple of State Department speeches and statements (Kerry 2013). Indo-Pacific terminology is even more frequent in the US military: for the commander of US Pacific

Command (PACOM), Admiral Samuel Locklear, and the leadership of the US 7th Fleet, the default definition of the region in which their forces operate is the Indo-Asia-Pacific (Miles 2012).

The United States under President Obama has not explicitly replaced Asia-Pacific with Indo-Pacific terminology at all levels or in all agencies. Even so, Indo-Pacific terminology and thinking now regularly crops up in State Department declarations of policy, and the Indo-Asia-Pacific formulation is now standard usage for Pacific Command and the 7th Fleet. Regardless of the continued use of Asia-Pacific language by the president and the vice president, it is apparent from such high-level expressions of policy as the Obama-Modi joint statement in January 2015 or Vice President Biden's speech on the eve of his travel to India and Singapore in July 2013 that the United States increasingly sees the region as Indo-Pacific in character if not necessarily in name, with India's eastward strategic and diplomatic engagement seen as integral to Asia's future (Biden 2013; White House, Office of the Press Secretary 2015). It is likely that US official statements and thinking will continue to use Asia-Pacific and Indo-Pacific formulations in parallel. Debate can be expected to continue about whether the United States, in an era of constrained defence budgets, is better advised to focus its strategic attentions on an East Asian or Asia-Pacific theatre rather than the wider Indo-Pacific (Bisley and Phillips 2013).

This increasing evidence of Indo-Pacific terminology and thinking among various governments is an evolution of parallel perspectives, albeit with some cross-fertilisation, rather than a formal coordination of positions. To be sure, there is some clear interplay and mutual encouragement, experimentation or emboldening at work here: some notable appearances of the term have been for instance in joint statements or press conferences such as in India's interactions with ASEAN, Australia or Japan, or Australia's interactions with the United States. There is also an accumulating body of literature from think tanks and academics that both reflects and perhaps influences the changing policy outlook (e.g. Khurana 2007; Auslin 2010; Medcalf 2012; Mohan 2012; Scott 2012).

An important question is whether the increased use of and prominence of Indo-Pacific rhetoric and frameworks around the period 2011–2015 will mark a high point for this concept. It is more likely that these are in fact intermediate usages foreshadowing the wider adoption and refinement of the concept, although probably not to the point of replacing the Asia-Pacific in international strategic and diplomatic discourse. In Australia, the use of Indo-Pacific was initially associated with the 2010–2013 Labor government of Prime Minister Julia Gillard and her Defence Minister Stephen Smith (who, as a West Australian, had an unsurprising inclination to privilege the Indian Ocean). It is notable, therefore, that the Abbott and Turnbull governments appear to remain reasonably supportive of an idea in which they have less political investment and which they could quite easily have abandoned in order to differentiate themselves from Labor. Foreign Minister Bishop initially referred to the 'Indian Ocean Asia-Pacific region', perhaps in order to maintain partisan difference (Rajendram 2013), but soon opted for Indo-Pacific (Bishop 2014a, 2014b). Defence Ministers Johnston and then Andrews, like Bishop and Smith a West Australian, have readily opted for an Indo-Pacific perspective (Johnston 2014; Andrews 2015). Wider questions about the fate of the Indo-Pacific concept, however, rest much more fundamentally on the perspectives, choices and behaviour of other countries, notably China.

Some observers suggest that the Indo-Pacific idea, particularly as presented by some American or perceived pro-American voices in the context of the US rebalance to Asia, is unlikely to appeal to China and could even in itself heighten Chinese perceptions that it is the target of a US-led containment strategy (Rumley, Doyle and Chaturvedi 2012). The same observers, and others, however note also that the Indo-Pacific itself need not be a politically or ideologically charged concept. Indeed, it would seem altogether odd and futile to employ the term as a tool for the wholesale exclusion of China from the regional order or to obstruct its legitimate interests, as a major maritime trading nation, in the Indian Ocean. None of this is to deny that an Indo-Pacific definition of Asia plays India into the power politics of China's neighbourhood and necessarily dilutes Chinese influence in regional forums. But the opposite must also be acknowledged: the concept also recognises China's role and interests in the Indian Ocean and thus questions Indian dominance there. That said, there will be a need to manage Chinese sensitivities about the fact that the Indo-Pacific idea is endorsed by – among others – Japan, India, Australia and the United States, the countries some of its analysts have previously accused of containment in the wake of their embryonic and short-lived quadrilateral dialogue in 2007. The continued socialisation of the Indo-Pacific idea by others, including Indonesia, will be important in this regard, as will active diplomacy to present it as an inclusive concept.

In understanding the future of the Indo-Pacific concept, it makes sense to monitor China's own responses. These have been mixed, and often wary, but are not entirely negative. Although some Chinese voices have warned that the US pivot strategy involves a broad definition of Asia that encompasses the Indian Ocean (Qi 2013), and some have claimed America is inventing a term to exclude China (Wei 2013), others still are open-minded about the concept, acknowledging that China's own interests are Indo-Pacific (Zhao 2013). As China's economic, strategic, diplomatic and soft power reach continues to extend across the Indian Ocean as well as into Southeast Asia, it will become increasingly hard for Chinese officials to avoid thinking or articulating along Indo-Pacific lines. Indeed, some of China's own military exercises and deployments in 2013 and 2014 have been Indo-Pacific in nature: not only the continued anti-piracy operations in the Gulf of Aden, but also a transit of the Sunda Strait and combat simulation near Christmas Island in February 2014 as well as a reported submarine patrol of the Indian Ocean in 2013.

In dealing with the growing usage of Indo-Pacific concepts by others, a thoughtful diplomatic response by China might therefore involve an effort to utilise Indo-Pacific terminology on occasion – for instance, in supporting China's case for admission to Indian Ocean diplomatic institutions – while continuing to privilege Asia-Pacific or Asian constructions. This kind of flexibility may be difficult for China, given its tendency to pursue uniformity of message as a way

Australia's new strategic geography 19

of demonstrating policy consistency and political cohesion. That said, China is already beginning to come to terms with a concept in some ways analogous to the Indo-Pacific: the Maritime Silk Road framework, as espoused by President Xi Jinping since late 2013 (Xi 2013). It has been initially presented as a geoeconomic initiative – intended to explain and conceptualise the growing economic and infrastructure links between China, maritime Southeast Asia and the Indian Ocean littoral states. However, it seems inevitable that the idea of advancing China's economic interests to its south and west will also involve some degree of attention to protecting those interests as well (Medcalf 2015). In this sense, it could be argued that the Maritime Silk Road may come to be seen as the Indo-Pacific with Chinese characteristics.

Towards an Indo-Pacific strategy for Australia?

The more immediate doubts about the future of the Indo-Pacific idea, ironically enough, relate to Australia's own ability or willingness to follow through on the endorsement of this concept in the 2013 Defence White Paper. A line of criticism that can be directed at the adoption of Indo-Pacific terminology is that it is largely rhetorical and does not fundamentally change Australia's defence posture. It would seem contradictory, and potentially harmful for the credibility of Australian defence and foreign policy, that Canberra seems to be widening its geography of strategic interest at the same time that it is not dramatically expanding its defence capabilities. After all, one of the reasons for the Labor government of Julia Gillard to bring forward the 2013 Defence White Paper (originally scheduled for 2014) was to provide the electorate with a rationale for the substantial cuts to the country's defence budget in 2012, which brought Australian military spending to its lowest level as a proportion of GDP – about 1.6 percent – since the 1930s. Against this background, there was an obvious dissonance between the introduction of a strategic framework, the Indo-Pacific, which expands Australia's zone of security interest, and the shift to lower levels of defence funding. In 2013 Australia, it would seem, was claiming responsibility for advancing the security of a wider region at the same time as it gave itself less resources to do so.

Closer examination suggests this contradiction is not as stark as it first seems. Admittedly, Australia will have trouble following through on an expansive definition of the strategic environment were it to continue to deprioritise defence spending. However, the decline in Australian defence spending has been arrested. As of 2015, both major Australian political parties had endorsed the objective of returning defence spending to about 2 percent of GDP. The Abbott government was elected on a platform of returning the defence budget to 2 percent of GDP, albeit within a decade. It remains to be seen whether or how Abbott's successor, Turnbull, will proceed with the defence spending increases needed to fulfil either the ambitious maritime force modernisation plan presented in former Prime Minister Kevin Rudd's 2009 Defence White Paper or the somewhat more modest and gradual variant of the same set forth in the 2013 iteration. The conservative government's forthcoming Defence White Paper aims at reconciling assessments of the strategic environment, force structure and budget limitations. Public statements, such as the August 2015 speech by Defence Minister Kevin Andrews, were clear that the Indo-Pacific maritime domain would be prioritised in developing new capabilities (Andrews 2015). Of course, whether the government can follow through given fiscal pressures remains to be seen.[2]

Still, even with constrained military spending, Australia is making some tangible Indo-Pacific shifts in strategic policy. Announcements in 2014 about the purchase of Triton drones and P-8 Poseidon aircraft confirmed an intensified interest in wide-area maritime surveillance. Australia's Indian Ocean naval presence has long been significant, with the submarine fleet, frigates and patrol boats based on the west coast, and ongoing participation in counter-piracy and other operations in the northwest Indian Ocean. As a force structure determinant for Australia, the effect of the Indo-Pacific concept will depend on how it is interpreted and applied. The 2013 White Paper lists 'a stable Indo-Pacific' as an Australian interest to be upheld, but also lists 'contributing to military contingencies in the Indo-Pacific region' as only the third of four priority tasks, with the caveat 'with priority given to Southeast Asia' (Commonwealth of Australia 2013, 25–26, 28). For a full understanding of how Australian security policy is implementing Indo-Pacific thinking, it is worth looking beyond force structure and self-assigned tasks to questions of force posture (including facilities and bases), alliance relations and wider defence diplomacy. In all three of these areas, change is evident.

The 2013 White Paper confirmed plans to upgrade air facilities on the strategically located Cocos Islands and at Learmonth in Western Australia, although in early 2014 it was still not clear that funding was forthcoming. If progressed, these steps will not only ensure the more sustained reach of Australian maritime surveillance and combat aircraft to Australia's northwest, but could allow for potential access by American military aircraft, including surveillance drones to Cocos Islands and bombers to Learmonth. Additionally, the intensified alliance with the United States involves the positioning of a space-tracking C-band radar at Exmouth in Western Australia. Meanwhile discussions have continued on possible enhanced US naval access to Australia's west coast fleet base, HMAS Stirling.

Moreover, Australia's defence and wider security diplomacy is acquiring a distinctly Indo-Pacific flavour. After all, the scale of the Indo-Pacific makes a greater emphasis on security partnerships not only logical, but essential for advancing and protecting the interests of any nation in the region. A priority here for Australia is stepping up engagement with India, until recently Australia's most neglected major power relationship. A visit to Australia by Indian Defence Minister A.K. Antony in mid-2013 has built on a 2009 security declaration and the warming of political ties following Canberra's removal of a uranium export ban at the end of 2011. Antony and Smith announced the beginning of regular Australia-India naval exercises, building on a strong array of security and defence dialogues. The first such exercise, involving high-end capabilities like submarines, was held in the Bay of Bengal in September 2015. Tentative steps have also been taken via coordination among Australia, India and Indonesia as a troika of past, present and former chairs of the Indian Ocean Rim Association (IORA). A second-track dialogue among the three countries also took place in September 2013. Progress towards a trilateral arrangement will require, among other things, further repair to Australia-Indonesia security relations, damaged in late 2013 by leaks about Australian espionage and by differences over the Abbott government's policy of turning back boats carrying asylum seekers and illegal migrants from Indonesia to Australia. An emphasis on their shared Indo-Pacific perspective could provide Australia and Indonesia with one foundation towards that repair.

At the multilateral level, too, Australia's security diplomacy is going Indo-Pacific. In 2014, Australia was chair of the Indian Ocean Naval Symposium (IONS) and IORA, using both as platforms for building maritime security cooperation in the Indian Ocean and beyond. The Perth-based international search for the missing Malaysian airliner MH370 in March 2014, at the same time as the IONS meeting, had something of an Indo-Pacific character, with major East Asian powers, China and Japan, plus the United States sending assets for an Australian-coordinated mission in Indian Ocean waters. Meanwhile Australia is active in the main Indo-Pacific security institutions: the East Asia Summit, the ASEAN Defence Ministers Meeting +8 and the ASEAN Regional Forum. These are now maritime Asia's three principal multilateral settings with a mandate to discuss strategic issues, and all include India, while the more Asia-Pacific focussed APEC, which does not include India, is in retreat as a strategic institution.

Even if Australia can sustain its own Indo-Pacific strategic pivot, however, the question arises whether this will have any negative consequences for regional stability, notably if this is seen in terms of uncritical support for a US-led strategy to contain China and to exclude it from the Indian Ocean. This misreads the nature of the US rebalance (which is a mix of balancing and engagement, not containment), the support for Indo-Pacific conceptions among countries that are not US allies (notably Indonesia), and the sophistication of Australia's own regional diplomacy.

Just as the Indo-Pacific as a region includes China by definition, so too can and should an Australian reorientation to the Indo-Pacific include a place for enhanced security diplomacy inclusive of China alongside the alliance and other arrangements that exclude China. Australia's Indo-Pacific geography, its US alliance and its activism in building defence engagement with Asian powers (including China) make this country in every sense well positioned to take the initiative as a hub for selective, functional security minilateralism bringing together key powers of the Indo-Pacific. This would involve parallel tracks and instances of enhanced security dialogue, exercises and operational coordination with different combinations of countries, and varying in function and levels of intensity. Sometimes these processes of engagement would include China and sometimes not. They would not all necessarily include the United States either, for that matter. Much would depend on partner nations' capabilities, interests, readiness to contribute and willingness to help shape and abide by rules and norms for regional and especially maritime security. These are basic standards for security cooperation in the era of the Indo-Pacific, and their embrace by others will be a factor Australia may seek to shape and influence but cannot in the end control.

Conclusion

Australian policy formulation has played an important role in developing and promoting Indo-Pacific conceptions of Asian security in recent years. That said, the wider international acceptance of an Indo-Pacific approach is not solely contingent on whether Australia sustains this shift in focus, since it appears on the cusp of acceptance as a valid geopolitical concept among policy makers and leaders in several key powers, notably India, Japan and Indonesia, as well as in the United States. Chinese acceptance of this term, or at least of its conceptual validity, would assist in developing a shared strategic vocabulary and perspective in Asia. That said, the continued expansion of Chinese and Indian economic and security interests beyond their neighbourhoods, such as through the Maritime Silk Road and Act East, means that Indo-Pacific thinking will continue regardless of who chooses to utter the phrase. For Australia, the challenge ahead will be to seize the opportunity of its redrawn geography and to follow its own Indo-Pacific rhetorical and policy pivot with suitable diplomatic initiatives and material adjustments to defence policy that maximise its centrality in this contemporary conception of Asia.

Notes

1 The author gratefully acknowledges research assistance from former Lowy Institute Research Associate Danielle Rajendram in the preparation of this chapter. Some of the arguments herein are developed further in: Medcalf, Rory (2013) 'The Indo-Pacific: What's in a Name?', *American Interest*, Vol. 9. No. 2, November/December, pp. 58–66; and Medcalf, Rory (2014) 'Mapping the Indo-Pacific: China, India and the United States', in Mohan Malik (ed.), *Maritime Security in the Indo-Pacific*, Lanham, MD: Rowman and Littlefield.
2 In the interest of full disclosure, the author is a member of the independent expert advisory panel to the Australian 2016 Defence White Paper.

References

Abe, Shinzo. 2007. 'The Confluence of Two Seas', Speech at the Parliament of the Republic of India, 22 August, http://www.mofa.go.jp/region/asia-paci/pmv0708/speech-2.html (accessed 8 October 2015).
Abe, Shinzo. 2013. 'Japan Is Back', Policy Speech at the Center for Strategic and International Studies (CSIS), Washington DC, 22 February, http://www.mofa.go.jp/announce/pm/abe/us_20130222en.html (accessed 8 October 2015).
Abe, Shinzo. 2014. 'Remarks by Prime Minister Abe to the Australian Parliament', Canberra, 8 July, http://japan.kantei.go.jp/96_abe/statement/201407/0708article1.html (accessed 8 October 2015).
Andrews, Kevin. 2015. 'Address to the American Chamber of Commerce in Australia', QT Hotel, Canberra, 27 August, http://kevinandrews.com.au/latest-news/2015/08/27/address-to-the-american-chamber-of-commerce-in-australia/ (accessed 8 October 2015).
Auslin, Michael. 2010. *Security in the Indo-Pacific Commons: Toward a Regional Strategy*, Washington, DC: American Enterprise Institute, https://www.aei.org/wp-content/uploads/2011/10/AuslinReportWedDec152010.pdf (accessed 8 October 2015).

Biden, Joe. 2013. 'Remarks by Vice President Joe Biden on Asia-Pacific Policy', Washington, DC: George Washington University, 19 July, http://www.whitehouse.gov/the-press-office/2013/07/19/remarks-vice-president-joe-biden-asia-pacific-policy (accessed 8 October 2015).
Bishop, Julie. 2014a. 'Helping Secure the Indo-Pacific Against Nuclear Terrorism', Media Release, 26 March, http://foreignminister.gov.au/releases/Pages/2014/jb_mr_140326.aspx (accessed 8 October 2015).
Bishop, Julie. 2014b. 'US-Australia: The Alliance in an Emerging Era', Speech at the Center for Strategic and International Studies, Washington, DC, 22 January, http://foreignminister.gov.au/speeches/Pages/2014/jb_sp_140122.aspx?ministerid=4 (accessed 8 October 2015).
Bisley, Nick, and Andrew Phillips. 2013. 'A Rebalance to Where?: US Strategic Geography in Asia', *Survival* 55:5, 95–114.
Buzan, Barry. 2003. 'Security Architecture in Asia: The Interplay of Regional and Global Levels', *Pacific Review* 16:2, 143–173.
Chacko, Priya. 2012. 'India and the Indo-Pacific: An Emerging Regional Vision', *Indo-Pacific Governance Research Centre Policy Brief* 5. University of Adelaide, November, http://www.adelaide.edu.au/indo-pacific-governance/policy/Chacko_PB.pdf (accessed 8 October 2015).
Clinton, Hillary. 2010. 'America's Engagement in the Asia-Pacific', Speech at the Kahala Hotel, Honolulu, 28 October, http://m.state.gov/md150141.htm (accessed 8 October 2015).
Clinton, Hillary. 2011. 'America's Pacific Century', *Foreign Policy*, 11 October, http://www.foreignpolicy.com/articles/2011/10/11/americas_pacific_century (accessed 8 October 2015).
Commonwealth of Australia. 2009. 'Defending Australia in the Asia-Pacific Century: Force 2030, Defence White Paper 2009', 2 May, http://www.defence.gov.au/CDG/Documents/defence_white_paper_2009.pdf (accessed 8 October 2015).
Commonwealth of Australia. 2012. 'Australia in the Asian Century (White Paper)', 28 October, http://www.murdoch.edu.au/ALTC-Fellowship/_document/Resources/australia-in-the-asian-century-white-paper.pdf (accessed 8 October 2015).
Commonwealth of Australia. 2013. 'Defence White Paper 2013', 3 May, http://www.defence.gov.au/whitepaper/2013/docs/wp_2013_web.pdf (accessed 8 October 2015).
Datta-Ray, Sunanda. 2009. *Looking East to Look West: Lee Kuan Yew's Mission India*, Singapore: Institute of Southeast Asian Studies and Penguin.
Defence Studies Project. 1965. *Proceedings of the Seminar on Nuclear Dispersal in Asia and the Indo-Pacific Region*, Canberra: Australian Institute of International Affairs and the Australian National University.
Defence Studies Project. 1966. *Proceedings of the Seminar on Commonwealth Responsibilities for Security in the Indo-Pacific Region*, Canberra: Australian Institute of International Affairs and the Australian National University.
Haushofer, Karl. 1924. *Geopolitics of the Pacific Ocean*, edited and updated by Lewis A. Tambs, translated by Ernst J. Brehm, 2002, New York: Edwin Mellen Press.
Jakarta Post. 2014. 'Jakarta Dialogue Stresses Maritime Peace', *Jakarta Post*, 20 March, http://www.thejakartapost.com/news/2014/03/20/jakarta-dialogue-stresses-maritime-peace.html (accessed 8 October 2015).
Johnston, David. 2014. 'Speech to the Jakarta International Defence Dialogue', Jakarta, 19 March, http://www.minister.defence.gov.au/2014/03/19/minister-for-defence-speech-jakarta-international-defence-dialogue/ (accessed 8 October 2015).

Kerry, John. 2013. 'Remarks on a 21st Century Pacific Partnership', Speech at Tokyo Institute of Technology, Tokyo, 15 April, http://www.state.gov/secretary/remarks/2013/04/207487.htm (accessed 8 October 2015).
Khurana, Gurpreet S. 2007. 'Security of Sea Lines: Prospects for India-Japan Cooperation', *Strategic Analysis* 31:1, 139–153.
Kushner, Jacob. 2013. 'As Africa Welcomes More Chinese Migrants, a New Wariness Sets In', *Christian Science Monitor*, 4 September, http://www.csmonitor.com/World/Africa/2013/0904/As-Africa-welcomes-more-Chinese-migrants-a-new-wariness-sets-in (accessed 8 October 2015).
Medcalf, Rory. 2012. 'Pivoting the Map: Australia's Indo-Pacific System', *The Centre of Gravity Series* 1 (November), Canberra: ANU Strategic and Defence Studies Centre, http://ips.cap.anu.edu.au/sites/default/files/COG1_Medcalf_Indo-Pacific.pdf (accessed 8 October 2015).
Medcalf, Rory. 2013. 'The Indo-Pacific: What's in a Name?', *American Interest* 9:2, 58–66.
Medcalf, Rory. 2015. 'Reimagining Asia: From Asia-Pacific to Indo-Pacific', *Asian Forum*, 26 June, http://www.theasanforum.org/reimagining-asia-from-asia-pacific-to-indo-pacific/ (accessed 8 October 2015).
Miles, Donna. 2012. 'Locklear, Regional Military Leaders Seek Closer Cooperation', US Department of Defense, American Forces Press Service, 8 November, http://archive.defense.gov/news/newsarticle.aspx?id=118485 (accessed 8 October 2015).
Modi, Narendra. 2014. 'Speech to the Australian Parliament', Canberra, 18 November, http://blogs.wsj.com/indiarealtime/2014/11/18/narendra-modis-speech-to-the-australian-parliament-in-full/ (accessed 8 October 2015).
Mohan, C. Raja. 2010. 'Return of the Raj', *American Interest*, May/June, http://www.the-american-interest.com/2010/05/01/the-return-of-the-raj/ (accessed 8 October 2015).
Mohan, C. Raja. 2012. *Samudra Manthan: Sino-Indian Rivalry in the Indo-Pacific*, Washington, DC: Carnegie Endowment for International Peace.
Natalegawa, Marty. 2013. 'An Indonesian Perspective on the Indo-Pacific', Speech, Washington, DC: Centre for Strategic and International Studies Indonesia Conference, 20 May, http://www.thejakartapost.com/news/2013/05/20/an-indonesian-perspective-indo-pacific.html (accessed 8 October 2015).
Neary, Adelle. 2014. 'Jokowi Spells Out Vision for Indonesia's "Global Maritime Nexus"', *Southeast Asia from Scott Circle* 5:24, November 2014, Center for Strategic and International Studies.
Panikkar, K.M. 1945. *India and the Indian Ocean*, London: G. Allen and Unwin.
Qi Jianguo. 2013. 'Article by LTG Qi Jianguo on International Security Affairs', *CNA China Studies*, April, https://www.cna.org/CNA_files/PDF/DQR-2013-U-004445-Final.pdf (accessed 8 October 2015).
Rajendram, Danielle. 2013. 'Indo-Pacific Word Games', *Interpreter*, 9 August, http://www.lowyinterpreter.org/post/2013/08/09/Julie-Bishop-Indo-Pacific-word-games.aspx (accessed 8 October 2015).
Richardson, Michael. 2005. 'Australia-Southeast Asia Relations and the East Asian Summit', *Australian Journal of International Affairs* 59:3, 351–365.
Rumley, Dennis, Timothy Doyle, and Sanjay Chaturvedi. 2012. '"Securing" the Indian Ocean? Competing Regional Security Constructions', *Journal of the Indian Ocean Region* 8:1, 1–20.
Scott, David. 2012. 'The "Indo-Pacific" – New Regional Formulations and New Maritime Frameworks for US-India Strategic Convergence', *Asia-Pacific Review* 19:2, 85–109.

Singh, Manmohan. 2013. 'PM's Address to Japan-India Association, Japan-India Parliamentary Friendship League and International Friendship Exchange Council', Tokyo, 28 May, http://pib.nic.in/newsite/mbErel.aspx?relid=96257 (accessed 8 October 2015).

Wei, Jing. 2013. 'Welcoming the US Into the Indo-Asia-Pacific', *Sohu*, 19 March, http://star.news.sohu.com/20130319/n369358343.shtml (accessed 8 October 2015).

White House, Office of the Press Secretary. 2015. 'US-India Joint Statement', 25 January, https://www.whitehouse.gov/the-press-office/2015/01/25/us-india-joint-statement-shared-effort-progress-all (accessed 8 October 2015).

Xi Jinping. 2013. 'Speech by President Xi Jinping to Indonesian Parliament', Jakarta, 2 October, http://www.asean-china-center.org/english/2013-10/03/c_133062675.htm (accessed 8 October 2015).

Zhao, Minghao. 2013. 'The Emerging Strategic Triangle in Indo-Pacific Asia', *Diplomat*, 4 June, http://thediplomat.com/china-power/the-emerging-strategic-triangle-in-indo-pacific-asia/ (accessed 8 October 2015).

2 Japan and the Indo-Pacific

Purnendra Jain and Takenori Horimoto

Japan has been somewhat neglected in studies of the geostrategic dynamic of the Indo-Pacific sphere now evolving in Asia. Japan is undoubtedly an integral and vital part of this geopolitical space as a global power economically, politically and strategically. Economically, as the third-largest world economy and the second largest in Asia, Japan's engagement is huge through trade, investment and aid disbursements to Asian nations. Politically, as well as through the politics of this economic engagement particularly through regional institutions, as a democratic 'pacifist state' Japan contributes to international peacekeeping activities under the auspices of the United Nations. Geostrategically, Japan the economic giant is a key ally of the United States while a neighbour of China, the Koreas and Russia, with all the consequences of that geographic positioning for the regional and international strategic landscapes.

Particularly significant for the present discussion is Japan's continuously difficult relationship with China, which has been rocky at best over the course of China's ascent as an Asian giant alongside Japan. This relationship is a primary motivation for Japan's interest in the Indo-Pacific as an additional, if not necessarily alternative, geostrategic region. The delicate balances involved in the basic geostrategic architecture of Asia at large changed little for decades. But now Japan, with support particularly from the United States and Australia, appears to be very much concerned to be involved in changing the balance by establishing, as a counterweight to China, a much denser alliance-type relationship with selected partners, including India.

This chapter casts an exploratory eye on this rather neglected aspect of Japan's strategic thinking in the twenty-first century, as the rising and declining of great powers dramatically reshapes the strategic landscape in which Japan rose as the first so-called Asian giant in the wake of World War II. Here we examine Tokyo's views on the Indo-Pacific, a term still with minimal currency in Japan; Asia-Pacific remains the primary concept and site for Japan's international diplomacy, and thus for its geostrategic manoeuvring. We argue that even though Japan is not abandoning its Asia-Pacific focus, its geostrategic thinking and action are now also orienting towards more active engagement beyond the Pacific, reaching southwest across the Indian Ocean. Tokyo is now firming up strategic relations with India alongside its foremost strategic ally, the United States, which is pursuing a strategy based on linking with India and other regional powers in pursuit of what it calls the Indo-Pacific concept. China has expressed deep concern about the Indo-Pacific as a geostrategic construct designed to contain China's strategic engagement within and beyond its neighbourhood. But while China recognises Japan's orientation towards the Indo-Pacific as 'anti-China', Tokyo is strongly supported in this move by a range of regional powers including most Southeast Asian nations and Australia. These nations are themselves part of both the Asia-Pacific and Indo-Pacific communities and, like Japan, to some extent they support the Indo-Pacific concept to signal to China their geostrategic priorities.

This chapter first explains the emerging concept of the Indo-Pacific and Japan's preference for the term *koiki Ajia* (broader Asia), which recognises geographic extension rather than replacement of strategic thinking. We then turn from concept to practice, considering in some detail Japan's evolving relationship with India in the new strategic environment and what this means for Japan's regional and global engagement. We then examine briefly the responses of major actors, especially China, the United States and Australia to Japan's broader Asia strategic reach into the Indian Ocean and subcontinent. Overall we argue that in the last decade Tokyo has drawn India into Japan's Asia focus in response to the region's strategic transformation with the rise of two more Asian giants, China and India, alongside the weakening of US influence. The consequent realignment of power across Asia and beyond has motivated Japan to gradually embrace a new broader Asia strategic framework in which India and the Indian Ocean as well as Asia-Pacific are significant for Japan's engagement with the world.

Japan's changing perceptions: Asia-Pacific and Indo-Pacific

Japan is a key element in the Indo-Pacific concept as articulated in American, Australian and Indian writings. Yet there is virtually minimal commentary by Japanese or other observers on Japanese views of the Indo-Pacific as a strategic concept for Japan. As the scholarly literature and official documentation reveal, the term has not come to life in Japanese strategic discourse. Takashi Shiraishi (2014), an eminent scholar specialising in Southeast Asia and the Asia-Pacific, is certainly a supporter, claiming that 'the Indo-Pacific region is emerging as a geographically strategic area, and Japan should pursue its Asian strategy with that in mind.' He claims that Japanese media mostly refers to *higashi Ajia* (East Asia). When speaking about Asia in a larger context, the media now generally speaks of *koiki Ajia* (broader Asia) or just *Ajia* (Asia), both of which include India and the Indian Ocean. Shiraishi claims that in recent years the Japanised version of Indo-Pacific, *Indo Pashifiku*, has been introduced to the Japanese discourse, in katakana script that signifies the term's foreign origin rather than in Japanese kanji characters, which would create an indigenous term.[1] Indeed, if we compare the Japanese term for Indo-Pacific (*Indo Pashifiku*) to the Japanese term for Asia-Pacific (*Ajia Taiheiyo*), we see how in the latter term Pacific is expressed in Japanese wording (*Taiheiyo*), which is not so in *Indo Pashifiku*.

Takashi Inoguchi, another Japanese international relations luminary, has also observed the term's absence from the international relations lexicon in Japan. He believes that *Indo Pashifiku* will gain some currency in Japan as a strategic concept given the present direction of regional geostrategic developments. Indo-Pacific is constructed as an extended narrative of Asia-Pacific. It reflects Asia more broadly since it reaches across two oceans of Asia rather than one, and stretches to include India and the Middle East theatre becoming even more important for Japan as the US retreats from that region and focusses on its 'pivot to Asia'. Asia for the US 'pivot' includes Asia in/on the Pacific as well as Asia in/on the Indian Ocean.[2]

The present Japanese preference for *koiki Ajia* (broader Asia) over *Indo Pashifiku* recognises the nation's geographic extension, rather than replacement, of strategic thinking. We can appreciate this preference as predisposition towards a term that more accurately reflects Japan's geostrategic stance. Even though in recent years Japan has begun to reach more broadly into geopolitical space southwest across the Indian Ocean, the focus of Japan's international engagements is still reaching southward and eastward, as captured by the familiar Asia-Pacific concept. The term Indo-Pacific positions the Indian Ocean before the Pacific Ocean and so can distort understanding of what remains Japan's primary geostrategic priority: the Asia-Pacific region, which includes the United States.

The course of modern Japan's international engagement helps to explain why Asia-Pacific is ingrained deeply in both official and scholarly texts concerning Japan's strategic policies. Security of economic relations has been the principal motivation, and Japan has long focussed these relations on partners in the Asia-Pacific. From the start of the Meiji period in 1867, Japan has focussed on the Pacific, gradually expanding its strategic sphere from East Asia to Southeast Asia, and its maritime reach to the western Pacific. Even after World War II, Japan's strategic sphere remained unchanged because the trade vital to its economic recovery and growth reached straight into markets in countries within these areas of the Pacific. The westward reach across the western Pacific including East and Southeast Asia was strategically cemented by the Japan-US alliance, under which Japan agreed to play a pivotal role in the region vis-à-vis the post-war communist regimes in the Soviet Union, China, and North Korea through hosting US forces in Japan, while accepting the strategic protection of the so-called US nuclear umbrella. From the 1980s Japan has been a great contributor to actualising the concept of the Asia-Pacific as an economic region, particularly through its important role in initiating and establishing the Asia-Pacific Economic Cooperation (APEC) forum. Japan still accepts the US security treaty, the US forces, and the US nuclear protection. The post–Cold War initially saw both the US reach for unipolar power in what it called a new world order, and Japan's willingness to stand with the United States as a Pacific power in that envisaged world order. However, as we discuss later, the twenty-first century has seen the evolution of a world order very different from what had then been envisioned. Especially from the end of that first decade, Japan saw the need to seriously reconsider its Asia policy, expanding its strategic reach westward from the Asia-Pacific to the Indo-Pacific region.

We can gain some sense of the recent emergence of Indo-Pacific and Asia-Pacific in official discourse through the appearance of these terms in documentary records. Japan's Parliamentary Debates Retrieval System (*Kokkai kaigiroku kensaku shisutem*)[3] identifies roughly 3,800 records from the period between 1947 and June 2015 that used 'Asia-Pacific'. In contrast, during the same period 'Indo-Pacific' yields only about 21 uses. A March 2015 search of the Ministry of Foreign Affairs (MOFA) website found 35,700 records using 'Asia-Pacific', whereas Indo-Pacific yielded 7,230 records. The following month, a search of the Ministry of Defence (MOD) website yielded some 16,400 records of 'Asia-Pacific' and 2,470 records of 'Indo-Pacific'. The MOFA and MOD are clearly using Indo-Pacific more frequently in recent years. The nature and pace of regional transformation and Japan's response to it suggest strongly that ever more participants and observers of Japan's strategic/security community will use Indo-Pacific in their spoken and written discussions, thus embedding the term and its acceptance within Japan's geostrategic discourse.

Already in recent years, Japanese analysts and diplomats have spoken on the theme of the Indo-Pacific in international conferences and seminars (e.g. Aspen Institute India 2011). Some in Japan's strategic studies community have begun to discuss the Indo-Pacific concept and explore Japan's relationship with the Indo-Pacific region in their writings (e.g. Kaneda 2013). Most significantly, in 2013 the Japan Institute of International Affairs (JIIA) completed a project examining the meaning and significance of Indo-Pacific in the context of the South China Sea and the Indian Ocean (JIIA 2013). JIIA is acknowledged internationally as one of Japan's premium think tanks on Japan's foreign and security policy, as it undertakes policy-related research, formulates government recommendations and promotes dialogues and joint studies with other institutions and experts at home and abroad. Given that the JIIA is funded by the MOFA, it is generally very cautious in its approach towards sensitive foreign relations issues as they might be easily construed as official policy statements by the MOFA.

Indeed, in 2011–2012 five reports have been published by Japanese think tanks discussing the Indo-Pacific concept.[4] Examining these reports, Professor Matake Kamiya of the National Defense Academy of Japan identified their shared perception, which mirrors dominant thinking within Japan's strategic community (Kamiya 2013). These reports all assess that while the United States remains a key actor in the region, Japan will find cooperation and partnership with India along the lines of the Indo-Pacific concept useful for coping with an assertive China. This is not to suggest Japan's need to abandon the concept of Asia-Pacific, but rather that Indo-Pacific usefully extends this concept by creating a new strategic environment in which Japan can feel better supported and more secure. In this sense we may see that the two concepts broadly meet different national needs: Asia-Pacific for economics (Japan's support for the Trans-Pacific Partnership is a good example) and Indo-Pacific for national security, with the necessary conceptual and practical integration of these concepts to maximise the benefits for Japan on both economic and security policy fronts.

Regional transformation inspiring the Indo-Pacific concept

Recognition by Japan and some other nations that they need to co-create a new strategic environment in Indo-Pacific to better suit their security needs has been inspired by regional transformation within Asia and beyond. For Japan this region is where its economic and geostrategic interests are concentrated. For all regional players, dramatic shifts in national capacities have altered their perceptions of both the extent and type of power that regional actors can exercise and their capacity and will to exercise it. Two striking realities are now reconfiguring this landscape concern. One is the rapid strengthening of China's economic power and consequently its capacity for international influence as an Asian giant. The other is the relative weakening of US power, particularly through declining economic strength and capacity for international influence. Both of these power shifts impact profoundly upon Japan as an international actor. Together with a third power shift – the slower rise of India as another Asian giant – their geostrategic ramifications have oriented Japan towards the Indo-Pacific concept.

China replaced Japan as the world's second-largest economy in 2012 and continues solidly to build national economic strength. Alongside this fresh economic strength, and like the United States and other nations in the region, China has begun to adopt increasingly assertive international policies, especially since the Xi Jinping leadership came to the national helm in 2013. China is now a crucially important economic partner for Japan. The United States was Japan's largest trading partner for half a century from post-war, but in 2002 China overtook the United States to become Japan's top import partner; in 2004 China became Japan's top export partner. Meantime, while Japan's economic relationship with China has become increasingly dependent, its politico-strategic relationship has become strained and sporadically worse, with an undertow of mutual ill will, particularly evident in their contested ownership of the uninhabited but strategically valuable and resource-rich Senkaku/Diaoyu Islands in the East China Sea. While China and the United States pursue proactive defence and diplomatic policies, strategic competition between them is delicate. So too, then, are Japan's policy choices, since like many other nations in the region, such as Australia, its economic interests are bound up just as intensely with China as its security interests are with the United States. Japan's strategic response has entailed engagement and hedging.

Japan has sought to bring more like-minded nations into its security networks alongside its alliance relationship with the United States. Australia and India are the foremost examples of Japan expanding its informal, 'soft security' networks. This approach led to a proposal for a quadrilateral (quad) framework comprising the four countries (Horimoto 2014, 82–83). The quad initiative originally began as a trilateral framework, but with the addition of India began to gain momentum around 2005. By 2007 Japan was actively involved in this strategic framework. The white paper, *Defense of Japan 2007* published in July, announced the Japanese government's intention to strengthen Japan's security cooperation with Australia and India as a counterbalance to the military rise of China and North Korea, and to help stabilise security balance within the region (Nikkei 2007). In early September the first leadership-level trilateral summit between Japan, the United States, and Australia was held on the sidelines of the APEC summit in Australia.

Simultaneous with the leadership-level trilateral summit in Australia, from 4–9 September, the United States, India, Japan, Australia, and Singapore conducted joint naval training in the Bay of Bengal ('Malabar 07-2'). The training was conducted from the centre of the bay near Myanmar's Coco Islands, which India regards as home to a Chinese naval facility. The massive exercise involved 20,000 participants, twenty-eight vessels, and approximately 150 aircraft. Previous Malabar training exercises entailed merely the United States and India; in 2007 Japan, Australia and Singapore also came on board. Governments of participating countries emphasised that the primary objective of the exercise was to increase interoperability among their navies. It was not to engender the creation of a 'democratic axis' in the Asia-Pacific region to contain China (Indian Express 2007). However, a *Kyodo News* article in Japan revealed otherwise. It identified the objective of the exercise as strengthening ties between the participating countries in their efforts to defend the sea lanes for transporting crude oil across the Indian Ocean to the Pacific, to counterbalance China's efforts to expand its own network of military cooperation by providing support to countries lining the Indian Ocean. The article also identified the exercise as part of the plan to increase dialogue among Japan, the United States, India and Australia, which was strongly endorsed by Prime Minister Shinzo Abe (*Kyodo News* 2007).

Shinzo Abe: prime ministerial support for the Indo-Pacific framework

Perhaps the most eminent Japanese supporter of the Indo-Pacific concept is Shinzo Abe, a conservative nationalist.[5] Since his first term as prime minister in 2006–2007 and even while out of the leadership position till December 2012, Abe has pursued his vision of broader Asia, perceiving China as threat to Japan and the region, and thus favouring the Indo-Pacific concept as a geopolitical framework with beneficial security implications for Japan. The Indo-Pacific as a geostrategic framework fits well with – indeed, gives legitimacy and practical life to – Abe's wish to further militarise Japan so that as a 'normal' state it can widen its engagement in collective self-defence operations and military cooperation with allies and partners beyond Japan's immediate maritime neighbourhood. Abe is also pleased to gain India as a crucial partner in Asia since unlike most major northeast states and those in the Association of Southeast Asian Nations (ASEAN), India does not have a history of serious military disputes with Japan; to the contrary, India was exceptionally generous with forgiveness and diplomatic acceptance for Japan in the early post-war period (Jain and Todhunter 1995).

Abe's three-day visit to India in August 2007 was heavy on strategic politics. By inviting India to participate in joint naval exercises, Abe was officially involved in initiating the Quadrilateral Security Dialogue (Quad) between Japan, the United States, Australia and India, which had begun as a trilateral grouping.

The Quadrilateral Security Dialogue did not continue officially, but the joint Malabar exercise that followed virtually only days after the dialogue was on an unprecedented scale, which China criticised as an act of hostile containment, as noted earlier. Abe also inaugurated a new bilateral alliance, building on the long history of amicable, if weak, bilateral relations between India and Japan. Abe's initiative was to establish the fifth bilateral link in an emerging scenario where US-Australia, US-Japan, Japan-Australia, and US-India links are already supportive strategic alignments; a sixth link between India and Australia would form the logical corollary of the quadrilateral strategic bulwark. Eventual expansion of this arrangement to include Vietnam, South Korea, the Philippines and Indonesia has been speculated in the media of those states. Chinese strategic experts have critically labelled the evolving geostrategic paradigm the 'Asian NATO' (*Nerve* 2007).

During his 2007 visit, Abe also presented to the Indian parliament a speech titled 'Confluence of the Two Seas', reaffirming his broader Asia message and the Japanese will for involvement in the Indo-Pacific concept:

> The Pacific and the Indian Oceans are now bringing about a dynamic coupling as seas of freedom and of prosperity. A 'broader Asia' that broke away geographical boundaries is now beginning to take on a distinct form. Our two countries [Japan and India] have the ability – and the responsibility – to ensure that it broadens yet further and to nurture and enrich these seas to become seas of clearest transparency.
>
> (Abe 2007)

Not long before he was voted back into office as prime minister in December 2012, Abe had additionally cemented his idea of the Indo-Pacific through his 2012 article in *Project Syndicate*. He claimed the *inseparability* of peace, stability and freedom of navigation in the Pacific and Indian Oceans, and the seriousness of a Chinese threat, with the South China Sea increasingly set to become a 'Lake Beijing' with the Chinese navy's attack submarines – capable of launching missiles with nuclear warheads – and newly built aircraft carriers. Referring to 'Asia's Democratic Security Diamond', he envisaged 'a strategy whereby Australia, India, Japan, and the U.S. state of Hawaii form a diamond to safeguard the maritime commons stretching from the Indian Ocean region to the western Pacific'. 'I am,' he claimed, 'prepared to invest, to the greatest possible extent, Japan's capabilities in this security diamond' (Abe 2012).

Following the landslide victory of the Liberal Democratic Party (LDP) in the 2012 general election, Abe assumed his second tenure as prime minister. Essentially the basic policy orientation of Prime Minister Abe is to expand Japan's strategic area from Southeast Asia to South Asia along the South China Sea to the Indian Ocean. The month after retaking office, Abe pursued this strategy through visits to Vietnam, Thailand and Indonesia. In Jakarta he pronounced the five principles of Japan's ASEAN diplomacy, conveying Japan's will to work together with ASEAN as its equal partner in pursuit of prosperity in the region through realising universal values such as freedom, democracy, basic human rights and the rule of law, and through a network of economic partnerships to ensure regional peace and prosperity in light of the changing strategic environment in this region (Abe 2013). Beyond the Southeast Asian region, Abe has shown a particular inclination to cultivate closer ties with India (discussed later). This inclination is evident in visits between the two countries at the highest political levels, and also by the visit of Japan's imperial couple to India in November–December 2013.

An important aspect of Abe's efforts to pursue an expanded proactive security policy involves efforts at home. Abe favours revising the Japanese constitution, particularly Article 9, which stipulates that the state formally renounces the sovereign right of belligerency and aims at an international peace based on justice and order, so to accomplish these aims, armed forces with war potential will not be maintained. Almost since post-war, Japan has maintained a de facto army – euphemistically called the Self-Defense Force (SDF),[6] signifying its objective only for Japan's defence. Article 9 has been strictly interpreted to deny Japan's right of collective self-defence.[7] Successive Japanese governments have upheld this interpretation of the article, which has been widely regarded as a symbol of Japan's pacifism.

The Abe government clearly seeks to amend Article 9 (Horimoto 2014), but finds this virtually impossible; an amendment to the constitution must be initiated by the Diet (parliament) through a concurring vote of two-thirds of both houses, which the LDP does not carry. In July 2014, the Abe government defiantly bypassed this constitutional restriction, despite domestic and international resistance, by reinterpreting the article to allow the SDF to provide military assistance to the United States and other strategically like-minded countries under attack, in the name of collective self-defence. And in April 2015, a meeting of Japanese and US foreign and defence ministers unveiled the new Defense Cooperation Guidelines eliminating the geographic restrictions that were limited to Japan's 'surrounding areas' under the 1997 Guidelines. Simply put, the SDF is now allowed to play a global role. Both Abe and US President Obama welcomed the new guidelines during Abe's US visit in April 2015. The Abe government has also proposed a package of security bills to be legislated in the first half of the 2015 parliamentary session to legally allow the SDF to handle new types of missions overseas.

In Japan, apprehensions and opposition to this package come from multiple sources, even within the LDP. For example, Taku Yamazaki, former vice president of the LDP, claims these laws might require Japan to work as a watchdog of the United States (Quoted in *Asahi Shimbun* 2015). Those who oppose the Abe government's security policy are apprehensive about changing the text or reinterpreting Japan's pacifist constitution. Mizuho Fukushima, vice president of the Social Democratic Party, even vilified the legislative package as a *war package* during an Upper House budget committee meeting on 1 April 2015, and refused a request from the LDP to withdraw or modify her claim (*Asahi Shimbun* (Editorial) 2015).

Seiji Maehara, of the opposition Democratic Party of Japan and former foreign minister, criticised the new guidelines when unveiled in Washington in April 2015.

He acknowledged the need to renew the guidelines and related security laws under changed security circumstances, but was concerned that the Japanese people might not support the new guidelines and the package. He also expressed doubt about the SDF's ability to upgrade its capability, equipment, and system to support the new guidelines, which would result in impairment in Japan's relations with the United States that may have excessive expectations (*Sankei News* 2015).

The United States welcomes Japan's new security approach, as expressed in John Kerry's (2015) welcome speech to Abe on 18 April 2015: 'The revised defense guidelines that we announced yesterday – the first in 17 years – establish important new frontiers for our alliance.' But as Sheila Smith (2015, 260), a respected American Japan scholar noted, 'the largest challenge for U.S. policymakers will be developing a cooperative relationship with Beijing while not undermining the United States' close alliance with Tokyo.'

In an opinion poll taken before the new Defence Guidelines were released, published in *Nihon Keizai Shimbun* (*Japan Economic Newspaper*) on 23 March 2015, 31 percent favoured new guidelines and 51 percent opposed them, even though the Abe government's approval rating was then 51 percent. A *Kyodo News* poll of 30 April 2015, after the guidelines were released, found similar responses: 47.9 percent opposed and 35.5 percent supported, while the Abe government's approval rating was 52.7 percent (*Japan Times* 2015). A vast majority of Japanese clearly oppose an amendment to Article 9, as demonstrated by a newspaper poll in May 2015, in which 63 percent were opposed while only 29 percent supported it (*Asahi Shimbun* 2015). A latest opinion poll also showed that only 13.6 percent supported the collective security bill and 80 percent opposed it (*Jiji Press* 2015).

The Abe government's high support ratings in opinion polls and its landslide victory in the December 2014 general election signify strong popular support for the party and the government despite opposition to the new security guidelines. A possible interpretation is that most Japanese are satisfied with the Abe government's economic performance, but they clearly feel anxious about this government's security policy. Since Japan's relationship with India is vital to Japan's involvement in the Indo-Pacific framework, let us turn to consider this relationship.

Japan-India relations and the Indo-Pacific

India had remained distant from Japan's foreign policy orientation for most of the post-war period. Although it has now taken a centre stage in Japan's Asia policy, it was long on the periphery of Japan's Asia vision – economically unattractive with a slow-growth economy, and strategically insignificant since Japan was focussed on its Northeast and Southeast neighbours and heavily dependent on US strategic orientation. Only in the early 2000s did Japan begin to turn its attention to India, inspired by India's growing economic appeal, improved relations with the United States, concerns shared with Japan about China, and perhaps most importantly India's strategic significance, especially because of its naval strength in the Indian Ocean region. These considerations finally led to Japan signing a joint statement with India, the Roadmap for Strategic and Global Partnership, in 2006 (Jain 2008; Mathur 2012).

Japan-India relations really took a new turn with Abe's visit to India in 2007 and his now renowned speech in the Indian parliament, 'Confluence of the Two Seas', as discussed earlier. Even after the defeat of Abe's party, the LDP, in the 2009 general elections, the momentum Abe had created continued under the Democratic Party of Japan (DPJ). None of the three DPJ prime ministers (Yukio Hatoyama, Naoto Kan and Yoshihiro Noda) showed the level of commitment and intense engagement with India that Abe has, but they did make incremental progress in networking with India. With the return of Abe as prime minister in December 2012 and the LDP in a stable position in both houses of parliament since July 2013, Abe's India agenda has accelerated. New Delhi noted Tokyo's increasing interest in India and responded positively. In January 2014, a Japanese prime minister was invited for the first time as the chief guest at India's Republic Day parade. With Narendra Modi as India's prime minister since May 2014, the Japan-India relationship has moved one notch higher. Abe sees that India is particularly important for Japan since India's support will strengthen Japan's strategic position in the region. This strategic role of India underpins all of Japan's other ties (including economic and diplomatic) with India.

Prime Minister Abe in his speech to the Indian Parliament in 2007 did not use the term Indo-Pacific but did introduce the idea of a 'broader' or 'expanded Asia' (*kakudai Ajia*) constituting Pacific and Indian Ocean countries that share the common values of democracy, freedom and respect for basic human rights. This was a prescient statement that Abe made well before leaders of the United States and other countries began to speak of linking the Indian and Pacific Oceans as one strategically significant geographical space, and in which India has a significant strategic role. While Abe's party was out of government for three years after 2009, Abe made a private trip to India in 2011. In his speech at the Indian Council of World Affairs he again articulated his vision of a broader Asia, situating India in a central position and New Delhi playing a crucial role in the maritime arena. He indeed used the word Indo-Pacific in this speech (Abe 2011, 5).

That India is becoming crucial in Japan's overall foreign policy is now mainstream thinking in Japan's policy and strategic communities as well as within various government departments, government-funded think tanks, business circles and academia. Japan's economic and trade links with India still languish, but with dramatic change in Japan's defence-security links with India – to the point where these links are now becoming paramount – economic links are also likely to strengthen. Japan now tends to consider India as part of East Asia, a shift from its earlier stance when Japan opposed India's membership in the APEC forum, for example, but subsequently supported India's membership in various East Asian groupings such as the East Asian Summit (EAS). Tokyo has already signed a number of agreements with New Delhi expanding their economic-security networks. Most notable are the Joint Declaration on Security Cooperation in 2008 when the LDP's Aso Taro was prime minister, and a Comprehensive Economic Partnership Agreement (CEPA) in February 2011 under the DPJ's Naoto Kan. It is noteworthy that Japan and India signed a bilateral security agreement before signing a bilateral free trade agreement, signifying Japan's emphasis on security aspects that led to follow-up in the economic partnership.

Two other key security-related issues are now on the negotiating table. One is Japan's co-development of weapons with India, which is now possible given Japan's de facto lifting of its prohibition on arms exports in December 2011. The other is development of a civilian nuclear technology agreement. Although some progress has been made, Japan remains hesitant due to strong domestic opposition, especially with anti-nuclear sentiment more pronounced after the Fukushima nuclear disaster. Both issues came up for discussion during Indian Prime Minister Manmohan Singh's visit to Tokyo in May 2013. But the nuclear agreement remains elusive, and little progress was made even during Modi's visit to Japan in September 2014. Nevertheless, Abe and his group are likely to push for both matters as India's strategic importance becomes more apparent and Japan is aware that India will regard a nuclear agreement as a high point in the bilateral relationship. Abe is keen to provide this sweetener to India to cement strategic partnership with Japan.[8] Many bilateral defence and other strategic ties have been developed in the last few years. As well as the 2007 multilateral Malabar exercises, Japan's Maritime Self-Defence Force conducted its first bilateral exercise with the Indian Navy in 2012, the Japan-India Maritime Exercise (JIMEX). The two coastguards have also been exercising since 2000, officially for counter-piracy and disaster relief situations, but with the potential to expand into more military types of operations.

The bilateral economic relationship has improved to a limited degree and a preferential trade agreement is now in place. Economic ties, along with cultural linkages and grassroots connections, all contribute to a rounded bilateral relationship. However, the India-Japan relationship today is bound by increasingly stronger ties in the strategic and defence realms. The further deepening that is likely here may also ultimately boost the economic relationship. For example, if a nuclear agreement goes ahead it will accelerate Japan's investment in India. Similarly, if joint development in arms production goes ahead, it will also impact on the two nations' trade in defence-related materials. This pattern of defence and security ties leading to other types of ties is rather unusual in a bilateral relationship where economic and grassroots linkages usually lead to security and defence ties. In Japan-India relations, however, the Indo-Pacific construct and new geostrategic dimensions are propelling in security and defence areas.

Responses of major powers to Japan's new strategic activism

Three powers will be considered briefly: China, the United States and Australia. The latter two countries, as partners with Japan in this framework, are proponents of the Indo-Pacific. China, to some extent the reason for this framework, looks at this geostrategic construct with concern, recognising it as essentially anti-China.

China

Chinese commentaries on Japan's approach to the Indo-Pacific appear to be few, ascribing this construct essentially to the United States seeking to redefine the Asia-Pacific and draw India into its networks of security partnership (Cai 2013; Kiracofe 2013). In one sense China and Japan share a perception of the Indo-Pacific as two linked oceans. For both, it is a vulnerable superhighway that transports their much-needed resources, and thus risk within this ocean region needs to be mitigated. The core tension arises from how these two nations appreciate this risk – its source and its reasons. Japan's new security and defence approach in the Indo-Pacific context has caused some apprehensions for the Chinese government as expressed in various commentaries. Writing in the pro-establishment *Global Times*, Lu Yaodong, director of diplomacy studies at the Institute of Japanese Studies, Chinese Academy of Social Sciences, has clearly drawn message from Abe's (2012) article in *Project Syndicate*, discussed earlier:

> Abe unveiled the concept of an 'Asia Democratic Security Diamond,' whereby Australia, India, Japan and the U.S. state of Hawaii form a diamond to 'safeguard the maritime commons stretching from the Indian Ocean region to the Western Pacific.' Abe vowed to invest Japan's capabilities to the greatest possible extent in this security diamond, highlighting Japan's intention to contain China's maritime strategy.
>
> (Lu 2014)

Lu critically appraises the overall tone of Abe's speeches as signifying China's containment, claiming that 'in the long run, Japan will continue to make shared values the basis of maritime security cooperation in the Indo-Pacific region and disrupt stability by driving wedges between countries in the region.'

It may be quite natural for China to guard against Abe's new security moves, which may jeopardise China's maritime strategy through the first and second island chains in Southeast Asia, the so-called string of pearls in South Asia, and the Belt and Road Initiative under President Xi. According to some Japanese strategists, China has criticised Japan for drawing India into Japan's strategic design, recognising that India is likely to play a key role in the Indian Ocean (Nagao 2014). Yet it can be argued that the strategic thinking of Japan's broader Asia Indo-Pacific concept dovetails with that of India's Look East policy, now revised as Act East under Prime Minister Modi. Beijing does not like this synchronicity, although it does understand that New Delhi maintains its 'strategic independence' stance in its foreign policy and will not be drawn into the orbit of its partner's strategic design.

United States

The United States has encouraged Japan to play a proactive strategic role globally, including contributions through Japan's Self-Defense Force. For the United

States, this role should be not just in overseas peacekeeping, but also through supporting Washington's efforts in fighting wars overseas, such as in Iraq and Afghanistan. Japan has generally complied with this expectation, through necessary legislation when required. Tokyo understands it is expected to 'share burden' with its chief ally. Naturally, Japan's increasing international activism receives the blessing of Washington, which considers Japan an important supporter of the Obama administration's 'pivot to Asia' and 'rebalancing'. Under both Abe administrations, Japan has proposed new initiatives such as the Quad to expand Japan's trilateral with the United States and Australia. Although the Quad was stillborn, the idea behind strategic cooperation among these four nations has not died. The revised US-Japan defence cooperation guidelines certainly aim to bring together the four parties as well as others from the Indo-Pacific region. Kotani has observed that the new guidelines' call for cooperation with other parties will enable the US-Japan alliance to work more effectively by partnering with Australia in the Pacific and India in the Indian Ocean, and can also enable more effective and efficient capacity building for countries like the Philippines and Vietnam (Kotani 2015).

In Washington's view, the Abe administration's move to legally allow and practically/technically enable Japan to participate in collective self-defence is in keeping with the changed strategic environment in the Indo-Pacific region, where the United States, Japan and other nations that are interested positively in the Indo-Pacific framework regard China as a strategic concern.

The very nature of the Indo-Pacific concept makes India a vital actor for all who support this concept as a strategic framework. The United States already has an official-level security dialogue process with Japan and India (Rogin 2011), and a push is under way to upgrade this dialogue to ministerial level, as is with Australia, Japan and the United States. Analysts Rossow, Ito, Srivastava and Glosserman (2015) suggest the time is ripe for a US-Japan-India trilateral framework, since the three countries 'are linked by the Indo-Pacific strategic construct that makes explicit the geographical connections and overlaps that each of them shares'. The apparent strength of US attachment to the Indo-Pacific concept suggests the United States will support any move by Japan that strengthens the US-Japan alliance and draws India and other Indo-Pacific-minded partners more closely into this framework process.

Australia

Australia supports Japan's contribution to broader security and its right to collective self-defence. Canberra is committed to deepening its defence ties with Japan and to enhancing the trilateral framework with the United States (Andrews 2015a). Even though China has replaced Japan as Australia's number-one trading partner, Australia holds serious concerns about China's military behaviour and assertiveness, which are often reflected in ministerial statements and defence white papers. Yet while Japan's economic appeal has diminished to a certain extent, Australia has strengthened and deepened its security and defence ties with Japan. Canberra and Tokyo are closely allied to the United States, and both view the changing geostrategic landscape through similar lenses. As indicated in the 2013 Defence White Paper and recent speeches, Canberra clearly shares the Japanese narrative of broader Asia and regards Japan as a very important partner in its Indo-Pacific strategy (Department of Defence 2013; Andrews 2015a). During his visit to Japan in June 2015, Australia's defence minister Kevin Andrews observed: 'Australia welcomes the new Japan-United States Defence Cooperation Guidelines and the opportunities this will provide for Australia, Japan and the United States to work together on capacity building initiatives in the Indo-Pacific' (Andrews 2015b).

Conclusion

Japan has long been a major Asian actor. This remains true in the era of significant power redistribution and strategic resets in the twenty-first century. China (a Pacific Ocean power and India (an Indian Ocean power) have risen together as Asian giants alongside Japan, with China as a challenge to Japan and India as a partner but not an ally. Evolution of this strategic environment has led some regional players in the Asia-Pacific to extend their geopolitical thinking to the new strategic concept of the Indo-Pacific. The narrative of broader Asia favoured by Prime Minister Abe and others in Japan is similar to the construction of Indo-Pacific articulated mainly by the United States and Australia. All three nations now regard the Pacific and Indian Oceans as a single geostrategic and geopolitical space. This new conceptualising responds to recognition that the rise of Asia's two new powers with growing capacity and thirst for influence is already shifting the power balance that underpinned the Asia-Pacific region in the latter half of the twentieth century.

While the Asia-Pacific still remains a dominant discourse in Japan's foreign and strategic community, the Indo-Pacific is gaining currency in Japan's strategic literature, with the Indo-Pacific increasingly regarded as a unified strategic area with which Tokyo should frame its Asia policy (Shiraishi 2014). Reports from Japanese think tanks and more frequent use of the term Indo-Pacific by Japanese senior ministers signal diffusion of this narrative in Japan's international relations discourse. More than any political leader in Japan, the realist and conservative Prime Minister Abe and his governments have embraced this new narrative. It justifies and legitimises the urge for Japan to stand up to the China challenge by strengthening security relations with the United States and building other security networks with like-minded nations such as India, Australia, Vietnam and the Philippines. To this end, Prime Minister Abe avowedly pursues his idea of revising Japan's 'pacifist constitution' to make Japan a 'normal' state that can participate in collective self-defence globally.

Mearsheimer's strategic framework of offensive realism foresees that China's rise will not be peaceful, compelling the United States to seek to contain China to prevent China from achieving regional hegemony in Asia. In this thinking, a war between China and the United States is inevitable (Mearsheimer 2014).

If Mearsheimer's prediction becomes reality, Japan will be involved inescapably in that war. Japan's Indo-Pacific strategic thinking surely carries this scenario in the background.

Notes

1 Purnendra Jain's personal meetings and correspondence with Professor Takashi Shiraishi, President of GRIPS, 16 May and 28 July 2013.
2 Purnendra Jain's personal meetings and correspondence with Professor Takashi Inoguchi, President, Niigata Prefectural University, 21 May and 29 July 2013.
3 http://kokkai.ndl.go.jp/
4 These reports, all in Japanese, are (as translated): (1) *Japan–US Alliance and Japan's Diplomacy in the Era of 'Smart Power'* (The Japanese Forum on International Relations, March 2011); (2) *Recommendations on Japan's Grand Strategy* (Policy Think Tank PHP Research Institute, June 2011); (3) *Policy Recommendations on 'International Order and Global Governance in the Era of Smart Power'* (The Japanese Forum on International Relations, March 2012); (4) *Medium- and Long-term Perspectives on Japan-US-China Relations* (The Japan Institute of International Affairs, March 2012); and (5) *Maritime Security and Safety* (The Japan Institute of International Affairs, March 2012).
5 In 2013 in an official address to a conservative US think tank, Abe offered that he once termed himself a right-wing militarist. 'Remarks by Prime Minister Shinzo Abe on the Occasion of Accepting the Hudson Institute's 2013 Herman Kahn Award, 25 September 2013'. http://japan.kantei.go.jp/96_abe/statement/201309/25hudson_e.html
6 Prime Minister Abe actually called the SDF *'need to give his exact words in Jese'* (our army) at a Budget Committee meeting on 30 March 2015. (source?) Despite strong criticism from opposition parties and newspapers, Abe has stuck firm to his words.
7 Japan's annual defence report for 2012 commented that under international law Japan as a sovereign state has the right of collective self-defence. 'Nevertheless, the Japanese government believes that the exercise of the right of collective self-defense exceeds the minimum necessary level of self-defense authorized under Article 9 of the Constitution and is not permissible.' http://www.mod.go.jp/e/publ/w_paper/e-book/2012/files/assets/basic-html/page131.html (accessed 4 May 2015).
8 In December 2015, India and Japan signed a memorandum of cooperation on nuclear energy cooperation although some of the technical and legal issues still need to be resolved before a final agreement is signed.

References

Abe, Shinzo. 2007. 'Confluence of the Two Seas', Indian Parliament, 23 August, http://www.mofa.go.jp/region/asia-paci/pmv0708/speech-2.html (accessed 27 June 2015).
Abe, Shinzo. 2011. 'Two Democracies Meet at Sea: For a Better and Safer Asia', New Delhi: Indian Council of World Affairs, 20 September.
Abe, Shinzo. 2012. 'Asia's Democratic Security Diamond', *Project Syndicate*, https://www.project-syndicate.org/commentary/a-strategic-alliance-for-japan-and-india-by-shinzo-abe (accessed 27 June 2015).
Abe, Shinzo. 2013. 'Prime Minister Abe's Visit to Southeast Asia' (Overview & Evaluation), http://www.mofa.go.jp/region/asia-paci/pmv_1301/overview.html (accessed 27 June 2015).

Andrews, Kevin. 2015a. 'Global Power Shifts to the Indo-Pacific', Melbourne, 22 May, http://www.minister.defence.gov.au/2015/05/22/minister-for-defence-australian-member-committee-of-the-council-for-security-cooperation-in-the-asia-pacific-aus-cscap-sofitel-25-collins-streeet-melbourne/ (accessed 27 June 2015).
Andrews, Kevin. 2015b. 'Inaugural Visit to Japan Concludes', Media Release, 4 June, http://kevinandrews.com.au/latest-news/2015/06/05/inaugural-visit-to-japan-concludes/?utm_source=rss&utm_medium=rss&utm_campaign=inaugural-visit-to-japan-concludes (accessed 27 June 2015).
Asahi Shimbun. 2015. 'Lessons of the Iraq Dispatch', *Asahi Shimbun*, 1 May, http://digital.asahi.com/articles/ASH4H4KBCH4HUZPS003.html (accessed 2 June 2015)
Asahi Shimbun (Editorial). 2015. 'Ruling LDP, Abe Administration Ratchet Up Pressure on Dissenting Voices', *Asahi Shimbun*, 21 April, http://ajw.asahi.com/article/views/editorial/AJ201504210038 (accessed 30 May 2015).
Aspen Institute India. 2011. 'India and Japan: Shaping the Indo-Pacific', New Delhi, 22 December, http://www.youtube.com/watch?v=7guMQNrGw3Q&list=UUIvdd1ncT8Z9OtE6gEXc8HQ&index=1&feature=plcp (accessed 5 April 2015).
Cai, Peng Hong. 2013. 'The Indo-Pacific: Its Geographical Implications for China', *Global Review* (Shanghai Institute for Strategic Studies), http://en.siis.org.cn/index.php?m=content&c=index&a=show&catid=68&id=127 (accessed 27 June 2015).
Department of Defence. 2013. '2013 Defence White Paper', http://www.defence.gov.au/whitepaper/2013/ (accessed 27 June 2015).
Horimoto, Takenori. 2014. 'Japan's Further Militarisation: Reinterpretation of Article 9 of the Constitution', *East Asian Monitor* 1:3, 15–16, http://www.idsa.in/system/files/page/2015/EAM_1-3.pdf
Indian Express. 2007. 'China's Self-serving Paranoia on "Malabar" Naval Exercise', *Indian Express*, 4 September, http://www.academia.edu/7726982/China_s_self-serving_paranoia_on_Malabar_Naval_Exercises (accessed 27 June 2015).
Jain, Purnendra. 2008. 'From Condemnation to Strategic Partnership: Japan's Changing View of India-1998–2007', Institute of South Asian Studies, National University of Singapore, http://goo.gl/WGNsuS (accessed 27 June 2015).
Jain, Purnendra, and Maureen Todhunter. 1995. '"India and Japan", Newly Tempering Relations', in *Distant Asian Neighbours: Japan and South Asia*, edited by Purnendra C. Jain, New Delhi: Sterling, pp. 85–107.
Japan Institute of International Affairs. 2013. *Ajia tokuni Minami Shina Indoyo ni okeru anzen hosho chitsujo* (Security Order in Asia With a focus on the South China Sea and the Indian Ocean), Tokyo: Kokusai Mondai Kenkyujo, http://www2.jiia.or.jp/ (in Japanese) (accessed 27 June 2015).
Japan Times. 2015. 'Nearly Half of Japanese Oppose New Joint Defense Guidelines With U.S.: Poll', *Japan Times*, 30 April, http://www.japantimes.co.jp/news/2015/04/30/national/politics-diplomacy/nearly-half-of-japanese-oppose-new-joint-defense-guidelines-with-u-s-poll/#.VqRCz2PeT9x (accessed 27 June 2015).
Jiji Press. 2015. 'Cabinet's Support Rate Drops to 45.8%', *Jiji Press*, 13 June, http://www.japantimes.co.jp/news/2015/06/12/national/politics-diplomacy/cabinets-support-rate-drops-to-45-8/#.VqRER2PeT9w
Kamiya, Matake. 2013. 'Indo Taiheiyo wa Nihon no chiiki anzen hosho seisaku no chukaku gainentarieruka', http://www2.jiia.or.jp/pdf/resarch/H25_Indo-Pacific/H25_Japanese_Diplomacy_in_the_Indo-Pacific_Age.php (accessed 27 June 2015).

Kaneda, Hideaki. 2013. 'Japan Should Strengthen Naval Cooperation With India', *Association of Japanese Institutes of Strategic Studies* 169, 17 January.

Kerry, John. 2015. 'Kerry's Remarks at a Luncheon in Honor of Prime Minister of Japan Shinzo Abe on April 28, 2015', US State Department, http://www.state.gov/secretary/remarks/2015/04/241236.htm (accessed 2 June 2015)

Kiracofe, Clifford A. 2013. 'US Keen to Revive Great Game Politics Through Imperial Return to Asia', *Global Times*, 24 September, http://www.globaltimes.cn/content/813617.shtml (accessed 4 April 2015).

Kotani Tetsuo. 2015. 'The Maritime Security Implications of the New U.S.-Japan Guidelines', http://amti.csis.org/the-maritime-security-implications-of-the-new-u-s-japan-guidelines/ (accessed 5 June 2015).

Kyodo News. 2007. 4 September.

LDP. 2012. Nihon wo torimodosu: juten seisaku 2012 Jiminoto (Regain Japan: LDP's Major Policy 2012), http://jimin.ncss.nifty.com/pdf/seisaku_ichiban24.pdf (accessed 27 June 2015).

Lu Yaodong. 2014 'Japan's Indo-Pacific Concept Another Platform for Containing China', *Global Times*, 13 October, http://www.globaltimes.cn/content/886012.shtml (accessed 27 June 2015).

Mathur, Arpita. 2012. *India-Japan Relations: Drivers, Trends and Prospects*, Singapore: Rajaratnam School of International Studies.

Mearsheimer, John A. 2014. *The Tragedy of Great War Politics* (updated ed.), New York: W. W. Norton.

Nagao Satoru. 2014. 'India Is Set to Play a Key Role in the Indian Ocean', ISPSW Strategy Series: Focus on Defense and International Security, November, http://www.isn.ethz.ch/Digital-Library/Publications/Detail/?id=185366 (accessed 27 June 2015).

Nerve. 2007. 'Abe Calls for Strategic Ties Between Japan, India', 22 August, http://www.nerve.in/news:25350081594 (accessed 27 June 2015).

Nikkei. 2007. 6 September (Evening edition).

Rogin, Josh. 2011. 'Inside the First Even U.S.-Japan-India Trilateral Meeting', *Foreign Policy*, 23 December, http://foreignpolicy.com/2011/12/23/inside-the-first-ever-u-s-japan-india-trilateral-meeting/ (accessed 3 June 2015).

Rossow, Richard, Toru Ito, Anupam Srivastava, and Brad Glosserman. 2015. 'A Trilateral Whose Time Has Come: US-Japan-India Cooperation', *National Interest*, http://nationalinterest.org/blog/the-buzz/trilateral-whose-time-has-come-us-japan-india-cooperation-11508 (accessed 27 June 2015).

Sankei News. 2015. 2 May, http://www.sankei.com/politics/news/150502/plt1505020016-n1.html (accessed 2 June 2015).

Shiraishi, Takashi. 2014. 'Abe's Diplomacy on the Mark in Indo-Pacific Era', *Japan News*, 14 October. [Del: (copy received from author)].

Smith, Sheila A. 2015. *Intimate Rivals: Japanese Domestic Politics and a Rising China*, Columbia: Columbia University Press.

3 India and the Indo-Pacific from Singh to Modi

Geopolitical and geoeconomic entanglements

Priya Chacko

India has always had a prominent presence in discussions on the Indo-Pacific. Two of the earliest (re)appearances of the Indo-Pacific concept were in a 2007 article by an Indian analyst, Gurpreet Khurana, and later that year in a speech by the Japanese Prime Minister Shinzo Abe to the Indian parliament, in which he raised the prospect of a 'broader Asia' fashioned out of the confluence of the Pacific and Indian Oceans (Abe 2007; Khurana 2007). Since then, the Indo-Pacific regional construction appeared sporadically in think-tank commentary before gaining prominence from 2011, after it was included in speeches by then US Secretary of State Hillary Clinton and then Australian Defence Minister Stephen Smith (Clinton 2011a, 2011b; Smith 2011). India featured prominently in these speeches as a key partner in regional-architecture building. According to Stephen Smith (2011), for instance, in addition to the need to ensure maritime security in the Indian Ocean, which has emerged as a crucial thoroughfare for global trade, it is India's 'rise' that is driving the emergence of the Indo-Pacific regional construction: 'So significant is India's rise that the notion of the Indo-Pacific as a substantial strategic concept is starting to gain traction.' Likewise, for Hillary Clinton (2011b), 'the stretch of sea from the Indian Ocean through to the Pacific contain the world's most vibrant trade and energy roots linking economies and driving growth' and 'India straddling the waters from the Indian to the Pacific Ocean is, with us, a steward of these waterways.' The emergence of the Indo-Pacific concept in international policy discourse was also welcomed by Indian officials, and it has since become a part of India's foreign policy lexicon. In this chapter I examine the debate on the Indo-Pacific as it developed under the previous United Progressive Alliance (UPA) government, led by the Congress Party, and as it is now evolving under the new National Democratic Alliance (NDA) government, led by the Bharatiya Janata Party.

The first part of the chapter presents an approach for understanding the emergence of the debate on the Indo-Pacific in India which draws on Marxist political geography and state theory. It argues that geoeconomic logics – the discourses and strategies which link political power to competitiveness in a global economy – are recasting geopolitical logics, which link political power with national territoriality, with regard to issues of security, spatialisation and citizenship. At the same time, geopolitical calculations persist and become entangled with geoeconomics and this reflects the relational nature of the state. Specifically, the state is not a fixed, unified entity, but is better understood as a social relation whose form at any given time is the outcome of the balance of power between different social forces which act through the state's institutional ensemble. This shapes the processes of recasting and entanglement in ways that create and reproduce social hegemonies and hierarchies. The second part of the chapter details the geoeconomic recasting of geopolitics in the 1990s, as India undertook liberalising pro-market and pro-business economic reforms, and focusses specifically on the respatialisation of India's regional imaginary towards an 'extended neighbourhood' conception during this period. Following Mitchell (2004, 8), 'respatialisation' is conceived of here as the 'back-and-forth reworking of spatial arrangements and its associated hegemonies'. This respatialisation involves both material and ideational processes which are intertwined. 'Imaginaries', following Jessop, are defined as 'semiotic systems that frame individual subjects' lived experience of an inordinately complex world and/or inform collective calculation about that world' (Jessop 2010, 344). In arguing for seeing the Indo-Pacific as the result of the respatialisation of India's regional imaginary, like Nieuwenhuis in this volume, I draw on work in Marxist political geography that regards space as political in both its construction and its effects (Elden 2007). The third section argues the Indo-Pacific explicitly took the form of a geoeconomic strategy and discourse under the previous UPA coalition government which was led by the Congress Party. The fourth part of the chapter analyses the further evolution of the Indo-Pacific under the new NDA coalition government, which is led by the Bharatiya Janata Party. I argue that growing perceptions of China's assertiveness have led to the surfacing of geopolitical discourses that position China as a threat and rival to India. These geopolitical discourses disrupt the geoeconomic discourse of the Indo-Pacific and lead to policy vacillation.

Geopolitics and geoeconomics: recasting and entanglement

In analysing the geopolitics and geoeconomics of the Indo-Pacific in India, this chapter draws on Cowen and Smith's (2009, 25) notion of the 'geopolitical social', which recognises that the emergence of modern 'national' societies 'occurred through the same practices, discourses – and importantly, *the acts of violence* – that allowed for the assemblage of national territory: geopolitics was as much a project of the making of "national society" as of national territory' (Cowen and Smith 2009, 25–26). This geopolitical social, which gave rise to the modern state system, national territories and national social orders, is now being 'recalibrated by market logics' such that the state is 'reframed as a geoeconomic agent' (Cowen and Smith 2009, 24). This definition of geoeconomics is distinct from more conventional definitions, such as that associated with Edward Luttwak (1990, 126), for whom geoeconomics is a term that describes inter-state rivalry and conflict conducted through the methods of commerce. In contrast, a Marxist political geography approach acknowledges that security relations and political economy have always been inextricably linked. However, whereas in a geopolitical social they are linked in ways that are reproduce developmental or welfare states and national economies, the notion of the geoeconomic social is an indication of the profound transformations wrought by the adoption of market rationalities and transnationalised economies. Hence, different forms of capitalism give rise to different configurations of geography and security. As Sparke (2013, 292) puts it:

> In place of orthodox geopolitics and its concerns for soldiers and citizens, this geoeconomic outlook tends to elevate the entrepreneurial interests of investors and customers; in contrast to a geopolitical focus on national borders and place, it privileges networks and pace; and instead of concentrating international politics on building alliances for 'security' against supposed 'evil empires,' geoeconomics is primarily concerned with building international partnerships that advance 'growth,' 'integration,' 'harmonization,' and 'efficiency,' against the threats of 'traditionalism,' 'isolationism,' 'anachronism,' and 'anarchy.'

Cowen and Smith suggest that geoeconomic forms, like the establishment of globalised systems of production, emerged as a result of attempts to resolve problems associated with geopolitics, such as the efficient production of military hardware (Cowen and Smith 2009, 32). However, as both Cowen and Smith (2009, 25) and Sparke (2007, 340) have argued, there is no straightforward historical succession between geopolitics and geoeconomics as suggested in other accounts of the emergence of geoeconomics, such as that of Luttwak. Rather, while geoeconomics seeks to 'recast' (Cowen and Smith 2009, 25) geopolitical calculations on issues related to security and citizenship, geoeconomic and geopolitical logics often remain 'entangled' (Sparke 2013, 289). The consequences and causes of the coexistence of the contradictory logics are not however, made clear in these accounts. I argue that the frequent entanglement of geopolitical and geoeconomic logics is due to the nature of the state, which is understood not as a fixed, unified entity, but as a social relation whose form at any given time is the outcome of the balance of power between different social forces which act through the state's institutional ensemble (Jessop 2003). I draw in particular on Jessop's (2003, 7473) notion of the 'state project' which consists of a state's 'internal unity and *modus operandi* (modes of policy making, and so on)'; a 'power bloc, supporting classes or other social forces and alliances'; and a 'set of discourses which define the illusory community whose interests and social cohesion are to be managed by the state within the framework of a given historic bloc and hegemonic project' which also provides 'political, intellectual and moral guidelines for the conduct of state policy'. State projects are challenged and contested as the result of ongoing processes of capitalist development which produce new economic and political imaginaries, including regional imaginaries like the Indo-Pacific. I suggest in this chapter that the emergence of the Indo-Pacific imaginary in India reflects both an attempt to recast the geopolitical into a geoeconomic social as a result of capitalist expansion and the ongoing entanglement of the two logics in this process. This is because the political and economic imaginaries empowered by geopolitical logics continue to exercise influence through factions of the power bloc and their supporting classes who still rely on geopolitical discourses and imaginaries for the exercise of hegemony. While in some cases geopolitical and geoeconomic discourses can be reconciled and successfully recast, in other cases they prove contradictory and can lead to policy incoherence.

State transformation and the respatialisation of India's regional imaginary

The Indo-Pacific is the latest in a series of efforts to respatialise India's region from the 1990s. This respatialisation is, in turn, the product of processes of state transformation, driven by economic reforms and political fragmentation, which have recast the geopolitical social but are also a product of the social system produced by geopolitics. Until the 1990s, the dominant regional construction placed India within a 'South Asian' region consisting of India, Pakistan, Bangladesh, Sri Lanka, Nepal, Bhutan and the Maldives. This spatialisation of India's region reflected a territorial logic which was shaped by the context of the Cold War and the developmentalist state project. This state project consisted of a unified but multi-ethnic and multireligious social democracy with a centrally planned economy based on import-substituting industrialisation (ISI), a federal political structure with independent institutions, a free press and civil society, and a separation of powers and a foreign policy based on active multilateral engagement and a non-aligned stance towards the emerging Cold War. The establishment of a system of parliamentary democracy, secularism, universal suffrage and the guaranteed protection of fundamental rights were all introduced to ensure the creation of a liberal state that was accountable to the people, unlike the British colonial state, while central planning and active social transformation through policies of redistribution were aimed at countering the 'ruralisation' and 'deindustrialisation' of India under the exploitative colonial economy established under British rule (Goswami 2004, 715; Muppidi 2004, 45–47; Alamgir 2009, 20). In the international sphere, ameliorating Cold War tensions and any prospects of neocolonialism, through close collaboration with other African and Asian post-imperial and postcolonial countries at the United Nations and a policy of nonalignment, was seen as being a way for India to maintain its political autonomy and capacity for endogenous economic development (Nehru 1961, 69, 47). Underpinning this state project was the nationalist ideology of anti-colonial nationalism through which the state could mobilise a cross-class coalition. Specifically, in the struggle against colonial rule, the Indian leadership, led by Jawaharlal Nehru, anchored the future independent Indian state's legitimacy to ideas and nationalist discourses about self-reliant economic development, an anti-imperial internationalism, and responsible and accountable governance (Nehru 1982 [1946]). Nehru's critique of colonial rule recognised Western modernity's deep imbrication with colonialism and located the problem not in modernity itself but in its Western manifestation (Nehru 1982 [1946], 554–555). The virulent nationalisms that emerged in the early to mid-twentieth century in Europe were seen as the product of the rise of industrial capitalism in Western Europe, and these nationalisms in turn gave rise to modern imperialism (Nehru 1996 [1934–1935], 399–402). Hence, while a selective appropriation of Western modernity was called for, a rejection and critique of certain aspects – such as the valorisation of 'realist' geopolitics and the 'competitive and acquisitive characteristics of modern capitalist society' – that reinforced and contributed to the rise of destructive nationalisms and imperialism was also necessary (Nehru 1982 [1946], 540–541, 554–546). Moreover, India was thought to be uniquely placed to develop an alternative, better modernity because Indian civilisation was 'based on a fearless search for truth, on the solidarity of man, even on the divinity of everything living, and on the free and co-operative development of the individual and the species' (Nehru 1982 [1946], 514–515).

The emergence of a distinctive regional imaginary was initially constrained by the commitment of India's first prime minister, Jawaharlal Nehru, to the necessity for a 'world community'. 'I have no liking for a division of the world into a few huge supra-national areas' he argued, 'unless these are tied together by some strong world bond' (Nehru 1982 [1946], 536). However, a focussed regional imaginary focussed on South Asia came to the fore in the 1970s and 1980s due to various domestic and international pressures which were seen to threaten the state project of national developmentalism. The then Prime Minister Indira Gandhi's leadership was increasingly contested by a range of domestic social forces, and her poor relationship with Richard Nixon and revelations of the CIA's involvement in the overthrow of Salvador Allende in Chile had made her increasingly apprehensive about American intentions in India (Dhar 2000, 254). Subsequently, as Gupta (1990, 712) argues, policy makers 'fancied external threats to the country from all corners. Relations with China were uneasy; Pakistan, despite Benazir Bhutto's democratically elected government, remained the chief adversary; even smaller neighbours were suspected of harbouring anti-India designs'; this 'climate of psychological insecurity' aided 'the ascendancy of the hawks in the formulation of neighbourhood policies'. While territorial aggrandisement did not become a feature of foreign policy, the idea of having India recognised as the preeminent regional leader did take hold, and India's overt and covert military and political involvement in Sri Lanka's civil conflict in the 1980s was an example of this shift (Krishna 1999).

By 1990, India's developmentalist state project had become increasingly politically and economically unsustainable, and this was exacerbated by the financial costs, political instability and challenges to legitimacy associated with a militaristic regional policy. Military intervention in Sri Lanka eventually resulted in India's longest-running and most expensive war, as its military contingent became bogged down in a counterinsurgency war with the militant group, the Liberation Tigers of Tamil Eelam (LTTE). Indian troops finally left Sri Lanka in 1990 tainted by allegations about the use of child soldiers and human rights abuses and without achieving the goal of disarming the LTTE (Krishna 1999). Although India experienced steady, if modest, industrial and economic growth during the Nehru era, the benefits of this growth were not evenly spread, which contributed to the erosion of support for the Congress Party and its model of development which was focussed on urban industrialisation. The emergence of 'populist' welfare programs in the 1970s, which included attempted land reforms, an expansion of the public sector and the nationalisation of major banks, represented a significant change in the dominant model of development, away from the notion of industrial growth with redistribution towards an emphasis on redistribution in its own right (Gupta 1998, 69). In the 1980s, as it became clear that these policies had done little to alleviate poverty and had contributed to the stagnation of economic growth, a further effort was made to overhaul the developmental state by paying greater attention to pro-business policies such as the reduction of corporate taxes, the provision of corporate subsidies, and increased public investment in certain areas like agriculture (Kohli 2004, 278–285). While these policies increased economic growth and stemmed the rise in rural poverty, the decline in revenue from direct taxes and heightened expenditures resulted in growing budget deficits and public debt (Kohli 2006, 1257). The subsequent balance of payments deficit in 1991 provided the opportunity for policy makers who were seeking more extensive economic reforms to point out the contrast between India's economic woes and East Asia's high growth economies and press the need for reforms. In the 1960s and 1970s the East Asian model was rejected as inappropriate given India's size and social and economic complexity. By the 1980s, as some pro-business reforms were implemented, East Asia's superior industrial growth rates were recognised against India's 3–3.5 percent growth rates; however, the Indian economy was still seen by many policy makers as too large and complex for the implementation of an East Asian-style export-oriented industrialisation model (Alamgir 2009, 98). Nonetheless, this position was an increasingly contested one, and in the 1990s pro-reform policy makers such as Jairam Ramesh repeatedly invoked the East Asian experience to delegitimise the ISI model (Alamgir 2009, 100). In addition to this, the 1990s saw the emergence of a new class of business interests that were technologically and globally oriented, and had benefitted from the pro-business policies of the 1980s as well as the protectionist policies and investments in professional and technical education of the developmental state (Pedersen 2000; D'Costa 2003). The apparent economic crisis, the emergence of a new capitalist class and the change in thinking among state elites laid the path for a shift in favour of the idea that economic development was best secured through policies of economic liberalisation (Mukherji 2008; Alamgir 2009, 101). An economic division, led by a senior bureaucrat, was created in the Ministry of External Affairs in the early 1990s, thereby institutionalising the new focus on open economy policies. Significantly, policy makers repeatedly raised the need to strengthen South Asia's regional engagement with East and Southeast Asia, thus respatialising India's regional imaginary (Faleiro 1992, 214).

The Look East and 'extended neighbourhood' policies were the policy outcomes of this process of respatialisation. The Look East policy emerged soon after the initiation of economic reforms and aimed to strengthen India's regional engagement with East and Southeast Asia in particular, so that, as the then Congress Prime Minister Narasimha Rao noted in 1994, 'the Asia-Pacific could be the springboard for our leap into the global market place' (Quoted in Jaffrelot 2003, 46). In 2003, in a reflection of broader concerns about Islamist militancy and disruptions to trade flows, India's external affairs minister in the BJP-led coalition government, Yashwant Sinha (Sinha 2003), noted the emergence of a 'new phase' in the Look East policy 'characterised by an expanded definition of "East", extending from Australia to East Asia, with ASEAN [Association of Southeast Asian Nations] at its core' and 'a shift from trade to wider economic and security issues, including joint efforts to protect the sea-lanes and coordinate counter-terrorism activities'. By the late 1990s, India's regional space was once again expanded through the promotion of the notion of the extended neighbourhood in the *Annual Report 1998–1999* by the Ministry of External Affairs, which proclaimed that India's 'concerns and interactions go well beyond South Asia. They include other neighbours, and countries immediately adjoining this region – our "extended neighbourhood,"' which includes 'countries in the ASEAN – Pacific region, Central Asia, the Gulf, West Asia and North Africa, and the Indian Ocean Rim' (Government of India 1999). The Look East policy was challenged by the East Asian financial crisis which hindered the expansion of trade and by India's failure in its bid for membership in the Asia-Pacific Economic Cooperation (APEC) forum in 1997. Yet neither the Look East policy nor the extended neighbourhood idea generated serious opposition among foreign policy elites and were subsequently embraced by the Congress-led coalition government that won power in 2004 (*Business Standard* 1997). Prior regional imaginaries have been definitively delegitimised through the processes of state transformation initiated in the 1990s, and the new regional imaginaries were further consolidated because policy makers could point to some tangible outcomes. In particular, India began achieving high economic growth rates in the 1990s, and the majority of its top trading partners now exist in its extended neighbourhood – including the top two, China and the United Arab Emirates – while trade with Asia and North Africa makes up the bulk of its overall trade (Exim Bank of India 2012).

The rise of the Indo-Pacific under the United Progressive Alliance government

The emergence of the Indo-Pacific concept in international policy discourse was welcomed by officials in the Congress Party-led UPA government because, as India's former ambassador to the United States, Nirupama Rao (2013, 9), put it, the Indo-Pacific concept gave international recognition to the shifts in India's regional engagement since the 1990s: 'The earlier concept of the Asia-Pacific had sought to exclude India'; in contrast, 'today the term, Indo-Pacific encompasses the subcontinent as an integral part of this eastern world.' As I have argued elsewhere, however, the Indo-Pacific concept was initially promoted most fervently in India by strategic analysts associated with prominent Indian think tanks, like the Observer Research Foundation and the Indian Council for Research on International Economic Relations, which are a part of a broader network of Australian and American think tanks that have also been at the forefront of the promotion of the Indo-Pacific concept (Chacko 2014). At the core of their arguments were assumptions based on a geopolitical logic, wherein the rise of India and China and their expanding reach into Asia and the Pacific and Indian Oceans, respectively, requires the revision of traditional geopolitical categories and stances. Analysts like C. Raja Mohan and Brahma Chellaney urged Indian policy makers to view the Indo-Pacific as a 'single geopolitical theatre' and abandon the tenet of nonalignment in order to ally with other states with concerns about China's rise (Chacko 2014, 12–13). The notion of the Indo-Pacific that was ultimately adopted by the government, however, was underpinned by a geoeconomic logic that recasts geopolitical discourses such as nonalignment.

Nonalignment, as noted earlier, was a product of anti-colonial nationalist ideology and emerged as a key part of India's developmental state project. As a discourse and a policy it contributed to the state elite's claims to legitimacy by helping to end the domination and marginalisation of Indian civilisation under the colonial regime. It did so by laying claim to an Indian ethos that repudiated the Manichean politics of the Cold War, since India's 'thinking and our approach do not fit in with this great crusade of communism or crusade of anti-communism' and creating a way for India to play a significant role in world affairs, for 'there is just a possibility . . . that at a moment of crisis our peaceful and friendly efforts might make a difference and avert that crisis' (Nehru 1961, 69, 47; 1982 [1946], 540). By contributing to the maintenance of global stability and India's domestic autonomy, moreover, nonalignment would allow India to pursue its model of endogenous economic development.

The case for recasting rather than replacing this key foreign policy tenet as India moves towards greater global economic integration was made most explicitly in a prominent report, *Nonalignment 2.0*, which was co-authored by scholars and former bureaucrats close to the UPA government, like Shyam Saran, a former foreign secretary and prime minister's special envoy. The report constitutes the most comprehensive effort to rework 'the fundamental principle that has defined India's international engagements since Independence' by linking one aspect of this principle, strategic autonomy, with India's new approach to economic development. According to the report, a policy of strategic autonomy gives 'India maximum options in its relations with the outside world – that is, to enhance India's strategic space and capacity for independent agency – which in turn will give it maximum options for its own internal development' (Khilnani et al. 2012, 8). In line with this objective, Saran (2011; quoted in Sharma 2013) adopted the view of the Indian and Pacific Oceans as constituting an 'inter-linked' space, viewing it as a 'logical corollary' to the Look East policy. He highlighted a growing strategic convergence with the United States, Australia, Japan, Indonesia and the Southeast Asian countries, while at the same time downplaying the threat of conflict with China and encouraging a 'more active Russian role in the newly emerging theatre of the Indo-Pacific' to 'help in creating more balanced security architecture in the region' (Saran 2011; quoted in Sharma 2013).

An examination of official statements referring to the Indo-Pacific, as well as foreign policy discourse and practice more broadly, shows that it was this recast geoeconomic conception of the Indo-Pacific that was adopted by the UPA government. Indian officials began using the Indo-Pacific terminology in 2012, particularly in speeches to American, Japanese and ASEAN audiences and on the issue of creating a regional architecture and stronger bilateral relationships (Mathai 2012; Rao 2012; Singh 2013). Hence, for instance, in his visit to Japan in 2013, Prime Minister Manmohan Singh praised the Japanese Prime Minister Shinzo Abe for his 'visionary' notion of the 'confluence of two seas' for providing a new framework for Japan and India's bilateral relationship and their regional cooperation for building interdependence, 'a more balanced regional architecture' and maritime security (Singh 2013). The predominant emphasis in these speeches, however, was on establishing 'an open, balanced, inclusive and transparent regional architecture', with ASEAN, in particular, as the 'lynchpin' of 'economic and security structures and institutions', which allows India to maintain its strategic autonomy (Singh 2012). The national security advisor in the UPA government, Shivshankar Menon (2013, 3–4), challenged the conceptualisation of the Indo-Pacific as a single geopolitical theatre; pointed to the dangers of pursuing a singular security prescription for the distinct areas of the Pacific, the Indian Ocean and the South China Sea; and rejected the assumption of Sino-Indian maritime rivalry. This conception of the Indo-Pacific moreover, fits well with nationalist narratives about India's history of anti-imperialist internationalism, and therefore with ideas about what constituted legitimate statehood: 'when we in India call for a plural, inclusive and open security architecture in the Indo-Pacific we are well within a tradition and culture of thought which was relativistic, idea driven and omni-directional' (Menon 2012).

Hence, although the UPA government made common cause with the United States on the issue of 'unhindered freedom of navigation in international waters', joined in trilateral defence dialogues and exercises with the United States and Japan, and increased naval spending which led to the addition of aircraft carriers and the development of a nuclear submarine, it also rejected third-party involvement in disputes in the South China Sea, called for a 'real concert of Asian powers', including China and the United States, to ensure maritime security in the Indian Ocean, and stressed the need to 'strengthen the multilateral security architecture in the Asia-Pacific and to move at a pace comfortable to all countries concerned' rather than focus on bilateral military partnerships (Menon 2009; Pubby 2012). The UPA government's defence minister, A.K. Antony, emerged as especially resistant to a closer military relationship with the United States despite demands to the contrary from the navy, in particular (Unnithan 2011). Antony, for instance, refused an American offer to post an Indian liaison officer in the US Pacific Command and rejected multilateral naval exercises, on the grounds that the previously held Malabar 2007 exercises involving India, the United States, Singapore, Australia, and Japan led to perceptions of an Asian NATO (North Atlantic Treaty Organization) to contain China. The latter, according to an unnamed bureaucrat constituted 'an overt display of force' which was 'against our government's policy' (Quoted in Unnithan 2011). Instead, the UPA government pursued new trilateral dialogues and military exercises with the United States and Japan, but sought to balance these with counter-piracy exercises with China. The UPA government also increased India's activities in the Pacific Ocean, particularly through the expansion of oil and gas exploration initiatives and military cooperation and with Vietnam, in the face of disapproval from China, which lays claim to the waters of the South China Sea (Brewster 2009). However, India's naval presence in the Pacific Ocean under the UPA government remained low-key, and the Maritime Security Strategy of 2007 defined the South China Sea as a secondary area of interest (Integrated Headquarters Ministry of Defence [Navy] 2007). Rather, the focus of India's Indo-Pacific engagements remained in the Indian Ocean and centred on naval diplomacy through the Indian Ocean Naval Symposium (IONS, founded in 2008), the Indian Ocean Rim Association (IORA) and a maritime security cooperation accord involving India, Sri Lanka and the Maldives with the Seychelles and Mauritius as guest countries. Thus, while the UPA government adopted the Indo-Pacific terminology, it took the form of a recast geoeconomic discourse and strategy that retained a focus on strategic autonomy and maritime diplomacy initiatives rather than military power.

The evolution of the Indo-Pacific under the National Democratic Alliance government

The UPA government lost power in May 2014 and was replaced by the NDA coalition led by the BJP. The BJP made little mention of the Indo-Pacific concept during the election campaign or in its election manifesto, but the concept has made occasional appearances in the NDA's foreign policy discourse while the focus on expanding India's engagements in the Indian Ocean region and the Asia-Pacific has been retained. The new government, headed by Narendra Modi and elected on a platform of economic growth and development, made attracting foreign investment into India to boost domestic manufacturing and infrastructure development key priorities. This reflected the anomalous path of India's open economy policies, which unlike China and East Asia has led to the growth of the services sector rather than industrial manufacturing. As a result, geoeconomic strategies such as the spatial rescaling of India's region as the Indo-Pacific were intensified, with a focus, in particular, on strengthening India's links with continental Asia and the Pacific Ocean while further developing the Indian Ocean initiatives started by the previous government. The Act East policy, for instance, is a revamped version of the Look East policy which aims to demonstrate the centrality of the Asia-Pacific in India's foreign policy, and has given rise to numerous bilateral visits by Modi to ASEAN countries, a renewed focus on maritime and land-based connectivity projects between India and Asia, India's participation in the China-led Asian Infrastructure and Investment Bank, a new India-Japan-Australia trilateral dialogue and the establishment of the Forum for India-Pacific Islands Cooperation. Project Mausam, to be run out of the Ministry of Culture and the Spice Route initiative spearheaded by the government of the state of Kerala, have been launched as 'soft power' initiatives aimed at reviving ancient trade routes and cultural linkages across the Indian Ocean.

At the same time, perceptions of China's growing unilateralism have surged in the past two years, due to incursions across the disputed India-China border, China's land reclamation in the disputed waters of the South China Sea, its Air Defence Identification Zone in the South China Sea and its One Belt One Road (OBOR) initiative for building land and maritime infrastructure. The OBOR initiative aims to connect underdeveloped regions of Western China, in particular, with Africa, Southeast Asia, the Middle East and Central Asia and the Mediterranean, and further internationalise Chinese capital. The current government, moreover, has sought to differentiate itself from its predecessor by laying claim to a more 'proactive' foreign policy (Parameswaran 2015). This has led to the revitalisation of older geopolitical narratives that portray China as a rival and threat to India. China has long been constructed as a rival by many Indian strategic thinkers. This characterisation of China dates to the turn of the twentieth century and the imperial geopolitics of colonial India, which portrayed China as a perpetual threat to India's territorial integrity (Alamgir 2009, 48–50). Nehru sought to contest this construction in the early years of India's independence through an emphasis on the shared experience of anti-colonialism. Yet, the 1962 border war, which remains unresolved; China's alliance with Pakistan, with which India has a serious and long-running territorial dispute; and China's rapid economic growth in the 1980s and 1990s has fuelled the dominance of discourses of rivalry and threat (Alamgir 2009; Chacko 2012, Ch. 3). China's rise and its perceived new assertiveness has revitalised these discourses. The OBOR initiative in particular has been criticised because 'it was not an international initiative they discussed with the whole world, or with the countries which in some way or the other have opinions (about it) or which are affected by it' (*Deccan Herald* 2015). A key concern is the proposed China-Pakistan economic corridor which is to pass through the disputed territory of Pakistan-occupied Kashmir. Implicitly referencing China during his visit to Tokyo, Modi noted:

> The 21st century is Asia's century . . . The question is – how will it be? There are two ways – one of 'Vistarvaad' (expansionism) and the other of 'Vikasvaad' (development). Those who walk on the path of Buddha, those who have faith in the path of development, they come with a guarantee of peace and progress. But we are witnessing today the expansionism that prevailed in the 18th century.
>
> (*NDTV* 2014)

This new focus on China has created a new prominence for the United States in India's Indo-Pacific discourse. During US President Barack Obama's visit to India in January 2015, the two countries announced:

> As the leaders of the world's two largest democracies that bridge the Asia-Pacific and Indian Ocean region and reflecting our agreement that a closer partnership between the United States and India is indispensable to promoting

peace, prosperity and stability in those regions, we have agreed on a Joint Strategic Vision for the region.
(Government of India and Government of the United States 2015)

China figures silently but prominently in the US-India Joint Strategic Vision for the Asia-Pacific and the Indian Ocean, which made special mention of 'ensuring freedom of navigation and over flight throughout the region, especially in the South China Sea', and asserted that 'in order to achieve this regional vision, we will develop a roadmap that leverages our respective efforts to increase ties among Asian powers, enabling both our nations to better respond to diplomatic, economic and security challenges in the region' (Government of India and Government of the United States 2015). The Joint Strategic Vision has laid out a five-year plan to strengthen regional integration, conduct regional dialogues, trilateral consultations with third countries, and explore opportunities for multilateral engagement. As India's Foreign Secretary S. Jaishankar made clear in March 2015, however, the Joint Strategic Vision does not amount to an alliance but rather, 'for us the fact that the US is both a source of supply and a military partner helps to create enough uncertainties that could actually strengthen security in Indo-Pacific region' (Quoted in *Economic Times* 2015). Jaishankar (2015) noted in a speech in Singapore in July that India aspired to be a 'leading power' rather than a 'balancing power' in a multipolar world, with 'shared power' at 'the heart of Asia's emerging security architecture'. This is not far removed from the UPA's notion of a plural, inclusive and open security architecture in the Indo-Pacific and suggests significant continuity.

Nonetheless, critics of the Joint Strategic Vision argue that, despite intentions to the contrary, it may associate India too closely with the United States and its alliance system (e.g. Varadarajan 2015). Thus far, China's reactions have been muted. China's foreign ministry spokesperson, Hua Chunying, responded to the Joint Strategic Vision announcement by repeating China's established position that South China Sea disputes needed to be resolved by the parties directly involved but rejected the idea that the announcement constituted an alliance to contain China: 'I do not think that kind of cold war mentality will work in the 21st century. And, India too is unlikely to be part of any such alliance' (Quoted in Patranobis 2015). Moreover, India and the United States are engaged in distinct regulatory and institutional projects in the Indo-Pacific which place limits on their partnership in the region. India is a member of a number of Chinese-centred organisations including the New Development Bank, the Shanghai Cooperation Organisation and the Asian Infrastructure Investment Bank, and it is also a party to the Regional Comprehensive Economic Partnership, the alternative to the United States–led Trans-Pacific Partnership which includes China. Moreover, shortly after the announcement of the Joint Strategic Vision, the three major states involved in these groupings, China, India and Russia, issued a statement at the thirteenth Russia-India-China foreign minister's trilateral meeting, which 'called for the development of an open, inclusive, indivisible and transparent security and cooperation architecture . . . in the Asia-Pacific region under the framework of the East Asia Summit' (Government of Russia, Government of India and Government of China 2015). The mention of the term 'indivisible' asserts the primacy of an ASEAN-centred security architecture in the Asia-Pacific as opposed to a US alliance system; however, the lack of mention of the Indian Ocean region in this statement reflects India's discomfort with China's Indian Ocean activities. Although China has sought to allay India's concerns by suggesting ways of linking the OBOR project with its Act East, Make in India, Mausam and Spice Route initiatives, formal talks have not commenced (Aneja 2015). If the OBOR project develops as envisaged by China and India remains aloof from it, there is a very real possibility that the geoeconomic discourse of the Indo-Pacific in India will evolve into a geopolitically charged one that pits India, the United States and its allies against China. Alternatively, if India develops a more substantial engagement with China in the Indian Ocean by linking its economic and connectivity projects with OBOR, then the Indo-Pacific may well become a geoeconomic strategy that brings India and China closer. Given, however, the much larger scale of OBOR, this potentially also involves placing India in a subordinate position to China, a move that would contradict its key foreign policy tenet of strategic autonomy as well as persistent geopolitical discourses that position China as a threat and rival. As Gurpreet Khurana has put it: 'We cannot tolerate the idea of playing second fiddle to China in something, even if it helps us' (Quoted in Kasturi 2015).

Conclusion

This chapter has sought to chart the evolution of the discourse on the Indo-Pacific and trace its origins back to the respatialisation of India's regional imaginary following its economic reforms of the 1990s. The emergence of the Indo-Pacific concept in international political discourse was welcomed by the UPA government because it gave legitimacy to the extended neighbourhood regional imaginary that emerged in the late 1990s. The UPA government fashioned the Indo-Pacific as a geoeconomic discourse and strategy of respatialisation that would facilitate the transformation of India's economy and maintain India's strategic autonomy through the establishment of a 'plural, inclusive and open security architecture'. Under the recently elected NDA government, the discourse on the Indo-Pacific has become less coherent. Heightened threat perceptions of an increasingly active China and the NDA's aspiration to assert a more proactive foreign policy have brought to the fore older geopolitical discourses that treat it as a territorial threat. China's OBOR initiative in particular poses a quandary for Indian policy makers. Engaging with the project has the potential to contribute to infrastructure development and therefore economic growth. However, cooperating with OBOR challenges key foreign policy tenets that are the product of nationalist narratives on which the state elite continues to rely for legitimacy. This suggests that the trajectory of the Indo-Pacific as a discourse and strategy in India is at a critical juncture.

References

Abe, Shinzo. 2007. 'Confluence of the Two Seas', Speech by H.E. Mr. Shinzo Abe, Prime Minister of Japan at the Parliament of the Republic of India, Ministry of External Affairs, http://www.mofa.go.jp/region/asia-paci/pmv0708/speech-2.html (accessed 14 June 2013).

Alamgir, Jalal. 2009. *India's Open-Economy Policy: Globalism, Rivalry, Continuity*, New York: Routledge.

Aneja, Atul. 2015. 'Western Elite Wary of India Moving Closer to China', *Hindu*, 17 May, http://www.thehindu.com/news/international/world/western-elite-wary-of-india-moving-closer-to-china/article7214803.ece (accessed 4 June 2015).

Brewster, David. 2009. 'India's Strategic Partnership with Vietnam: The Search for a Diamond on the South China Sea?', *Asian Security* 5:1, 24–44.

Business Standard. 1997. 'Meet Criticises Gujral Doctrine, Tells Pak to Curb ISI Activities', *Business Standard*, 9 August, http://www.business-standard.com/article/economy-policy/meet-criticises-gujral-doctrine-tells-pak-to-curb-isi-activities-197080901068_1.html (accessed 30 September 2013).

Chacko, Priya. 2012. *Indian Foreign Policy: The Politics of Postcolonial Identity From 1947 to 2004*, London: Routledge.

Chacko, Priya. 2014. 'The Rise of the Indo-Pacific: Understanding Ideational Change and Continuity in India's Foreign Policy', *Australian Journal of International Affairs* 68:4, 433–452.

Clinton, Hillary. 2011a. 'America's Pacific Century', *Foreign Policy*, 10 November, http://www.foreignpolicy.com/articles/2011/10/11/americas_pacific_century (accessed 26 January 2012).

Clinton, Hillary. 2011b. 'Secretary of State Hillary Rodham Clinton on India and the United States: A Vision for the 21st Century', *IIP Digital*, 20 July, http://iipdigital.usembassy.gov/st/english/texttrans/2011/07/20110720165044su0.7134014.html#ixzz1UxWVNLPL (accessed 18 March 2011).

Cowen, Deborah, and Neil Smith. 2009. 'After Geopolitics? From the Geopolitical Social to Geoeconomics', *Antipode* 41:9, 22–48.

D'Costa, Anthony P. 2003. 'Uneven and Combined Development: Understanding India's Software Exports', *World Development* 31:1, 211–226.

Deccan, Herald. 2015. 'One Belt, One Road Not International Venture: India', *Deccan Herald*, 21 July, http://www.deccanherald.com/content/490656/one-belt-one-road-not.html (accessed 12 August 2015).

Dhar, P.N. 2000. *Indira Gandhi, The Emergency and Indian Democracy*, New Delhi: Oxford University Press.

Economic Times. 2015. 'If American "Trumpet" Was More Certain in Asia-Pacific, It's Helpful: India', *Economic Times*, 16 March, http://articles.economictimes.indiatimes.com/2015-03-16/news/60174859_1_south-china-sea-asia-pacific-region-asia-pacific (accessed 15 June 2015).

Elden, Stuart. 2007. 'There Is a Politics of Space Because Space Is Political', *Radical Philosophy Review* 10:2, 101–116.

Exim Bank of India. 2012. *Catalysing India's Trade and Investment*, Export-Import Bank of India, http://www.eximbankindia.com/fore-trade.pdf (accessed 23 August 2012).

Faleiro, Eduardo. 1992. 'Changing World Order', *Foreign Affairs Record* 38:5, 211–214.

Goswami, Manu. 2004. *Producing India: From Colonial Economy to National Space*, New Delhi: Permanent Black.

Government of India. 1999. *India's Foreign Relations, 1998–99*, Embassy of India, Washington, DC, http://www.indianembassy.org/policy/Foreign_Policy/FP_1999/Introduction_ FP_98–99.html (accessed 23 August 2012).
Government of India and Government of the United States. 2015. 'U.S.-India Joint Strategic Vision for the Asia-Pacific and Indian Ocean Region', White House, https://www.whitehouse.gov/the-press-office/2015/01/25/us-india-joint-strategic-vision-asia-pacific-and-indian-ocean-region (accessed 4 June 2015).
Government of Russia, Government of India and Government of China. 2015. 'Joint Communiqué of the 13th Meeting of the Foreign Ministers of the Russian Federation, the Republic of India and the People's Republic of China', Ministry of Foreign Affairs, the People's Republic of China, http://www.fmprc.gov.cn/mfa_eng/wjdt_665385/2649_665393/t1233638.shtml (accessed 4 June 2015).
Gupta, Akhil. 1998. *Postcolonial Developments: Agriculture in the Making of Modern India*, Durham, NC: Duke University Press.
Gupta, Anirudha. 1990. 'A Brahmanic Framework of Power in South Asia?', *Economic and Political Weekly* 25:14, 711–714.
Integrated Headquarters Ministry of Defence [Navy]. 2007. *Freedom to Use the Seas: India's Maritime Military Strategy*, New Delhi: Ministry of Defence.
Jaffrelot, Christophe. 2003. 'India's Look East Policy: An Asianist Strategy in Perspective', *Asian Review* 2:2, 35–68.
Jaishankar, S. 2015. 'India Wants to Be a Leading Power Rather Than Just a Balancing Power', *Wire*, 20 July, http://thewire.in/2015/07/20/india-wants-to-be-a-leading-power-rather-than-just-a-balancing-power-6903/ (accessed 4 August 2015).
Jessop, Bob. 2003. *State Theory: Putting the Capitalist State in Its Place*, Cambridge: Polity Press.
Jessop, Bob. 2010. 'Cultural Political Economy and Critical Policy Studies', *Critical Policy Studies* 3:3–4, 336–356.
Kasturi, Charu Sudan. 2015. 'Call to Embrace China Projects – Don't Veto Connectivity Plans: Experts', *Telegraph*, 14 May, http://www.telegraphindia.com/1150514/jsp/nation/story_20029.jsp#.VhPFJvmqqko (accessed 4 September 2015).
Khilnani, Sunil, Rajiv Kumar, Pratap Bhanu, Mehta, Prakash Menon, Nandan Nilekani, Srinath Raghavan, Shyam Saran, and Siddharth Varadarajan. 2012. *Nonalignment 2.0: A Foreign And Strategic Policy for India in the Twenty First Century*, New Delhi: National Defence College and Centre for Policy Research.
Khurana, Gurpreet S. 2007. 'Security of Sea Lines: Prospects for India-Japan Cooperation', *Strategic Analysis* 31:1, 139–153.
Kohli, Atul. 2004. *State-Directed Development: Political Power and Industrialisation in the Global Periphery*, Cambridge: Cambridge University Press.
Kohli, Atul. 2006. 'Politics of Economic Growth in India, 1980–2005: Part I: The 1980s', *Economic and Political Weekly* 41:13, 1251–1259.
Krishna, Sankaran. 1999. *Postcolonial Insecurities: India, Sri Lanka, and the Question of Nationhood*, Minneapolis: University of Minnesota Press.
Luttwak, Edward. 1990. 'From Geopolitics to Geoeconomics: Logic of Conflict, Grammar of Commerce', *National Interest* 20, 17–23.
Mathai, Ranjan. 2012. 'Speech by Foreign Secretary of India, Mr. Ranjan Mathai at the Center for Strategic and International Studies (CSIS), Washington, DC on 6 February 2012 on "Building on Convergences: Deepening India-U.S. Strategic Partnership"', Embassy of India: Washington, DC, http://www.indianembassy.org/prdetail1860/speech-by-foreign-secretary-of-india,-mr.-ranjan-mathai-at-the-center-for-strategic-

and-international-studies-(csis),-washington-dc-on-february-6,-2012-on-andquot; building-on-convergences:-deepening-india-u.s.-strategic-partnershipandquot; (accessed 20 March 2012).

Menon, Shivshankar. 2009. 'Speech on Maritime Imperatives of Indian Foreign Policy (National Maritime Foundation), 11 September 2009', India Habitat Centre, http://www.indiahabitat.org/download/Maritime_Imperatives.pdf (accessed 12 October 2013).

Menon, Shivshankar. 2012. 'Speaking Notes at Workshop on Kautilya – Kautilya Today, Institute for Defence Studies and Analysis', http://www.idsa.in/keyspeeches/ShivshankarMenon_KautilyaToday (accessed 19 October 2012).

Menon, Shivshankar. 2013. 'Speech on Sino-Indian rivalry in the Indo-Pacific', Observer Research Foundation, http://www.orfonline.org/cms/export/orfonline/documents/Samudra-Manthan.pdf (accessed 19 March 2013).

Mitchell, Katharyne. 2004. *Crossing the Neoliberal Line: Pacific Rim Migration and the Metropolis*, Philadelphia, PA: Temple University Press.

Mukherji, Rahul. 2008. 'The Political Economy of India's Economic Reforms', *Asian Economic Policy Review* 3:2, 315–331.

Muppidi, Himadeep. 2004. *The Politics of the Global*, Minneapolis: University of Minnesota Press.

NDTV. 2014. 'PM Modi Takes Swipe at China Before Talks With Japanese Premier Abe', *NDTV*, 1 September, http://www.ndtv.com/india-news/pm-modi-takes-swipe-at-china-before-talks-with-japanese-premier-abe-657457 (accessed 10 August 2015).

Nehru, Jawaharlal. 1961. *India's Foreign Policy: Selected Speeches, September 1946–April 1961*, Delhi: Publications Division, Ministry of Information and Broadcasting, Government of India.

Nehru, Jawaharlal. 1982 [1946]. *The Discovery of India*, Calcutta: Signet Press.

Nehru, Jawaharlal. 1996 [1934–1935]. *Glimpses of World History: Being Further Letters to His Daughter Written in Prison, and Containing a Rambling Account of History for Young People*, New York: Jawaharlal Nehru Memorial Fund.

Parameswaran, Prashanth. 2015, 'India Needs a More Ambitious Foreign Policy, Says Country's Top Diplomat', *Diplomat*, 21 July, http://thediplomat.com/2015/07/india-needs-a-more-ambitious-foreign-policy-says-countrys-top-diplomat/ (accessed 23 September 2015).

Patranobis, Sutirtho. 2015. 'China Reacts Sharply to India-US Statement on South China Sea Dispute', *Hindustan Times*, 26 January, http://www.hindustantimes.com/india/china-reacts-sharply-to-india-us-statement-on-south-china-sea-dispute/story-WOL8UOd3PsG1PMV0qxXaJO.html (accessed 4 June 2015).

Pedersen, JØrgen Dige. 2000. 'Explaining Economic Liberalization in India: State and Society Perspectives', *World Development* 28:2, 265–282.

Pubby, Manu. 2012. 'US Says India "Lynchpin" of Rebalancing Strategy', *Indian Express*, 7 June, http://www.indianexpress.com/story-print/958842/ (accessed 12 September 2013).

Rao, Nirupama. 2012. 'Speech on Indian Foreign Policy in the 21st Century: Challenges and Opportunities', Hudson Institute, http://www.hudson.org/index.cfm?fuseaction=publication_details&id=8826 (accessed 24 August 2012).

Rao, Nirupama. 2013. 'Speech on America's "Asian Pivot": The View from India' (Brown University, 4 February 2013), Brown India Initiative, http://brown.edu/initiatives/india/sites/brown.edu.initiatives.india/files/uploads/NirupamaRao-America's'AsianPivot'The ViewfromIndia-Brown-IndiaInitiativeSeminar2.4.2013.pdf (accessed 5 March 2013).

Saran, Shyam. 2011. 'Mapping the Indo-Pacific', *Indian Express*, 29 October, http://www.indianexpress.com/news/mapping-the-indopacific/867004/ (accessed 4 June 2015)

Sharma, Rajeev. 2013. 'More Proactive Russian Role Needed in Indo-Pacific: Shyam Saran', *Russia-India Report*, 14 October, http://indrus.in/world/2013/10/14/more_proactive_russian_role_needed_in_indo-pacific_shyam_saran_30125.html (accessed 12 November 2013).

Singh, Manmohan. 2012. 'PM's Opening Statement at Plenary Session of India-ASEAN Commemorative Summit', Government of India, http://www.aseanindia.com/pms-opening-statement-at-plenary-session-of-india-asean-commemorative-summit/ (accessed 23 October 2013).

Singh, Manmohan. 2013. 'PM's Address to Japan-India Association, Japan-India Parliamentary Friendship League and International Friendship Exchange Council', Ministry of External Affairs, http://pmindia.nic.in/speech-details.php?nodeid=1319 (accessed 20 June 2013).

Sinha, Yashwant. 2003. 'When Elephants Move', *Outlook*, 1 October, http://www.outlookindia.com/article.aspx?221594 (accessed 20 September 2013).

Smith, Stephen. 2011. 'Speech by Stephen Smith MP Minister for Defence, Australia and India Building the Strategic Partnership', at the Asia Society. Mumbai, Department of Defence, http://www.minister.defence.gov.au/2011/12/10/minister-for-defence-australia-and-india-building-the-strategic-partnership/ (accessed 1 September 2013).

Sparke, Matthew. 2007. 'Geopolitical Fears, Geoeconomic Hopes, and the Responsibilities of Geography', *Annals of the Association of American Geographers* 97:2, 338–349.

Sparke, Matthew. 2013. *Introducing Globalization: Ties, Tensions, and Uneven Integration*, Chichester: Blackwell.

Unnithan, Sandeep. 2011. 'Lone Dissenter', *India Today*, 11 April, http://indiatoday.intoday.in/story/defence-minister-a-k-antony-reins-in-military-ties-with-the-us/1/134697.html (accessed 4 June 2015).

Varadarajan, Siddharth. 2015. 'China or US? India Must Have a Master Strategy in This Poker Game', *Hindustan Times*, 29 January, http://www.hindustantimes.com/ht-view/china-or-us-india-must-have-a-master-strategy-in-this-poker-game/story-SMr6R3YG9BjDPKJOGNd71J.html (accessed 4 June 2015).

4 Climate change as comprehensive security in the continuum

Geostrategy and geoeconomics in the time and place of the Indo-Pacific

Timothy Doyle[1]

As global fault lines multiply and variegate in the twenty-first century, new regional networks and constellations are proliferating, each one built on alternate constructions of geoeconomic and geopolitical (in)securities. The rise (and return) of the Indo-Pacific region has brought with it new and contested forms of map-making, using multiple dimensions of time and space to redefine the relationships between domestic and regional governance, alongside transnational markets. Countries within the region usually mark out the region using more traditional, although differentiating, more ephemeral territorial borders to suit their geoeconomic and geostrategic needs. Borders and boundaries, therefore, are shuffled appropriately. This chapter, however, focusses on a new form of *intermittent globalisation* – a form of deterritorialisation which is, in fact, the creation of the Indo-Pacific region (IPR) as a *liquid continuum, super-region*, or *non-region*. As argued in the first part of the chapter, this version of the IPR has emerged as one dominant but competing view, largely promulgated within United States defence circles. Moreover, as shown in the second part of the chapter, it becomes particularly powerful in both geostrategic and geoeconomic terms when coupled with the dynamics and markets of global climate change which provide the perfect narrative space for this neo-liberal 'de/reterritorialisation'. Although the Cold War, as Mastanduno (1998) argued, saw connections between economy and geopolitics (in security terms) emerge forcefully, the entrenchment of neo-liberalism in the decade of US-led multilateralism which followed the demise of the Soviet Union further entrenched both the discourses of realpolitik and real markets. In economic terms, particularly from the 1980s, global financial institutions implemented major macro-economic restructuring, and embraced the so-called open economy. After the collapse of the Soviet Union, neo-liberal ideology has emerged as the triumphant hegemonic discourse – a kitbag of doctrines, values and policy prescriptions – applied globally by extremely powerful international institutions, regimes (such as the International Monetary Fund and the World Bank) and private corporations. In security terms, as Luciani (1989, 151) writes, 'National security may be defined as the ability to withstand aggression from abroad' within the context of economic, and not just territorial aggression. This is particularly pertinent when discussing the power of transnational corporations (TNCs) (and nations

Climate change as comprehensive security 61

such as the United States, Japan and China with large stakes in TNCs) and their relationships with nation-states. Moreover, as Ullman (1983, 133) argues:

> A threat to national security is an action or sequence of events that (1) threatens drastically and over a relatively brief span of time to degrade the quality of life for the inhabitants of a state, or (2) threatens significantly to narrow the range of policy choices available to the government of a state or to private, nongovernmental entities (persons, groups, corporations) within the state.

This definition of national security is a vital premise for later arguments on economic, human and environmental insecurities in nations within the region, and across the IPR as a whole.

The argument pertaining to the increasing inseparability of geopolitics and geoeconomics – particularly during times of rapidly changing cartographies of power – is central to this chapter. In this 'new' time and space, the US military has embraced the climate bandwagon (in fact, it has become one of climate change's biggest supporters in financial terms). Climate re-endorses the military's strategic entry into all places and spaces, as climate change is constructed globally as omniscient, and an enemy to all – a *conflict multiplier* (in a realist sense). But better than this, although sometimes contextualised within these green moral arguments, it makes both economic and security sense, as climate is also constructed by the military through the lens of energy security and, in doing so, morphing into a *force multiplier*. Finally, these Indo-Pacific practices provide a powerful illustration as to how the temporality of climate change is being harnessed to legitimate the US military's strategic involvement in the region.

Mapping the Indo-Pacific: the creation of the US-led liquid continuum

Persisting uncertainties over the spaces and spatialities of the modern era and the corresponding contestation over the cartographies of globalisation are graphically captured by Matthew Sparke (2013) in his insightful analysis of the interplay between geopolitics and geoeconomics (Chaturvedi and Doyle 2015). In his view, despite the growing appeal of the geoeconomic arguments, 'their globalist vision remains deeply entangled with nationalist geopolitics at the same time' (Sparke 2013, 295). He continues:

> we cannot look at contemporary geoeconomic maps of the world without noticing their entanglement with geopolitical ideas and engagements. We cannot pretend that we have entered some sort of post-geopolitical era. Instead, geoeconomic perspectives ranging from Luttwak's new grammar to the Pentagon's discourse of disconnection defines danger as existing in uneasy tension with ongoing geopolitical assertions about national interests, national homelands, and national security. Instead, just as the early efforts to articulate geoeconomic outlooks at the start of the twentieth century were attended by

some of the starkest geopolitical expressions of nationalism the world has ever seen, today's proponents of geoeconomics also frequently betray their own geopolitical interests. After all, Luttwak conceptualized his own grammar primarily for the purposes of national state-craft, and it is geopolitical leaders that he therefore calls upon to protect 'vital economic interests by geo-economic defenses, geo-economic offenses, geo-economic diplomacy, and geo-economic intelligence'.

While acknowledging the primacy of nation-states, another way in which place and space are now celebrated within a more globalised world order is in the re-emergence of geoeconomic regionalisms. Regions, regionalisms and regionalisations are at once a result of globalisation and a challenge to it. Regions have long been part of the international system (and non-systems), but it must be acknowledged that in this progressively more translateralist world, the concept and symbol of region has been increasingly used to challenge the power and existence of any uniform model of macro-geopolitics.

Nation-states remain the most vociferous players, each one jostling from different and often ambiguous positions, as to which countries should be included within and without these new regional cartographies (see Nieuwenhuis in this volume). A book currently in preparation (Doyle, Rumley and Chaturvedi, forthcoming) lists the properties of these emergent positions with special reference to the United States, India, Japan, China and Australia. Due to the nascent nature of these regional constructions, it must be stressed at the outset that these positions are not universally adopted by particular nation-states. In some countries, it may be a particular think tank, a specific political party, or one branch of the governmental bureaucracy which advocates a version of Indo-Pacific regionalism. This fits in nicely with Jayasuriya's (2008) concept of a regulatory regionalism: that certain constructions are championed by actors, networks, and specific bureaucratic and epistemic communities within and outside of governments, rather than being examples of a whole-of-government understanding.

Despite this lack of coherence, however, there is no doubt that among think tanks, national policy making and epistemic communities, these concepts are in their ascendancy, and on occasion, certain positions become dominant. These attempts at regional framing are usually sparse, with real intent to develop pan-regional co-operative identities, securities or economies (although these exist as subservient traditions). Rather these regional conceptual maps are usually understood by regionally situated nation-states as depicting new bilateral and multilateral relationships and allegiances designed to draw lines *in the sea* denoting 'natural' borders and 'no-go zones', past which other specific nation-states are either admitted or excluded entry.

In the case of the United States, a super-region like the Indo-Pacific is sometimes also imagined in exactly the opposite way – as a non-region or liquid continuum which (at least in narrative terms) denies the existence of the formal politics and histories drawn on maps by nation-states. Instead, a super-region demands free and smooth movement through time and place – national and regional borders

Climate change as comprehensive security 63

are bypassed or passed through, as the continuum is a globally referent object of security. Instead of constantly protecting and securitising regions and borders, it is now flows, routes and sea lanes which become important in efforts to secure geo-economic spaces in a more fluid and time-specific manner (Ryan 2013). Whereas traditional nation-statist regions were more perennial, this form of securitising space as non-region is more intermittent, more temporal.

The United States has been undergoing a reassessment of the strategic importance of the Indian Ocean region in recent years due, in part, to the growth in a range of non-traditional threats, and the growing economic and military importance of both China and India which challenge US dominance in the region. Indeed, it has been asserted that 'the Indian Ocean may be the essential place to contemplate the future of US power' (Kaplan 2010, xiv), and that 'only by seeking at every opportunity to identify its struggles with those of the larger Indian Ocean world can American power finally be preserved' (Kaplan 2010, 323).

It is claimed that the sixtieth annual Australia-United States Ministerial Consultations (AUSMIN) meeting in San Francisco in September 2011 marked the 'pivot point' at which both Australia and the United States began to 'redefine their region not as the Asia-Pacific, but as the Indo-Pacific' (Sheridan 2011). Buzan has recently argued that these regionalised reactions to the ongoing rise of China have led to the generation of 'a weak but definite Asian supercomplex' (Buzan 2012, 2). This trend, he suggests, is being reinforced both by China's turn to a harder line policy since 2008, and by an increase in the strength of United States regional linkages as part of its role as an intervening external power in South and East Asia. Buzan goes on to state:

> The idea of an 'Indo-Pacific region' sometimes mooted by the Obama administration, is so vast as to make a nonsense of the concept of 'region'. As I have argued elsewhere, this fits with a longstanding and very clever anti-regional diplomatic tactic of the US (Buzan 1998, 84–85). By defining itself as part of various super-regions (the Atlantic, Asia-Pacific, the Americas) the US both legitimizes its intrusions into them and gives itself leverage against the formation of regional groups that exclude it (respectively Europe, East Asia, Latin America). This pattern is repeated if one looks more narrowly at strategic balancing behavior, the two being related aspects of the Asian supercomplex.
>
> (Buzan 2012, 1)

Admiral Samuel J. Locklear, former commander of PACOM, would view Indo-Pacific more in terms of the continuum of security spectrum and invoke the more fluid geographies of flows:

> Whether the name is Indo-Pacific or something else, when I am sitting in my office looking at a pretty detailed chart of my entire jurisdiction, *I view it as a continuum of security requirements, not broken down by historical perspectives of the different oceans. I think 'one continuum' is a good concept.*

However, it's not just about the Indian Ocean. It's about the connectivity of these large economies, the large core populations, and how things have to move. Take that to the next level and you have the cyber commons and the space commons. Ships and airplanes travelling across the Indian Ocean, whether it be to the Arabian Gulf or through the Straits of Malacca, are critical for trade and flow of energy sources. The PACOM helps protect these routes.

(Quoted in DeSilva-Ranasinghe 2013, emphasis added)

As discussed earlier in this chapter, the Indo-Pacific, when viewed as a super-region, 'maritime commons' or 'the continuum' allows a global power access to all areas, at specific junctures in time. By invoking the existence of such a super-region, or non-region, this conception of the Indo-Pacific actually denies the existence of regions as drawn on maps, or forms of regionalism which are essentialist in terms of hard-and-fast borders (as some countries, some peoples physically live near others). The US continuum denies any 'special relationship' forged between neighbouring peoples. Indeed, if such a special relationship should prove an impediment to the smooth flow of trade, or the exchange of information necessary to secure the homeland, then it will be dispersed. This is, of course, the key difference between a vision of the Indo-Pacific from the point of view of a superpower, when compared with its construction when understood from the gaze of smaller or middle powers such as India or Japan. (Interestingly, the Japanese concept of the Indo-Pacific usually includes the coast of Southern and Eastern Africa and the west Indian Ocean, whereas the US and Indian constructions usually end at the perimeters of the US PACOM command-structure zone, to the immediate west of India.)

The notion of the declining power of the United States (or its depleted hegemonic reach) needs to be further developed here. In attempting to hold its hegemonic position to a more limited budget, within a very nuanced and ever-changing series of geostrategic games, the United States has had to respond in a number of ways. Despite the existence of a still large expenditure, defence spending has declined from approximately 60 percent to 20 percent of total US resources. These reductions in defence spending have been further exacerbated by the global financial crisis in 2008–2009. In short, the United States can no longer exclusively play (or afford) traditional geostrategic games. Whereas in the Cold War the lines were usually visible (sometimes manifesting themselves literally as walls dividing 'us' from 'them'), this new geostrategic game is more amorphous, ultimately flexible, temporal and many-sided. It is geostrategic string theory. Desperate to uncover and disavow the secrets of global black holes, it sees geopolitical space in ten dimensions, not the usual four (three spatial and one temporal). The United States has globalised and deterritorialised (and, when it suits the perpetrators, post-politicised) more permanent boundaries *outside* its borders, whereas its homeland boundaries and borders are further strengthened, politicised and securitised in a more realist sense.

There are a number of other geopolitical narratives from the past which ring true here. First of all, in some ways, in order to protect its commerce on seaways, on land and in airspace, the military now resembles the antebellum cavalry

Climate change as comprehensive security 65

protecting the migration routes of the early white settlers moving westward across the American plains. And these western metaphors ring true when we imagine this Indo-Pacific space as yet another push to the west (beyond California). The US Navy and Air Force are, in effect, 'riding with the wagons' to protect them from the savagery of 'the natives' who have already been stripped of their livelihoods. At this juncture in global colonialism, however, no treaty will be necessary as sovereign space does not exist outside the homeland, the national borders of temporary 'burden sharers' and the drifting trade flows they protect. This is invasion of the Commons using *Mare Nullius* ('Nobody's Sea') as its doctrine.

Next, as the United States is declining in real terms in relation to both its financial and military might, it seems to be deploying strategies and tactics used for centuries by comparatively powerless minorities. To fight Goliath (China in another life), the old ways of land armies with distinct battle lines can only mean annihilation for the United States. The move to the air and the sea is, in part, a response to this. The military – often the 'Navy Seals' (Ryan 2013) – has the ability to enter the fray at will, securing their markets and trade routes at certain times of passage (and then retreating), thus becoming more guerrilla-like, more terrorist-like, in its activities. It is reminiscent of the Naxalites in South Asian forests, guarding their roads as their enemies enter their domain, striking in relative darkness, and then retreating.

Finally, in many ways (and sometimes paradoxically), its strategic form can be viewed as more post-political (at least pertaining to its dominant narrative). As US power recedes in relation to the power of China, it can be understood to be deploying strategies and tactics more reminiscent of new social movements (NSMs) than nation-states. Characteristics of NSMs are many, but some relate to a form of politics which allows social movements to cross beneath, around and over more traditional nation-state borders. Social movements play a politics which is at once local and global; social movements play the long game, not the short game; social movements are multi-headed, and their goals are ambiguous, ever-shifting. The temporal nature of goal-oriented networks with broader social movements allows strange bedfellows to make alliances, as the territories and issues are shifting constantly. So, as I will argue later, apart from the military taking the issue of climate change from the global environment movement (after years of rejecting it), it may also have adopted some of its organisational structures and strategies, which allowed the movement to sustain its moral force as one of the leading social and political movements across the globe for forty years or more.

These transient geostrategic partners and bedfellows (bilateral monogamy seems to be a thing of the past) provides significant burden-sharing (and cost-saving) advantages. New regional constructions such as the IPR provide promiscuous forms of cooperative security such as that shared between India, Japan and Australia. In an article entitled 'Building Bridges over the Sea', Tetsuo Kotani (working for Japan's premier security think tank, the Japan Institute of International Affairs) reinforces Prime Minister Abe's 'democratic security diamond', 'as a key enabler for good order at sea' (Kotani 2014). Furthermore, this vision, ably supported during three meetings of the Japan-India-US Trilateral Strategic

Dialogue on Security Issues in the Indo-Pacific Region (held between November 2011 and March 2013), includes the Indo-Pacific geopolitical/geoeconomic zone as a construction which 'maintain(s) a liberal rule-based maritime order'.

In fact, this version of the Indo-Pacific is more reminiscent of a neo-liberal and neo-securitised dis/order. Although neo-liberalism champions movements of resources, trade and finance across borders, it only does so when this 'free movement' does not impact upon the interests of the powerful – so too with the case of neo-securitisation.

Climate as omniscient neo-security

> It is quite ironic and sometimes self-defeating because what we are ultimately talking about is comprehensive security. There are other security challenges facing citizens: such as food, water, energy and a host of others. So we have to balance our security spending to ensure our people are safe . . . But many people realise that we have to reduce spending on hard military and build more resilience and a comprehensive security strategy.
>
> (Hilton, interviewing Major General Muniruzzaman of Bangladesh 2011)

As the Pentagon loses its outward control, its *inward* power is being heightened. In an article entitled 'The Amazing Expanding Pentagon', Cambanis (2012) details the manner in which the Pentagon has captured US foreign policy through 'mission creep'. Cambanis writes:

> What 'military' means has changed sharply as the Pentagon has acquired an immense range of new expertise. What began as the world's most lethal strike force has grown into something much more wide-ranging and influential. Today, the Pentagon is the chief agent of nearly all American foreign policy, and a major player in domestic policy as well. Its planning staff is charting approaches not only toward China but toward Latin America, Africa, and much of the Middle East. It's in part a development agency, and in part a diplomatic one, providing America's main avenue of contact with Africa and with pivotal oil-producing regimes. It has convened battalions of agriculture specialists, development experts, and economic analysts that dwarf the resources at the disposal of USAID or the State Department . . . The world's most high-tech navy runs counter-piracy missions off the coast of Somalia, essentially serving as a taxpayer-funded security force for private shipping companies . . . Super-empowered and quickly deployable, the Pentagon has become a one-stop shop for any policy objective, no matter how far removed from traditional warfare.
>
> (Cambanis 2012)

Climate change is just one of these non-traditional policy/security areas under the increasing influence of the military. As the US military learns from, heeds and utilises the strategic lessons and structural forms of new social movements (like

Climate change as comprehensive security 67

the environmental movement), it has also co-opted the language and moral superiority of the environmental movement. Particularly, the politics of climate change have now been increasingly used by militaries around the world to broaden their policy reach. Climate issues are usually seen through the dominant realist prism of 'national interests' within the context of an anarchical world system – as another set of issues pertaining to the struggle for power among nation-states. In addition, climate, as a form of environmental security, is usually seen as a 'threat multiplier', rather than a base or fundamental threat. In this vein, climate can exacerbate tensions but, as an alternative form of security (and, therefore, not as a fundamental one such as race, religion, ethnicity, finances, etc.), it acts as an accelerator or catalyst for existing tensions between nation-states (for examples of this dominant realist – and usually militarist – approach, see Myers 1993; Salehyan 2005). Interestingly, not only does it imagine an anarchical world system, but it also views natural processes themselves as anarchical. In this world view, humanity has not only declared a war against itself, but is also locked into mortal combat with the earth itself – Nature as enemy.

In this view of climate security, nation-states are seen as having to protect their borders from climate refugees of the Indo-Pacific, driven from the global (and particularly Global South) periphery; protecting their 'natural comparative advantage' (in the terms of the classical economist, David Ricardo) of coal, uranium and other markets (Doyle and Chaturvedi 2010). Ever since the concept of global climate change rose to prominence in the 1980s, a series of metaphors has been deployed at the service of imaginative geographies of chaotic and catastrophic consequences of climate change, including 'mass devastation', 'violent weather', 'ruined' national economies, 'terror', 'danger', 'extinction' and 'collapse'. A number of security experts and analysts are convinced that the United States will be the first responder to numerous national security threats generated by climate change (see Podesta and Ogden 2008). In April 2007, the CNA Corporation (2007), a think tank funded by the US Navy, released a report on climate change and national security by a panel of retired US generals and admirals that concluded: 'Climate Change can act as a threat multiplier for instability in some of the most volatile regions of the world, and it presents significant national security challenges for the United States.'

One of the specific and key pressure points in the realist and largely militarist reconstructions of environmental issues (using climate as a political metaphor) relates to *the blood-dimmed tides*, the washing up of the Indo-Pacific's climate refugees – and even climate terrorists – upon the shores of the affluent world, due in part to rising sea levels. If anything, this imagined ecological Armageddon sees the Global North re-engaging with the Global South, not through choice, but through necessity.

Cambanis contends that the Pentagon has emerged as 'a surprisingly progressive voice in energy policy, openly acknowledging climate change and funding research into renewable energy sources'. He goes on to state:

> With little fanfare, the Pentagon – currently the greatest single consumer of fossil fuels in all of America, accounting for 1 percent of all use – has begun

promoting fuel efficiency and alternate energy sources through its Office of Operation Energy Plans and Programs. Using its gargantuan research and development budget, and its market-making purchasing power, the Defense Department has demanded more efficient motors and batteries. Its approach amounts to a major official policy shift and huge national investment in green energy, sidestepping the ideological debate that would likely hamstring any comparable effort in Congress.

This move towards more efficiency (and an increasing interest in extra-carbon technologies) is of particular interest here. In this manner, climate change moves from just a threat multiplier to a force multiplier, allowing the US military to operate in external fields more efficiently, for longer periods away from the homeland. This is critical, as conflict points are increasingly unpredictable as to their location, outside of more costly, more permanent bases. The adoption of greener, more mobile 'combat headquarters' allows force to be deployed for longer and more flexibly.

In an article which largely focusses on the Australian military's response to green initiatives, Press, Bergin and Garnsey list some of the green combat initiatives deployed by North American defence forces:

> The US Army is developing an electric vehicle fleet in order to reduce its reliance on fuel on the battlefield. The US Department of Defense is increasingly turning to microgrids to ensure self-contained energy generation and assuredness during critical operations. There are 454 renewable energy initiatives currently underway or under development by the department. The development of more efficient and longer lasting batteries and fuel cells to provide portable power systems for troops is a US defence priority. In 2010, the US Air Force conducted the first successful test flight of an aircraft powered by a biofuel blend. It aims to use alternative fuels for 50% of its domestic needs by 2016. Increased use of alternative fuels in US tactical fleets and systems is an important consideration for ADF capability planners seeking fuel interoperability between national platforms.
>
> (Press, Bergin and Garnsey 2013, 27)

Also, in a report released by the US Department of Defense in 2011, commonly referred to as the 'Pew Project on National Security, Energy and Climate', arguments pertaining to the morality and rhetoric of cleaner carbon futures, coupled with force multipliers, were both evident (Schario and Pao 2011):

> The U.S. Department of Defense (DoD) is accelerating clean energy innovations in an effort to reduce risks to America's military, enhance energy security and save money, according to a report released today by The Pew Charitable Trusts. 'From Barracks to the Battlefield: Clean Energy Innovation and America's Armed Forces' finds that DoD clean energy investments increased 200 percent between 2006 and 2009, from $400 million to $1.2 billion, and are projected to eclipse $10 billion annually by 2030. 'As one of

Climate change as comprehensive security 69

the largest energy consumers in the world, the Department of Defense has the ability to help shape America's energy future,' said Phyllis Cuttino, director of the Pew Clean Energy Program. 'DoD's efforts to harness clean energy will save lives, save money and enhance the nation's energy and economic future. Their work is also helping to spur the growth of the clean energy economy.'

The work of Emily Gilbert is of particular interest here. She argues the US 2010 Quadrennial Defense Review builds on the previously mentioned Center for Naval Analyses (CNA) report of 2007, which connects climate change with failed states, humanitarian aid, terrorism and mass migration scenarios (Gilbert 2012, 2). She critiques this trend for several reasons. Firstly, the military take a narrow, traditional view of security, as described earlier. This is based on nationalistic, defensive, territorial lines, viewed in statist terms. It is furthermore a model of external threats, based on the idea of resource conflict, which

> coheres easily with the competitive frame that has been established between China and the US, as they vie not only for economic ascendency and resource-acquisition, but also for energy security and environmental policies and initiatives. In this vein, Thomas Freidman [*sic*] has proposed a militant green nationalism, something along the lines of a triumphalist Green New Deal that will recapture US global hegemony.
>
> (Friedman 2009; quoted in Gilbert 2012, 3)

In this manner, the military is further legitimised, 'to the detriment of formal and informal politics' (Gilbert 2012, 4). In their expanded roles as providers of disaster and humanitarian relief, they are given entrée to, or encroach upon, the roles of civilian development and aid: 'This is part of a worrisome trend of the rise of an "aid-military complex" and military "encroachment" on civilian-sponsored development' (Hartmann 2010, 240). Furthermore, the militarisation of the phenomenon does not address the causes of climate and environmental insecurities in any way. There is never any discussion of the fact that the vast majority of the earth's resources are consumed by an ever-decreasing few. It merely entrenches the role of the military in defining the problem – in the worst possible outcome/ worst case scenario sort of way – and this becomes 'the basis for actions in the present' (Gilbert 2012, 4).

Gilbert's second major concern is that the environment is being mobilised and cast as the enemy. She argues that this has the useful effect of resurrecting and perverting a view of 'the commons' which now actually serves to defend national interests, as opposed to genuinely common ones:

> Either way, nature is an externality to be managed as the resurrection of the concept of 'the commons' in these debates affirms (see Posen 2003). Advocacy groups and government representatives alike are using the 'commons' to inform their perspectives on climate change security. Abraham Denmark and James Mulvenon explicitly delineate the concept's legacy to Garrett Hardin's

controversial piece, 'The tragedy of the commons', and his argument that 'Freedom in a commons brings ruins to all' (Denmark and Mulvenon 2010, 7–8). Rather than privatization, the contemporary version of the polemic posits that military force is necessary to prevent the misuse and abuse of navigable passageways.

(Gilbert 2012, 5)

Gilbert refers to the 'complex web of collaborations' addressing climate change, which she describes as a 'military-industrial-academic-scientific complex' (2012, 6). Transformative technological innovations are presented as being of immense social benefit, and hence, it becomes easier to justify enormous amounts of money being transferred to the military and its privatised civilian partners to work on these carbon-friendly technologies. The problem, of course, of funnelling resources (however green) through the military is that resources are drained from other sectors, 'unless they are working in partnership with the military' (Gilbert 2012, 8). Meanwhile, returned military personnel are reintegrated into civilian life through various green mechanisms, like 'green training' and 'green jobs' initiatives. This is just another way of legitimating spending on the military:

> Domestic measures to address energy security are put forward as calculable, rational and even compassionate measures, while the 'foreign' threat is presented as non-state, elusive, and undetermined – and hence coherent with much of the discourse around diffuse 'new wars' and terrorist threats (Kaldor 2013). At the same time, there is also greater convergence between the inside and the outside, and between the environment and the military in the ways that the discourses are mobilized and mapped out (Cooper 2006). Indeed, as Mikkel Vedby Rasmussen notes, there is a coherence between pre-emptive military doctrines and precautionary environmental strategies: both are based upon a rationale for urgent action based on anticipated future disaster scenarios (Rasmussen 2006, 124). Notably, however, it is only when environmental issues are harnessed to security claims that the precautionary approach gains traction.
>
> (Gilbert 2012, 10)

Ferguson would argue that this is typical of militarism's 'double move': on one side of the coin, war is constructed as being 'over there', while on another side, the 'second move saturates our daily lives with warness' (Ferguson 2009, 478).

Conclusion

Climate change in the *liquid continuum* constructs global spaces – in this case the Indo-Pacific – using specific notions of time and globalisation, as connected threads of gold through lawless darknesses; as networks, pathways and trading song-lines through black waters and evil airs held together by strings of liberal values. The depiction of nature is still a realist one – the essential *nature of nature* is a maelstrom, is still anarchical – and nation-states (at least 'the good and the true' ones) must order it, and call its marauding tribes to account.

This is omniscient security. It secures the earth using a climate narrative which cannot be seen, smelled or touched in the lifetimes of humans. It strikes everywhere and nowhere at once. It is arbitrary and can be deployed only by the most powerful and their piecemeal coalitions to protect the 'free flow' of capital. It is both a conflict and force multiplier. This latter interpretation allows the US military and its temporal allies to strike harder for longer (through greener, noncarbon energy intensive warfare) when fighting in intermittent conflict spaces away from more ephemeral combat bases and headquarters and, of course, the homeland. In this vein, the Indo-Pacific is now largely understood (in US defence terms) as a series of geoeconomic routes and elastic time zones which need to be secured; sovereignty (at least in an external affairs sense) becoming something amorphous and arbitrary (although no less powerful); and climate change is used in a manner which accentuates this idea of comprehensive security in a continuum or super-region (non-region), sometimes called the Indo-Pacific. Accordingly, while advocating climate crisis imperatives, the military can now make preemptive strikes, as it is the only one which has 'the lift capacity' to secure trade flows; 'protect' the most 'climate vulnerable' by 'swarming' to secure 'storm surges'; and to utilise both armed and unarmed 'intervention relief' in order to establish 'neo-Malthusian anticipatory regimes' (Chaturvedi and Doyle 2015). As a consequence, Indo-Pacific citizens and their leadership are now being made markedly insecure, disciplined by predominantly foreign geoeconomic forces.

This is simply plutocracy – the rule of a wealthy global elite – desecuritising and disciplining weaker domestic economies and democracies. This is a very different kind of 'foreign policy'. In its place, there is a *re*-securitisation, but one which only further secures the power of the elite to the detriment of the many. New geoeconomic lines, new geopolitical maps are drawn marking new borders and boundaries between the haves and the have-nots, crossing and then erasing the histories, cultures and politics of troublesome nation-states and non-states. This is a new type of colonisation: a transition from state-led to TNC-led colonisation, ably supported and protected by powerful (but at the same time declining) military regimes such as the United States.

Note

1 This chapter is derived from research and writings contributing to two major book-length treatments: Doyle, T., Rumley, D. and Chaturvedi, S. (forthcoming), *The Return of the Indo-Pacific* (Oxford: Oxford University Press); and Chaturvedi, S. and Doyle, T. (2015), *Climate Terror: A Critical Geopolitics of Climate Change* (London: Palgrave Macmillan). The author also wishes to acknowledge that this research is funded in part by the Australian Research Council (ARC) Discovery Projects Scheme, 'Building an Indian Ocean Region' (DP120101166).

References

Baldwin, David. A. 1985. *Economic Statecraft*, Princeton: Princeton University Press.
Buzan, Barry. 1998. 'The Asia Pacific: What Sort of Region in What Sort of World?', in *Asia-Pacific in the New World Order*, edited by Anthony McGrew and Christopher Brook, Abingdon: Routledge, pp. 68–87.

Buzan, Barry. 2012. 'Asia: A Geopolitical Reconfiguration', *Politique Etrangère* 77:2, 331–343.
Cambanis, T. 2012. 'The Amazing Expanding Pentagon', *Boston Globe*, 27 May, http://thanassiscambanis.com/2012/05/25/the-amazing-expanding-pentagon/ (accessed 27 May 2012).
Chaturvedi, S., and T. Doyle. 2015. *Climate Terror: A Critical Geopolitics of Climate Change*, London: Palgrave Macmillan.
CNA Corporation. 2007. *National Security and Threat of Climate Change*, Alexandria, VA: CNA Corporation.
DeSilva-Ranasinghe, Sergei. (2013). '"A Continuum of Security Requirements": The US Pacific Command and the Rise of the Indian Ocean', *South Asian Masala*, 3 April, http://asiapacific.anu.edu.au/blogs/southasiamasala/2013/04/03/a-continuum-of-security-requirements-the-us-pacific-command-and-the-rise-of-the-indian-ocean/ (accessed 23 April 2014).
Doyle, T., and S. Chaturvedi. 2010. 'Climate Territories: A Global Soul for Global South?', *Geopolitics* 15:3, 516–535.
Doyle, Timothy, Dennis Rumley, and Sanjay Chaturvedi. Forthcoming. *The Rise and Return of the Indo-Pacific*, Oxford: Oxford University Press.
Ferguson, K. E. 2009. 'The Sublime Object of Militarism', *New Political Science* 31:4, 475–486.
Gilbert, Emily 2012. 'The Militarization of Climate Change', *ACME: An International E-Journal for Critical Geographies* 11:1, 1–14.
Hartmann, B. 2010. 'Rethinking Climate Refugees and Climate Conflict: Rhetoric, Reality and the Politics of Policy Discourse', *Journal of International Development* 22:2, 233–246.
Hilton, Isabel. 2011. 'Militarising Climate Change', 4 July, http://www.chinadialogue.net/article/show/single/en/4388 (accessed 22 August 2011).
Jayasuriya, Kanishka. 2008. 'Regionalising the State: Political Topography of Regulatory Regionalism', *Contemporary Politics* 14:1, 21–35.
Kaplan, Robert. 2010. *Monsoon: The Indian Ocean and the Future of American Power*, New York: Random House.
Kotani, Tetsuo. 2014. 'Building Bridges Over the Sea: Shinzo Abe's Visit Is a Good Time to Operationalise the India-Japan Maritime Partnership', *Indian Express*, 14 January, http://indianexpress.com/article/opinion/columns/building-bridges-over-the-sea/ (accessed 23 April 2014)
Luciani, G. 1989. 'The Economic Content of Security', *Journal of Public Policy* 8:2, 151–173.
Mastanduno, Michael. 1998. 'Economics and Security in Statecraft and Scholarship', *International Organization* 52:4, 825–854.
Myers, N. 1993. 'Environmental Refugees in a Globally Warmed World', *Bioscience* 43:11, 752–761.
Podesta, John, and Peter Ogden. 2008. 'The Security Implications of Climate Change', *Washington Quarterly* 31:1, 115–138.
Press, M., A. Bergin, and E. Garnsey. 2013. 'Special Report: Heavy Weather. Climate and the Australian Defence Force', Australian Strategic Policy Institute, http://www.aspi.org.au/publications/publication_details.aspx?ContentID=354 (accessed 3 June 2013).
Ryan, Barry. 2013. 'Zones and Routes: Securing a Western Indian Ocean', *Journal of the Indian Ocean Region* 9:2, 1–16.

Salehyan, I. 2005. 'Refugees, Climate Change and Instability', presented at Human Security and Climate Change: International Workshop, Oslo, 21–23 June (conference).
Schario, T., and S. Pao. 2011. 'Pew Study: Department of Defense Accelerates Clean Energy Innovation to Save Lives, Money', Press Release 21 September 2011 Pew Project on National Security, Energy and Climate, http://www.pewenvironment.org/news-room/press-releases/pew-study-department-of-defense-accelerating-clean-energy-innovation-to-save-lives-money-85899364102# (accessed 2 June 2012).
Sheridan, Greg. 2011. 'New Australia-US Push Deals India in to Pacific', *Australian*, 17 September, http://www.theaustralian.com.au/news/opinion/new-australia-us-push-deals-india-in-to-pacific/story-e6frg76f-1226139302534 (accessed 22 October 2012).
Sparke, Matthew. 2013. *Introducing Globalization: Ties, Tensions, and Uneven Integration*, Chichester: Wiley.
Ullman, R. H. 1983. 'Redefining Security', *International Security* 8:1, 129–153.

5 Indonesia's new geopolitics
Indo-Pacific or PACINDO?[1]

David Willis

> Indonesia should not become an 'object' in the international political struggle. On the contrary, it should become a 'subject' which has the right to make its own choice.
>
> Mohammad Hatta (Quoted in Leo Suryadinata (1996))
> Prime Minister and Founding Father, 1948

> The way you define the map defines how you behave internationally.
> Rizal Sukma (2014), Presidential Advisor on Foreign Policy 2014

This chapter argues that Indonesia's approach to the Indo-Pacific regional construct will depend heavily on the extent to which it serves Indonesia's security interests and leadership aspirations. Jakarta's approach to regionalism has long been driven by an adherence to the foundational doctrine of Indonesian foreign policy independent-active, espoused in the nation's pre-independence debates (see Hatta quoted in Suryadinata 1996, 25), and the need to mitigate a sense of 'vulnerability' and satisfy a sense of 'regional entitlement', identified by Michael Leifer (1983). As a result, regionalism is embraced by Indonesia only when it fulfils these two objectives. This has been demonstrated by its rejection of foreign-led, pro-Western and anti-communist architecture before 1967 and its later embrace of its own proposal – the Association of Southeast Asian Nations (ASEAN), with its norms of non-interference, supported during the New Order. It also explains the emergence of a 'post-ASEAN' discourse in the country given its rising stature since the return of democracy in 1999 and increasing divisions within the grouping (Sukma 2009). Regional architecture that is imposed from the top down, led by the Indo-Pacific Rim democracies (the United States, Japan, India and Australia) and perceived to be aimed at containing a re-emerging China will not be welcomed in Jakarta. Indonesia's discomfort with the proposed Indo-Pacific is important; because as a key 'pivot state', the success or failure of the new regional construct may rest on the support it receives from regional states like Indonesia (Bremmer 2012, 120).[2]

Indonesia has long declared that it will not be an object in international affairs, but a subject that determines its own fate. As such it has expressed unease at the idea of an Indo-Pacific construct imposed from the top down. This is most evidently demonstrated in the new government of President Joko 'Jokowi' Widodo's (2014a) rebranding of the expanded regional concept as PACINDO: the Pacific and Indian Ocean region. Recognising the importance of geopolitical concepts in constraining and focusing foreign policy choices, former Presidential Advisor on Foreign Policy Rizal Sukma (2015) stated that 'we tried to find a new term, as Indo-Pacific has been claimed by Americans and Australians.' Indonesia has so far approached the idea of the Indo-Pacific by trying to reshape it in ways that would allow it to play a leadership role and maintain its strategic independence through the mitigation of regional conflict. This was evident in both former Foreign Minister Marty Natalegawa's (2013) call for an 'Indo-Pacific wide treaty of friendship and cooperation' based on the ASEAN-like Bali Principles in 2013 and new president Jokowi's plan to reassert Indonesia's regional centrality as a *poros maritim dunia* (global maritime fulcrum) (Widodo 2014a).[3] The chapter asserts that the concerns expressed that Indonesia may be turning away from ASEAN and towards bilateralism are overstated (Parameswaran 2014). Instead I argue that Indonesia's consternations over ASEAN are indicative of a concern about the right medium for the regionalist foreign policy that has thus far served it so well. Given the current approach of the Indonesian government, Jakarta may be willing to embrace the Indo-Pacific, although only if it meets the twin objectives of its regionalist foreign policy: allaying its strategic vulnerability and acknowledging its regional stature.

In exploring Indonesia's approach to the Indo-Pacific, this chapter will begin with an overview of Indonesia's regionalist foreign policy. It will show how regionalism has been used as a foreign policy tool by Indonesia since the New Order regime of President Suharto. The chapter then examines how Indonesia has historically been responsive to geopolitical change and where the Indo-Pacific fits in this dynamic, charting the journey between Prime Minister Hatta's description of Indonesia's foreign policy approach as 'rowing between two reefs' in 1948 to Sukma's reframing of the approach as 'sailing in two oceans' in 2014. The following section provides an explanation of Indonesia's interests in a broader region. It argues that a rising Indonesia has a strong interest in playing a central role in the Indo-Pacific, in terms of supporting both the aims of its regionalist foreign policy, as well as its developmental goals. The next section examines Indonesia's Indo-Pacific discourse. It identifies the relative lack of serious discussion about the Indo-Pacific concept in Indonesia and the centrality of the South China Sea territorial disputes in Indonesian thinking about regional affairs. The chapter ends with an exploration of the implications of Indonesia's approach for the Indo-Pacific Rim democracies, China and ASEAN. It concludes that Jakarta's approach to the Indo-Pacific so far indicates an anxiety about the prospects of a region that is no longer centred on Indonesia's interests and aspirations.

Regionalism in Indonesian foreign policy

Indonesia's approach to the Indo-Pacific concept will depend on the extent to which it can be utilised to support Jakarta's regional interests. Indonesia's foreign policy has long centred on using regionalism as a tool to hedge against its vulnerability vis-à-vis the major powers and enhance its regional leadership ambitions. As such, regionalism is embraced by Jakarta only when it satisfies these two objectives. At the heart of Indonesian foreign policy is the concept of *bebas-aktif* (independent-active), which stipulates that Indonesia should be both free to chart its own course in world affairs and active in shaping a benign global order. It finds its origins in the speeches and writing of former Mohammad Hatta, former prime minister (1948–1950) and vice president (1945–1956). In a 1953 *Foreign Affairs* article, at the height of the Cold War, Hatta declared:

> Indonesia plays no favourites between the two opposed blocs and follows its own path through the various international problems. It terms this policy 'independent,' and further characterizes it by describing it as independent and 'active.' By active is meant the effort to work energetically for the preservation of peace and the relaxation of tensions generated by the two blocs.
>
> (Hatta 1953, 444)

Dewi Fortuna Anwar (2003, 2), scholar and advisor to both former President Habibie and former Vice President Boediono, has stressed that *bebas-aktif* has become so entrenched in Indonesia as to 'become part of [its] national identity'. Similarly, former diplomat and advisor to former President Susilo Bambang Yudhoyono, Dino Patti Djalal (2012) has argued that 'generations of policy makers have accepted it without question.' The concerns at the root of *bebas-aktif* are mirrored in Michael Leifer's (1983, 173) observation that Indonesian foreign policy at its core is driven by a 'need to overcome an intrinsic vulnerability' which 'paradoxically, however [is] combined with an equally continuous sense of regional entitlement'. This manifests itself in a strong suspicion of outside powers. Franklin Weinstein (1976, 42) has observed that Indonesian foreign policy elites have described Indonesia's geopolitical situation as 'analogous to that of a pretty maiden constantly being approached by men who wanted to take advantage of her'. This view, that has remained constant over the last four decades, is ultimately concerned with Indonesia's 'weakness and vulnerability vis-à-vis the outside world' (Novotny 2010, 217). As a postcolonial state that struggled for its independence against the Dutch, Indonesians value their independence highly, and 'efforts by outside powers to dominate the region and to exclude Indonesia from deliberations about its fate are viewed as an infringement of this independence' (Weinstein 1976, 30).

The twin objectives of Indonesia's foreign policy have always dictated its approach to regionalism. It will not accept regional constructions organised by other states that do not support its leadership aspirations or organisations that would jeopardise its non-aligned stance. As a result Indonesia rejected early attempts at region-building at both the Philippines-led Baguio Conference of 1950 and the US-led Southeast Asian Treaty Organization, both being perceived as pro-Western and anti-communist (Anwar 1994, 18). Indonesia instead turned its focus towards a broader Third World grouping of primarily postcolonial states

Indonesia's new geopolitics 77

in Africa and Asia. The Bandung Conference of 1955, an initiative of Indonesian Prime Minister Ali Sastroamidjojo, put Indonesia centre-stage in shaping global politics. Indonesia's goals for the conference were nothing short of lofty; Secretary-General of the Conference Ruslan Abdulgani (Quoted in Acharya 2009, 54–55) stated that the aims of the meeting were 'to continue the struggle toward a full materialization of national independence' and 'to determine ... the standards and procedures of present-day international relations'. For President Sukarno the Bandung Conference was a chance to model Indonesia as a Third World leader against colonialism. He opened the conference with a warning to fellow delegates:

> And I beg of you, do not think of colonialism only in the classic form which we in Indonesia and our brothers in different parts of Asia and Africa knew. Colonialism has also its modern dress, in the form of economic control, intellectual control, actual physical control by a small but alien community within a nation.
>
> (Quoted in Leifer 1983, 52)

Bandung was the beginning of Sukarno's 'Light House' foreign policy that sought internationalist answers to the vulnerability/entitlement paradox (Anwar 2008, 189). This was based on an obvious feeling of success by Indonesia post-Bandung, summarised by Prime Minister Ali's comment that 'it was because of the Bandung Conference that our country soon acquired a respected place on the map of world politics' (Quoted in Leifer 1983, 39).

Indonesia did not demonstrate any further interest in regionalism until Sukarno was deposed in 1966. Attempts at regionalism by Malaysia in the shape of the Association of Southeast Asia (ASA) proposed in 1957 was criticised by Indonesia 'as a "Western-inspired", anti-communist bloc' which it refused to join (Acharya 2012, 153). The Philippines' proposal of a 'Malay' confederation under the acronym MAPHILINDO (Malaysia, Philippines, Indonesia) also met with failure. Despite Sukarno's willingness to join a meeting with government heads from Malaysia and the Philippines in 1963, aimed at resolving the perceived issue of a neocolonial Malaysian Federation, it was ultimately subsumed by Jakarta's policy of *konfrontasi* (confrontation) against Malaysia (Acharya 2012, 154). South Korea's proposed Asia-Pacific Council in 1964, which included Japan and Australia, met a similar fate (Acharya 2015, 52). Indonesia under Sukarno preferred to pursue its agenda through the internationalist anti-colonial struggle and Third World forums such as the Non-Aligned Movement.

Konfrontasi had been a diplomatic disaster for Indonesia; it isolated Indonesia both regionally and internationally and the new government of Major General Suharto moved towards regional cooperation as a way to 'exorcize the ghost of confrontation' (Anwar 1994, 45). ASEAN, as an Indonesian proposal, served Indonesia's foreign policy objectives well, unlike alternate regional constructions initiated by other states, like ASA, to which 'Indonesia was too proud to become a junior member' (Anwar 1994, 50). This new forum was seen 'as having the potential "to serve as a forum for the expression of Indonesia's leadership in Southeast

Asia"' (Weinstein 1969; quoted in Acharya 2012, 157). Being under Indonesian leadership also allowed Jakarta to try and shape the region into its preferred model, one that would keep out the tensions that come with external powers' involvement. As Anwar (1994, 46) states, from an Indonesian security perspective, 'the creation of a shield of friendship around Indonesia meant moving the immediate danger zone further away from the Indonesian perimeter.' A secure and stable region under Indonesian purview suited the political goals of the New Order in its quest for domestic legitimacy; it saw 'regionalism as a vital adjunct to its national development plan' (Acharya 2012, 157). ASEAN located Indonesia at the heart of regional affairs and kept foreign influence to a minimum. It was designated the 'cornerstone' of Indonesia's foreign policy in the 1970s (Djalal 1990, 171).

As the region expanded to become the Asia-Pacific and include the United States in the region after the end of the Cold War, ASEAN remained at the centre of Indonesia's approach. The Australian-proposed Asia-Pacific Economic Cooperation (APEC) in the early 1990s was supported by Indonesia, despite initial concerns about it sidelining ASEAN, as it could be used to 'project the Indonesian leadership position' (Suryadinata 1996, 179). In the same vein the ASEAN Regional Forum was supported, despite initial concerns about giving too big a role to external powers in Southeast Asia, as it was centred on ASEAN, 'which quelled Indonesian fears of being marginalized' (Vatikiotis 1995, 226). However, the Malaysian-proposed East Asia Economic Group, which excluded both the United States and Australia, was opposed when Malaysia failed to consult with, and therefore, show deference to Indonesia's leadership (Vatikiotis 1995, 226). After the Asian Financial Crisis, Malaysia again proposed another exclusive East Asian grouping – the East Asian Community, which would comprised the ASEAN plus the three East Asian economies of Japan, China and South Korea (ASEAN+3). Indonesia resisted this approach preferring the broader East Asia Summit (EAS), which expanded to include India, Australia and New Zealand in 2005 and later the United States and Russia in 2011. Jakarta was worried that 'Chinese dominance in the ASEAN+3 did not make for a stable regional order in East Asia' (Tan 2015, 294). Crucially for Indonesia, the EAS was ASEAN-led and dominated by no one.

The commitment to ASEAN, however, has frayed in recent years as Indonesia's democracy has consolidated and its economy strengthened. In 2009, then Executive Director of the Centre for Strategic and International Studies (Jakarta) Rizal Sukma wrote that Indonesia needed a 'post-ASEAN foreign policy'. Sukma (2009) argued 'ASEAN should no longer be treated as the only cornerstone of Indonesia's foreign policy . . . ASEAN should constitute only one of the available platforms through which we can attain and fulfill [sic] our national interests.' Indonesia's post-ASEAN discourse is driven by changing geopolitical dynamics and a new-found confidence and assertiveness. These have exacerbated the twin dynamics of Indonesian foreign policy in which there is a new sense of vulnerability and a new determination to meet its long-held leadership aspirations. What this is not, however, is a rejection of regionalism. As Evelyn Goh (2015, 8) argues, 'the post-ASEAN argument is more an argument for going beyond ASEAN *centrality*, not ASEAN per se' (italics in original). Geopolitical changes rather than foreign policy changes have precipitated the rise of the Indo-Pacific in Indonesia's strategic thinking.

Indonesia's changing geopolitical landscape

While Indonesia has continually pursued both strategic independence and regional leadership, it has also been consistently responsive to geopolitical change. The consideration of the Indo-Pacific concept in Indonesian foreign policy is an updated response to its new strategic environment. Perceptions of Indonesia's changing geopolitical landscape have always prompted new strategic concepts in Jakarta from the burgeoning Cold War to the current Sino-American rivalry, the first instance of which was Hatta's metaphor *mendayung antara dua karang* (rowing between two reefs). As prime minister, in 1948 he argued:

> Should the Indonesian people who are fighting for their independence choose between the pro-Soviet and pro-American stand? Can we have any other stand in pursuit of our goal?
> (Quoted in Suryadinata 1996, 25)

He continued:

> The policy of the Republic of Indonesia must be resolved in the light of its own interests and should be executed in consonance with the situations and facts it has to face . . . The line of Indonesia's policy cannot be determined by the bent of the policy of some other country which has *its* own interests to service.
> (Quoted in Hatta 1953, 446, italics in original)

Hatta and subsequent leaders during the parliamentary democracy era (1949–1957) pursued a policy of geopolitical nonalignment, although not neutrality, between the major powers.

President Sukarno's annulment of parliamentary democracy and autocratic rule during the Guided Democracy period (1957–1966) was characterised by the concept of NEFOS versus OLDEFOS (New Emerging Forces versus Old Established Forces). Sukarno saw an Indonesia that was dominated by Western influence and imperialism, and as Weinstein states Sukarno's 'anti-imperialist ideology clearly predisposed him toward policies emphasizing independence' (Weinstein 1976, 296). The geopolitics of imperialism was perceived by Sukarno to be the greatest threat to an independent-active foreign policy, as opposed to the superpower rivalry of the Cold War. Sukarno declared at the first conference on the Non-Aligned Movement in 1961:

> There is a conflict which cuts deeper into the flesh of man, and that is the conflict between the new emergent forces for freedom and justice and the old forces of domination.
> (Quoted in Leifer 1983, 58)

Sukarno thought Indonesia's interests were best served through a global internationalist struggle; this was almost completely reversed by the Suharto regime that took power from President Sukarno in 1966.

The New Order regime (1966–1998) of President Suharto instead reframed Indonesia's geopolitics in terms of the concept of the *mandala* or 'concentric circles'. Under the concentric circles doctrine, Indonesia would order its priorities in spatial terms: Southeast Asia would take priority and constitute the first circle, East Asia would form the second circle and the Asia-Pacific would be the final and least important circle (Anwar 2014). Indonesia's regionalist foreign policy since the mid-1960s is at least partially a product of the geopolitical reframing of the New Order. Suharto's foreign policy stressed the idea of 'national resilience' and later 'regional resilience'. For the New Order government, regional security was addressed through 'regional resilience . . . a consolidation of the national resilience of every domestic regional actor' (Sebastian 2006, 18). Under Indonesia's leadership, regional resilience was formally adopted by ASEAN in 1976 and became the central component of the organisation's preferred model of relations: the Treaty of Amity and Cooperation (Anwar 1994, 178).

The end of the Cold War saw critical changes in an expanded Asia-Pacific region for Indonesia, namely the re-emergence of China, concerns over the continuation of the US security role and the appearance of India as a potential major power. Indonesia's initial response to this was a complex hedging strategy shared with other Southeast Asian states (see Goh 2005). With the fall of Suharto in 1998 and the advent of *reformasi*, Indonesia went through a period of weakness and inwardness with a succession of short-lived presidents: B.J. Habibie, Abdurrahman Wahid and Megawati Sukarnoputri. This ended with the arrival of Indonesia's first directly elected president Susilo Bambang Yudhoyono (2004–2014), colloquially known as SBY. In his first foreign policy speech after being inaugurated, the freshly elected SBY suggested the metaphor of 'navigating a turbulent ocean' as a revision of Hatta's Cold War-era metaphor (Yudhoyono 2005, 386). SBY identified that Indonesia faced new geopolitical challenges in a transformed post-Cold War world. His foreign minister Marty Natalegawa expressed a similar sentiment in 2010 when he stated:

> Nowadays we think the world today is no longer a world of two reefs but it's of multiple reefs. We have so many; it's a very multi-polar world, with different kind of challenges, no longer East and West.
>
> (Natalegawa 2010)

President SBY's response was for Indonesia to follow a policy of diversification, having a broad range of economic and security partners to avoid reliance on any one. Upon winning a second term in office, the president developed his ideas further, declaring that Indonesia was to have an 'all directions' foreign policy of 'a million friends and zero enemies' (Yudhoyono 2009). Natalegawa (2010) added to this with his 'dynamic equilibrium' doctrine, in which he stated that Indonesia

Indonesia's new geopolitics 81

seeks a region 'where not one country is preponderant . . . we wish to see inclusivity, more countries, the merrier'.

The most recent expansion of the region's geopolitics – the Indo-Pacific – has similarly seen Indonesia respond with the development of new strategic doctrine. Natalegawa argued that his dynamic equilibrium idea should be applied to the Indo-Pacific. The foreign minister declared his preference for an Indo-Pacific

> marked by an absence of preponderant power not through the rigidity, rivalry and tensions common to the pursuit of a balance of power model. Instead, through the promotion of a sense of common responsibility in the endeavor to maintain the region's peace and stability.
>
> (Natalegawa 2013)

The normative and multilateral approaches of the SBY/Natalegawa era have met with rejection by the new government of Joko Widodo, which has sought to replace the previous diversification approach with the more self-interested notion of *pro-rakyat* (pro-people) or *diplomasi membumi* (down-to-earth diplomacy). New foreign minister Retno Marsudi (Quoted in Wardhy 2014) stated soon after Jokowi's inauguration in a clear repudiation of the SBY era that 'Indonesia's foreign policy must be down-to-earth; it should not be detached from the people's interests . . . Therefore, the kind of diplomacy that the Foreign Ministry will do is a pro-people diplomacy, diplomacy for the people.' For the new government, an expanded Indo-Pacific region that includes a rising India is seen as a new reality for Indonesia and both a challenge and an opportunity for the pursuit of its regionalist foreign policy. In the most recent update of Indonesia's geopolitical thinking, Rizal Sukma (2014, 2015), a former key advisor to President Jokowi, has stated that in his view Indonesia is now *berlayar di dua samudera* (sailing in two oceans). The idea behind which is that Indonesia is geographically central to the Indo-Pacific and must orient its foreign policy as such. Therefore, the new government's *poros maritim dunia* (global maritime fulcrum) doctrine sets a list of five 'pillars' spanning the sociocultural, economic and geostrategic fields (Widodo 2014a).[4] The new policy aims to 'rebuild the country's maritime culture and expand its economy' in addition to projecting 'Indonesia to become a maritime power with considerable diplomatic influence' (Gindarsah and Priamarizki 2015b, 2). Indonesia has responded to the new regional environment of the Indo-Pacific, as it has with previous geopolitical changes, by creating new doctrines to manage the risks and opportunities inherent within them; as the broadest conception yet, the Indo-Pacific offers a uniquely challenging set of dynamics in which Indonesia must pursue its interests.

Indonesia's interests in the Indo-Pacific

The concept of an expanded Indo-Pacific region has been promoted in Indonesia, as it offers Jakarta a new way to pursue the goals of its regionalist foreign policy and pursue the developmental goals of respective governments. Given the intensifying competition among the major powers in the Asian theatre and the increasing divisions plaguing ASEAN, Indonesia has much to gain from a broadened concept of its region. Indonesia has promoted the Indo-Pacific as it offers Jakarta an opportunity to focus on, in Sukma's (2014) words, the 'expansion [of] its space of engagement'. First, Indonesia's sense of vulnerability and need to reassert its independence has once again come to the fore as the major powers have expressed an increasing interest in Indonesia and its immediate region. This sense of vulnerability is exacerbated by the increasingly obvious failure of ASEAN to manage Southeast Asia's relations with the great powers, most notably in its failure to release a joint communiqué during Cambodia's Chair in 2012 over the territorial disputes of some members with China in the South China Sea (SCS) (Acharya 2015, 57). The intensifying involvement of the region's two major powers, the United States and China, has had implications for Indonesia's security at both the national and regional levels. Beijing's new-found assertiveness since 2009, marking an end to China's 'Charm Diplomacy', concerns Indonesia as its SCS claims overlap with the Exclusive Economic Zone (EEZ) and the promising D-Alpha gas block of the Natuna Islands of Riau province (Weatherbee 2013, 86). Weatherbee (2013, 78) asserts that within the region China's behaviour has begun to shred ASEAN unity between those states more friendly to Beijing Cambodia and Laos on one side and those states more hostile to Beijing Vietnam and the Philippines on the other.

Washington has responded in turn with the announcement of its 'pivot to Asia' in 2011, indicating a new willingness to be directly involved in regional affairs (Obama 2011). The previous year Secretary of State Hillary Clinton declared in Hanoi that the United States has 'a national interest in freedom of navigation, open access to Asia's maritime commons and respect for international law in the South China Sea' (Clinton 2010). And just this year at Asia's premier security conference – the Shangri-La Dialogue – Defense Secretary Ashton Carter (2015) directly criticised China for its land reclamation activities in the SCS and declared, 'the United States will fly, sail, and operate wherever international law allows.' In addition to this, US ally Australia has agreed to host a rotation of US Marines in the northern Australian port city of Darwin, close to its border with Indonesia. The behaviour of both Beijing and Washington has been a source of concern in Jakarta. In a warning to both powers, General Moeldoko (2014), commander of the *Tentara Nasional Indonesia* (TNI; the Indonesian National Armed Forces), wrote in a piece for the *Wall Street Journal* that 'Southeast Asian countries would not welcome the appearance of a sphere of influence in the region tied to the military rise and leadership aspirations of any country.' Natalegawa (Quoted in McDonnell and Brown 2011) had already expressed, in response to the Darwin announcement: 'What I would hate to see is if such developments were to provoke a reaction and counter-reaction precisely to create that vicious circle of tensions and mistrust or distrust'. For Indonesian strategic thinkers, an expanded Indo-Pacific which brings India into the region adds a positive source stability to the regional balance of power. This is because Indonesia has long held benign views of India (Novotny 2010, 279–281). As Gindarsah and Priamarizki (2015b, 13) state, Indonesia's engagement with Indian Ocean powers on security

Indonesia's new geopolitics 83

matters is done 'with a view to balance the U.S. pivot position and the growing power of China'. Balancing Chinese influence was a core rationale behind Indonesia's determination and crucial support to include India in the East Asia Summit (Storey 2011, 207).

Second, the proposal of an Indo-Pacific region has emerged at a time in which Indonesia's traditional method of leadership – ASEAN – has begun to fracture, and with it, its prized role as a mediator of regional issues. The Indo-Pacific proposal may offer Indonesia an opportunity to play a role in any new regional architecture, given its status in Southeast Asia. Including the Indian Ocean in Indonesia's area of interest is seen as a potential new avenue for regional leadership. Awidya Santikajaya (2014) has suggested such a role for Indonesia, noting its historic leadership role in ASEAN as well as the dearth of regional institutions in the region. Under Jokowi's new government, Indonesia has set the Indian Ocean Rim Association (IORA) – of which it assumed leadership in 2015 – as a foreign policy priority (Marsudi 2015). Another aspect of Indonesia's sense of regional entitlement has been its 'urge to mediate in regional disputes' (Vatikiotis 1995, 231). Indonesia has a long role in mediating regional issues in Southeast Asia, from the Malaysia-Philippines dispute over Sabah in 1968 to the more recent Preah Vihear temple conflict between Thailand and Cambodia in 2011 and the ASEAN crisis of 2012 (Widyaningsih and Roberts 2015, 264–286). The South China Sea is critical in this, and Greta Nabbs-Keller (2014b, 14) has argued that 'Indonesia's regional leadership and national prestige is invested in its mediation role between Beijing and the four ASEAN claimant states.' This is perhaps why Indonesia's foreign ministry is loath to declare that is has a potential territorial dispute with China, where the EEZ of its Natuna Islands overlaps China's 'nine-dashed line' that SCS claims and what has been called Indonesia's 'invisible border' (Arsana and Schofield 2012, 19–36). Mediation is a key part of both Indonesia's aspired regional and global leadership roles. Beyond its immediate region Indonesia has sought to play a mediating role between the Islamic world and the West, with President SBY reportedly offering to mediate between Iran and Western states (BBC 2006). It is highly likely that Indonesia will seek to renew both its leadership as a facilitator of regional cooperation and as a mediator in the Indo-Pacific when and where territorial disputes and potential conflicts arise.

Finally, an extended region also serves Indonesia's developmental interests, which require significant amounts of investment beyond what can be offered by any one partner. Jokowi's plan to develop Indonesia into a global maritime fulcrum should be understood first as 'an overarching development doctrine, which seeks to augment Indonesia's prosperity and welfare through economic development of the maritime domain' (Nabbs-Keller 2014b, 5). As the quintessential Indo-Pacific state, the new regional concept elevates Indonesia's role in a potentially advantageous central position. Indonesia recognises that the broadened region places Indonesia in the centre of 'an area encompassing some of the most dynamic economies in the world' (Natalegawa 2013). While Indonesia is deeply concerned about the effects of conflict between the major powers in the region, it is supportive of them competing economically, recognising the potential benefits for Indonesia. President Yudhoyono (2012) encouraged this dynamic, stating that while once Southeast Asia was torn by superpower conflict, 'today, extra-regional powers compete for more trade, investment exchanges and education . . . It is a good thing – we like it and we welcome it.' As such Indonesia welcomes trade competition from as many states as possible. The new government of Jokowi has identified foreign investment as a crucial part of achieving the objectives of the global maritime fulcrum plan. Jokowi (2014) himself declared weeks after being inaugurated to the APEC CEO Summit in November that 'we are waiting for you to come to Indonesia. We are waiting for you to invest in Indonesia.' Unsurprisingly then, Jokowi's first bilateral overseas visits were to Japan and immediately followed by China, the two states seen as the leading sources of foreign investment (Sentana 2015). It has been suggested that Indonesia is now playing China and Japan off against each other as a way to maximise their investment potential (Brummitt 2015). Indonesia has also identified the Indian Ocean region and the IORA as having perspective developmental benefits, supporting its global maritime fulcrum plan (Saragih 2015). Indonesia has important economic interests in the region such as oil imports from the Middle East and coal exports to India (Supriyanto 2013, 221). However, neither India nor the Indian Ocean has yet to factor strongly in Indonesia's developmental plans, which have to date focussed on the two big East Asian economies: China and Japan.

Fundamentally, Jakarta's geopolitical outlook remains focussed on the Pacific Ocean, and the Indian Ocean only really factors in when the risk of the strategic rivalries of the Pacific spreading to the Indian Ocean is raised.[5] This is not a wholly new concern in Jakarta; as early as 2012, President SBY warned at the Shangri-La Dialogue that:

> There is every likelihood that in the twenty-first century the Indian Ocean will grow in geostrategic importance. We must make sure that the Indian Ocean does not become an area of new strategic contest and rivalry.
>
> (Yudhoyono 2012)

Strategic analysts Iis Gindarsah and Adhi Priamarizki (2015a, 133) have identified the potential for India and China to 'engage in maritime competition over the Indian Ocean and South China Sea', as a considerable future strategic challenge for Jakarta. In the event of the Indian Ocean succumbing to the dynamics of the Pacific, Indonesia would be surrounded by the type of great power tensions it has spent its entire independent existence trying to avoid. Although India is an appealing partner to Indonesia in potentially resolving some Pacific security issues, and the Indo-Pacific offers Jakarta a low-risk way to support some of the aspirations of its regionalist foreign policy, talk of Indonesia returning to the two-ocean geography originally espoused by Mohammad Hatta (Shekhar and Liow 2014) has little evidence to date to support it. This may change now that Indonesia has assumed the chair of the IORA, but for now Indonesia's geopolitics remain focussed on the Pacific, with the South China Sea perceived as the primary strategic concern.

Indonesia's Indo-Pacific discourse

The chapter now turns to the discourse, or lack of it, about the Indo-Pacific concept in Indonesia. It is worth noting that Indonesia's foreign policy has long been driven by the elite (for examples see Weinstein 1976; Novotny 2010; Bower 2011). Despite the re-emergence of democracy in Indonesia since 1999, 'foreign policy decision-making largely remains the prerogative of a relatively small elite group' (Novotny 2010, 63). As a result the public discourse on the Indo-Pacific has been limited to a handful of academics and think-tankers. Natalegawa's (2013) proposal of an 'Indo-Pacific wide treaty of friendship and cooperation' received some limited attention. Rizal Sukma (2013), in his capacity as executive director of the Centre for Strategic and International Studies (Jakarta), commented that the proposal would be useful as a starting point to discuss the regional security dilemma, but overall was lacking in detail. Professor Bantarto Bandoro (2013, 6) of the Indonesia Defence University sounded a similar note, but added a more sceptical tone: 'there is no guarantee that these powers [US, Japan, China] will behave as Indonesia expects nor does Indonesia have the capacity to dictate their strategic direction.' The difficulty of getting China on board, given Chinese intransigence over ASEAN's attempts to negotiate a code of conduct in the South China Sea, was also a consistent concern (see for example Jemadu quoted in Khalik and Aswim 2013; Handoyo 2014). Former diplomat Awidya Santikajaya (2013) raised concerns over ASEAN's consistency and clarity, arguing 'in this current age of uncertain geopolitical change, ASEAN has to become more cohesive, relevant and effective if Southeast Asian nations do not want to become objects of competition for influence among major powers.' The lack of response to Natalegawa's contribution can be interpreted as the widespread view that it did not represent a serious reorientation of Indonesia's foreign policy focus.

The Indo-Pacific did not make its re-emergence a strategic concept until May 2014, with the release of then Jakarta Governor Jokowi's election manifesto and its four foreign policy priorities, which included expanding Indonesia's regional engagement in the Indo-Pacific (Jokowi 2014, 12–14).[6] The foreign policy section of the governor's election manifesto, as well as his preparations in the foreign policy debate, were led by Rizal Sukma, one of the academics that had criticised Natalegawa's (2013) proposal and described as having 'the ear of the President' (Connelly 2015, 11). However, the Indo-Pacific region has not been the recipient of much attention since then, except in the speeches of Sukma, when presidential advisor on foreign policy. This may be largely a result of the intense focus on the global maritime fulcrum doctrine and its implications for the future of Indonesia's foreign policy. For example, Indonesia's strategic orientation was never even brought up in the 2014 presidential elections between Governor Jokowi and former-Kopassus Commander Prabowo Subianto, even with a presidential debate focussed on foreign policy (Sulaiman 2014). Moreover a 450-page English-language book on Indonesia's strategic future, *Toward 2014–2019: Strengthening Indonesia in A Changing World*, published by the *Badan Intelijen Negara* (Indonesian State Intelligence Agency) refers to Indo-Pacific only once in reference to the strengthening security relationship between Australia and the United States (Hikam 2014). The reason for the lack of engagement with the Indo-Pacific as an idea has been suggested to the author as being due to the relative lack of seriousness of the proposals themselves. To the extent they reveal anything, it is Indonesia's concerns about the regional security implications of the SCS disputes.[7]

Indonesia's strategic outlook is dominated by the disputes in the SCS, as nothing threatens Indonesia regional interests as much as the conflict between China and the other claimant states in Southeast Asia – Vietnam, the Philippines, Malaysia and Brunei – and increasingly the United States and its partners. It is no surprise then that there has been far more written on this prominent, ongoing security issue than the Indo-Pacific. The debate in Indonesia over the SCS splits along both institutional and ideological lines. As Greta Nabbs-Keller (2014a) argues, the debate is often between the TNI, which 'like all militaries, is essentially realist in orientation', and *Kemlu* (*Kementerian Luar Negeri*, the Ministry of Foreign Affairs) which 'is more liberal-institutionalist in inclination'. Diplomat Arif Havas Oegroseno (2014) gives a typical *Kemlu* position, describing arguments that Indonesia has a territorial dispute with China in the SCS as 'laughable' in terms of international law. Rejecting the validity of China's claims under its 'nine-dashed line', Oegroseno states 'as a matter of law, fact and logic make it simply unfathomable that Indonesia would start overlaying its highly precise and legally correct work with an incomplete, inaccurate, inconsistent and legally problematic map.' This contrasts starkly with the realpolitik view of General Moeldoko (2014), who states that 'China has included parts of the Natuna Islands within the nine-dashed line, thus apparently claiming a segment of Indonesia's Riau Islands province as its territory.' The failure of ASEAN to address these issues has led one commentator to suggest that Natalegawa's 2013 proposal for an Indo-Pacific-wide treaty of friendship and cooperation was an attempt to bring the disputes to a 'new, higher layer' (Weatherbee 2013, 81). This sentiment was echoed by Jusuf Wanandi (Quoted in Amirio 2015) at the recent Foreign Policy Community of Indonesia conference: 'The East Asian Summit, for example, should be a platform for resolution, but ASEAN has yet to make full use of it. It should be the main architect of regional security.' Although never officially stated, the Indo-Pacific is seen as offering an alternate way for Jakarta to address an essentially Pacific Ocean security question – the SCS disputes – but for it to work Indonesia requires an inclusive concept of the region that must accommodate all regional powers.

Conclusion: the implications of Indonesia's new geopolitics

This chapter has explored the relationship between Indonesia's long-held regionalist foreign policy and Indonesia's burgeoning response to the concept of an expanded Indo-Pacific region. I have argued that Indonesia's approach to regional affairs has been driven by a need to address both a sense of its own vulnerability through asserting its strategic independence and an aspiration for regional leadership through taking an activist role in the development and promotion of regional architecture, as was asserted by Michael Leifer in 1983. I have argued that the Indo-Pacific will be embraced or rejected by Indonesia primarily on these criteria. This chapter has shown that Indonesia has been historically very geopolitically responsive and that its foreign policy approach to regional questions is not static but pragmatic. It has identified Indonesia's interests in the Indo-Pacific in meeting the requirements of its regionalist foreign policy as well as meeting the developmental goals of successive governments. The chapter then identified the weak and elite-driven debate over the Indo-Pacific in Indonesia and the importance of the SCS in understanding Indonesian geopolitical thinking.

Facing an increasingly complex and dangerous geostrategic environment, Indonesia seeks to maintain its strategic independence, promote itself as a leader and pursue its developmental agenda. A new regional order led by the Indo-Pacific Rim democracies and aimed at containing the re-emergence of China will not be acceptable to Jakarta. Indonesia has shown no desire to join an alliance of democracies, despite its democratisation agenda within ASEAN. Indonesia has been a far greater projector of democracy than promoter of it, which boosts its regional leadership stocks in the eyes of many (Sukma 2011, 110–123). The idea that Indonesia should join the club of regional democracies, as has been expounded by envoys like former Ambassador to Indonesia Paul Wolfowitz, is unlikely to materialise (Bakrie 2013). As Donald E. Weatherbee (2013, 27) has noted, while Indonesia has joined groups like the American-led Community of Democracies it has maintained its distance, displaying a 'reluctance to fully engage with a proactive American lead in the organization'. While the United States has been very supportive of the developmental agenda of the global maritime fulcrum doctrine; US Ambassador to Jakarta Robert Blake stated, 'we stand ready to boost maritime collaboration, to complement the vision of President Jokowi' (Blake quoted in Nelson and Sulaiman 2015). This is not nearly as attractive as managed competition between the regional major powers. It is difficult to see how the Indo-Pacific in the form currently being promoted in some quarters can meet Jakarta's foreign policy requirements.

Importantly, Indonesia's conception of the region would not exclude China. Although Indonesia is concerned about China's actions in the SCS, it does not want to see it ostracized for fear that it would merely exacerbate existing insecurities, turning China further away from pursuing the multilateral resolution Indonesia desires.[8] Indonesian elites are aware of the 'security dilemma' China faces from the US presence in the region and its harmful effect on both regional security and ASEAN unity (Gindarsah and Priamarizki 2015a, 137). Indonesia also needs Chinese investment to meet its developmental goals. As such, the Jokowi government has been cautious towards China; for example, in its first six months it refrained from destroying any Chinese vessels as part of its assertive anti-illegal fishing policy (*Economist* 2015). When it did finally sink a Chinese boat, after previously indicating that it would, the vessel in question was one that had been detained since 2009 (*Rappler.com* 2015). This approach was favoured by Jokowi's 'realist' advisors like Sukma and former Cabinet Secretary Andi Widjajanto who have no confidence in a normative approach to resolving regional issues and see close relations with China as Indonesia's best bet.[9] China likewise has courted good relations with Indonesia; in a renewed charm offensive President Xi Jinping chose the Indonesian legislature to announce China's Maritime Silk Road initiative, which has been well received in Indonesia, especially under the leadership of Jokowi (Wu and Zhang 2013). Indonesia's inclusive regionalist foreign policy precludes the exclusion of China, as Jakarta wishes to both manage regional tensions and project its leadership of the region as a whole.

What this means for the future of ASEAN is that it is increasingly seen by policy makers in Jakarta to no longer meet the requirements of Indonesia's regionalist foreign policy. ASEAN is currently struggling to manage itself, let alone the region, and it no longer befits Indonesia's stature as a potential major power. As Weatherbee (2013, 8) argued, 'its utility as an instrument of Indonesian foreign policy has diminished.' But Indonesia does not face a binary choice between ASEAN and alternative regional architecture; Indonesian foreign policy has never been focussed on ASEAN 'to the exclusion of other pathways and pillars' (Tan 2015, 297). As recently as 1999, under the admittedly erratic leadership of Abdurrahman Wahid, Indonesia proposed that ASEAN be replaced with a West Pacific Forum centred on Indonesia, Malaysia and the Philippines, when Singapore failed to support Indonesia's proposal for Timor Leste's accession to the grouping (Widyaningsih and Roberts 2015, 277). Even the bilateral turn in Jakarta's policies in the last few years, with Indonesia signing a raft of 'strategic partnerships' with regional powers, is aimed at achieving the objectives outlined in the regionalist foreign policy this chapter identifies (Gindarsah and Priamarizki 2015a, 138). ASEAN no longer meets these needs and as a result has been demoted rather than abandoned. As Rizal Sukma (2014) has said, 'we used to say ASEAN is *the* cornerstone of our foreign policy, now we change it to *a* cornerstone of our foreign policy' (emphasis added).

All of this informs Indonesia's fundamental unease at some of the core regional security dynamics, in which the Indo-Pacific regional construct proposed by the rim democracies is seen as another potential source of concern. The prospect of a region that is no longer centred on Indonesia's interests and aspirations is a cause for deep anxiety among Indonesian policy makers, as both the concepts of 'pacific' Indo-Pacific and PACINDO are indicative. On the other hand, Jakarta can be relatively confident that no realistic Indo-Pacific architecture can work without the inclusion of the quintessential Indo-Pacific state, Indonesia. Jakarta promotes its conception of the Indo-Pacific as a way to 'reassert its position as the diplomatic hub of the two vast maritime regions' (Gindarsah and Priamarizki 2015a, 138). Any alternative regional architecture that is to include Indonesia must be willing to satisfy the twin objectives of its regionalist foreign policy: it cannot jeopardise regional stability nor demote Indonesia's core role, for as anyone with a map can clearly see, without the Indonesian archipelago there can be no Indo-Pacific.

Notes

1 The author would like to thank the following individuals, who read and commented on drafts of this chapter: Associate Professor Michael Barr, Emily Bienvenue, Dr. Priya Chacko and Dr. Maryanne Kelton.
2 See also Dewi Fortuna Anwar, 'A Problem of Mixed Messages', *Asialink Essay*, August 2012 (http://asialink.unimelb.edu.au/asialink_diplomacy/commentary-and-research/

the_asialink_essays/past/a_problem_of_mixed_messages) for an Indonesian perspective on the same idea.
3 The Indonesian word *poros* has been variously translated as 'nexus', 'axis' and 'pivot'. Former Presidential Advisor on Foreign Policy Rizal Sukma makes clear in his speech to the United States–Indonesia Society in 2014 that the correct translation is 'fulcrum' – the 'point of support where the burden of the two oceans actually rest'. See Sukma (2014), *Speech on Panel: Indonesia's Foreign Policy and Security Issues: Continuity, Evolution, or Change?*, The Jokowi Administration: Prospects for Indonesia's Economic Development, Democratic Governance, and International Engagement, Washington, DC, 11 December, https://vimeo.com/115271536.
4 The five pillars of the global maritime fulcrum are: rebuilding Indonesia's maritime culture; guarding Indonesia's marine resources and building marine food sovereignty; prioritising the development of infrastructure and maritime connectivity; cooperating in the maritime field; and becoming a fulcrum of the two oceans (Indian and Pacific) and establishing a maritime defence force.
5 I am indebted to Priya Chacko for pointing this out.
6 The four priorities outlined are: promoting Indonesia as an archipelagic state; increasing Indonesia's global role through middle-power diplomacy; expanding Indonesia's regional engagement in the Indo-Pacific; and formulating and implementing foreign policy which engages the character, aspirations and interests of the people.
7 Email correspondence with a former Indonesian diplomat, 21 June 2015.
8 Email correspondence with a former Indonesian diplomat, 21 June 2015.
9 Email correspondence with a former Indonesian diplomat, 6 July 2015.

References

Acharya, Amitav. 2009. *Whose Ideas Matter?: Agency and Power in Asian Regionalism*, Ithaca, NY: Cornell University Press.

Acharya, Amitav. 2012. *The Making of Southeast Asia: International Relations of a Region*, Singapore: Institute of Southeast Asian Studies.

Acharya, Amitav. 2015. *Indonesia Matters: Asia's Emerging Democratic Power*, Singapore: World Scientific.

Amirio, Dylan. 2015. 'RI Can Play More Decisive Role in South China Sea Conflict: Experts', *Jakarta Post*, 15 June, http://www.thejakartapost.com/news/2015/06/15/ri-can-play-more-decisive-role-south-china-sea-conflict-experts.html (accessed 15 June 2015).

Anwar, Dewi Fortuna. 1994. *Indonesia in ASEAN: Foreign Policy and Regionalism*, Singapore: Institute of Southeast Asian Studies.

Anwar, Dewi Fortuna. 2003. 'Key Aspects of Indonesia's Foreign Policy', in *Indonesia: Foreign Policy and Domestic Politics*, edited by Dewi Fortuna Anwar and Harold Crouch, Trends in Southeast Asia, no. 9. Singapore: Institute of Southeast Asian Studies, pp. 1–10.

Anwar, Dewi Fortuna. 2008. 'Indonesia and the Bandung Conference: Then and Now', in *Bandung Revisited: The Legacy of the 1955 Asian-African Conference for International Order*, edited by See Seng Tan and Amitav Acharya. Singapore: NUS Press, pp. 180–197.

Anwar, Dewi Fortuna. 2014. 'Indonesia's Foreign Relations: Policy Shaped by the Ideal of "Dynamic Equilibrium"', *East Asia Forum*, 4 February, http://www.eastasiaforum.org/2014/02/04/indonesias-foreign-relations-policy-shaped-by-the-ideal-of-dynamic-equilibrium/ (accessed 15 June 2015).

Arsana, I., Made Andi, and Clive Schofield. 2012. 'Indonesia's "Invisible" Border With China', in *Beijing's Power and China's Borders: Twenty Neighbors in Asia*, edited by Bruce A. Elleman, Stephen Kotkin and Clive Schofield, Armonk, NY: M. E. Sharpe, pp. 19–36.

Bakrie, Connie Rahakundini. 2013. 'US Pivot: The Future of the Indo-Pacific (Part 2 of 2)', *Jakarta Post*, 13 September, http://www.thejakartapost.com/news/2013/09/13/us-pivot-the-future-indo-pacific-part-2-2.html (accessed 15 June 2015).
Bandoro, Bantarto. 2013. 'Will Good Intentions in Indonesia's Blueprint for Asia-Pacific Security Collide With Harsh Realities?', *ISEAS Perspectives* 54, 3 October.
BBC News. (2006). 'Indonesia Offers Iran Mediation', *BBC News*, 10 May, http://news.bbc.co.uk/2/hi/asia-pacific/4756757.stm
Bower, Ernest Z. 2011. 'Great, But Unfocused: Indonesian Assessments of U.S. Power', in *Capacity and Resolve: Foreign Assessments of U.S. Power*, edited by D. Cohen, Center for Strategic and International Studies, June, pp. 44–45. http://csis.org/files/publication/110613_Cohen_CapacityResolve_Web.pdf
Bremmer, Ian. 2012. *Every Nation for Itself: Winners and Losers in a G-Zero World*, New York: Portfolio/Penguin.
Brummitt, Chris. 2015. 'Desperate for Investment, Indonesia Plays China vs. Japan', *Bloomberg Business*, 20 May, http://www.bloomberg.com/news/articles/2015-05-19/desperate-for-investment-indonesia-plays-china-vs-japan (accessed 15 June 2015).
Carter, Ashton. 2015. 'The United States and Challenges of Asia-Pacific Security: Ashton Carter', IISS Shangri-La Dialogue 2015, First Plenary Session, Singapore, 30 May, https://www.iiss.org/en/events/shangri%20la%20dialogue/archive/shangri-la-dialogue-2015-862b/plenary1-976e/carter-7fa0 (accessed 2 July 2015).
Clinton, Hillary. 2010. 'Comments by Secretary Clinton in Hanoi, Vietnam', National Convention Center, 23 July, http://iipdigital.usembassy.gov/st/english/texttrans/2010/07/20100723164658su0.4912989.html#axzz3j84W44qS (accessed 15 June 2015).
Connelly, Aaron L. 2015. 'Sovereignty and the Sea: President Joko Widodo's Foreign Policy Challenges', *Contemporary Southeast Asia* 37:1, 1–28.
Djalal, Dino Patti. 1990. *Geopolitical Concepts and Maritime Territorial Behavior in Indonesian Foreign Policy*, Master of Arts Thesis, Simon Fraser University, Burnaby, BC.
Djalal, Dino Patti. 2012. 'An Independent, Active and Creative Foreign Policy for Indonesia', *Strategic Review*, 2:1, January–March.
Economist. 2015. 'A Thousand Jilted Friends', *Economist*, 2 May, http://www.economist.com/news/asia/21650173-new-president-charts-markedly-different-course-thousand-jilted-friends (accessed 15 June 2015).
Gindarsah, Iis, and Adhi Priamarizki. 2015a. 'Politics, Security and Defense in Indonesia: The Pursuit of Strategic Autonomy', in *Indonesia's Ascent: Power, Leadership and the Regional Order*, edited by Christopher B. Roberts, Ahmad D. Habir, and Leonard C. Sebastian, Basingstoke: Palgrave Macmillan, pp. 130–154.
Gindarsah, Iis, and Adhi Priamarizki. 2015b. *Indonesia's Maritime Doctrine and Security Concerns*, RSIS Policy Report, 9 April.
Goh, Evelyn. 2005. 'Meeting the China Challenge: The U.S. in Southeast Asian Regional Security Strategies', Policy Studies 16, East-West Center, Washington, DC.
Goh, Evelyn. 2015. 'Indonesia's New Strategic Policy Under Jokowi: Change, Continuity, and Challenges', in *A Strategy Towards Indonesia*, edited by Andrew Carr. Centre of Gravity Series, ANU Strategic and Defence Studies Centre, May, pp. 4–9. http://ips.cap.anu.edu.au/sites/default/files/COG%20%2320%20Web.pdf
Handoyo, Wiryono Sastro. 2014. 'Befriending China Through Cultural Soft Power (Part 2 of 2)', *Jakarta Post*, 20 June, http://www.thejakartapost.com/news/2014/06/20/befriending-china-through-cultural-soft-power-part-2-2.html (accessed 15 June 2015).
Hatta, Mohammad. 1953. 'Indonesia's Foreign Policy', *Foreign Affairs* (April), 441–452.

Indonesia's new geopolitics 91

Hikam, Muhammad A. S. Ed. 2014. *Toward 2014–2019: Strengthening Indonesia in a Changing World*, cv. rumah buku, Jakarta.

Jokowi, Jusuf Kalla. 2014. *Jalan Perubahan Untuk Indonesia yang Berdaulat, Mandiri dan Berkepribadian, Visi Misi, dan Program Aksi*, Jakarta, May, http://kpu.go.id/koleksigambar/VISI_MISI_Jokowi-JK.pdf (accessed 15 June 2015).

Khalik, Abdul, and Dessy Aswim. 2013. 'Marty Urges Treaty to Ward Off Indo-Pacific Conflict', *Jakarta Globe*, 2 August, http://jakartaglobe.beritasatu.com/news/marty-urges-treaty-to-ward-off-indo-pacific-conflict/ (accessed 15 June 2015).

Leifer, Michael. 1983. *Indonesia's Foreign Policy*, London: Allen & Unwin.

Marsudi, Retno L. 2015. 'Annual Address', Ministry of Foreign Affairs of the Republic of Indonesia, Jakarta, 8 January, http://www.kemlu.go.id/Documents/PPTM%202015/PPTM%202015%20ENG%20FINAL%20PDF.pdf (accessed 15 June 2015).

McDonnell, Stephen, and Helen Brown. 2011. 'China, Indonesia Wary of US Troops in Darwin', *ABC News*, 17 November, http://www.abc.net.au/news/2011-11-17/china-indonesia-wary-of-us-troops-in-darwin/3675866 (accessed 15 June 2015).

Moeldoko. 2014. 'China's Dismaying New Claims in the South China Sea', *Wall Street Journal*, 24 April, http://www.wsj.com/articles/SB10001424052702304279904579515 69283517224 (accessed 15 June 2015).

Nabbs-Keller, Greta. 2014a. 'Is Indonesia Shifting Its South China Sea Policy?', *Lowy Interpreter*, 16 April, http://www.lowyinterpreter.org/post/2014/04/16/Indonesia-Natuna-shift-south-china-sea-policy.aspx (accessed 15 June 2015).

Nabbs-Keller, Greta. 2014b. 'Strategic Clarity, Political Uncertainty: Prospects for Defence and Security Under President Joko Widodo', in *New Perspectives on Indonesia: Understanding Australia's Closest Asian Neighbour*, 2–24. Perth: Perth USAsia Centre.

Natalegawa, Marty. 2010. 'A Conversation with Marty Natalegawa, Minister of Foreign Affairs, Republic of Indonesia' [transcript], Council of Foreign Relations, 20 September, http://www.cfr.org/indonesia/conversation-marty-natalegawa/p34820 (accessed 15 June 2015).

Natalegawa, Marty. 2013. 'An Indonesian Perspective on the Indo-Pacific Treaty', Keynote Address, Conference on Indonesia, Washington, DC, 16 May, http://csis.org/files/attachments/130516_MartyNatalegawa_Speech.pdf (accessed 15 June 2015).

Nelson, Brad, and Yohanes Sulaiman. 2015. 'The Implications of Jokowi's Global Maritime Axis', *Strategic Review*, April–June, http://www.sr-indonesia.com/in-the-journal/view/the-implications-of-jokowi-s-global-maritime-axis (accessed 15 June 2015).

Novotny, Daniel. 2010. *Torn Between America and China: Elite Perceptions and Indonesian Foreign Policy*, Singapore: Institute of Southeast Asian Studies.

Obama, Barack. 2011. 'Remarks By President Obama to the Australian Parliament', Parliament House, Canberra, 17 November, https://www.whitehouse.gov/the-press-office/2011/11/17/remarks-president-obama-australian-parliament (accessed 15 June 2015).

Oegroseno, Arif Havas. 2014. 'Indonesia, South China Sea and the 11/10/9-Dashed Lines', *Jakarta Post*, 9 April, http://www.thejakartapost.com/news/2014/04/09/indonesia-south-china-sea-and-11109-dashed-lines.html (accessed 15 June 2015).

Parameswaran, Prashanth. 2014. 'Is Indonesia Turning Away From ASEAN Under Jokowi?', *Diplomat*, 18 December, http://thediplomat.com/2014/12/is-indonesia-turning-away-from-asean-under-jokowi/ (accessed 15 June 2015).

Rappler.com. 2015. 'Indonesia Sinks 41 Foreign Boats to Deter Illegal Fishing', *Rappler.com*, 21 May, http://www.rappler.com/world/regions/asia-pacific/indonesia/93918-indonesia-sinks-41-foreign-boats-illegal-fishing (accessed 15 June 2015).

Santikajaya, Awidya. 2013. 'Countries at the Crossroads', *Jakarta Post*, 3 June, http://www.thejakartapost.com/news/2013/06/03/countries-crossroads.html (accessed 15 June 2015).
Santikajaya, Awidya. 2014. 'Indonesia: A Potential Leader in the Indian Ocean', *Diplomat*, 12 December, http://thediplomat.com/2014/12/indonesia-a-potential-leader-in-the-indian-ocean/ (accessed 15 June 2015).
Saragih, Bagus B.T. 2015. 'RI's Maritime Axis to Pivots Westward Through IORA', *Jakarta Post*, 26 February, http://www.thejakartapost.com/news/2015/02/26/ri-s-maritime-axis-pivots-westward-through-iora.html (accessed 15 June 2015).
Sebastian, Leonard C. 2006. *Realpolitik Ideology: Indonesia's Use of Military Force*, Singapore: Institute of Southeast Asian Studies.
Sentana, I. Made. 2015. 'Jokowi to China, Japan: Show Me the Money', *Wall Street Journal*, 22 April, http://blogs.wsj.com/indonesiarealtime/2015/04/22/jokowi-to-china-japan-show-me-the-money/ (accessed 15 June 2015).
Shekhar, Vibhanshu, and Joseph Chinyong Liow. 2014. 'Indonesia as a Maritime Power: Jokowi's Vision, Strategies, and Obstacles Ahead', *Brookings*, November, http://www.brookings.edu/research/articles/2014/11/indonesia-maritime-liow-shekhar (accessed 15 June 2015).
Storey, Ian. (2011). *Southeast Asia and the Rise of China: The Search for Security*, Abingdon: Routledge.
Sukma, Rizal. 2009. 'Indonesia Needs a Post-ASEAN Foreign Policy', *Jakarta Post*, 30 June, http://www.thejakartapost.com/news/2009/06/30/indonesia-needs-a-postasean-foreign-policy.html (accessed 15 June 2015).
Sukma, Rizal. 2011. 'Indonesia Finds a New Voice: Do New Democracies Support Democracy?', *Journal of Democracy* 22:4, 110–123.
Sukma, Rizal. 2013. 'Insight: Friendship and Cooperation the Indo-Pacific: Will a Treaty Help?' *Jakarta Post*, 28 May, http://www.thejakartapost.com/news/2013/05/28/insight-friendship-and-cooperation-indo-pacific-will-a-treaty-help.html (accessed 15 June 2015).
Sukma, Rizal. 2014. 'Speech on Panel: Indonesia's Foreign Policy and Security Issues: Continuity, Evolution, or Change?', Washington, DC: Jokowi Administration: Prospects for Indonesia's Economic Development, Democratic Governance, and International Engagement, 11 December, https://vimeo.com/115271536 (accessed 15 June 2015).
Sukma, Rizal. 2015. 'The Global Maritime Fulcrum and Indonesia's Foreign Policy', Singapore: RSIS Distinguished Public Lecture, 4 March, https://www.youtube.com/watch?v=EG3yurxmst4 (accessed 15 June 2015).
Sulaiman, Yohanes. 2014. 'Foreign Affairs a Stranger to Indonesia's Presidential Hopefuls', *New Mandala*, 23 June, http://asiapacific.anu.edu.au/newmandala/2014/06/23/foreign-affairs-a-stranger-to-indonesias-presidential-hopefuls/ (accessed 15 June 2015).
Supriyanto, Ristian Atriandi. 2013. 'Indonesia and India: Toward a Convergent Mandala', *India Review* 12:3, 207–224.
Suryadinata, Leo. 1996. *Indonesia's Foreign Policy Under Suharto: Aspiring to International Leadership*, Singapore: Times Academic Press.
Tan, See Seng. 2015. 'Indonesia Among the Powers: Will ASEAN Still Matter to Indonesia?', in *Indonesia's Ascent: Power, Leadership and the Regional Order*, edited by Christopher B. Roberts, Ahmad D. Habir and Leonard C. Sebastian, Basingstoke: Palgrave Macmillan, pp. 287–307.
Vatikiotis, Michael. 1995. 'A Giant Treads Carefully', in *East Asia in Transition: Toward a New Regional Order*, edited by Robert S. Ross. New York: M.E. Sharpe, pp. 216–234.

Wardhy, Robertus. 2014. 'Jokowi Signals Break With "Thousand Friends" Foreign Policy', *Jakarta Globe*, 17 November, http://jakartaglobe.beritasatu.com/news/jokowi-signals-break-thousand-friends-foreign-policy/ (accessed 15 June 2015).

Weatherbee, Donald E. 2013. *Indonesia in ASEAN: Vision and Reality*, Singapore: Institute of Southeast Asian Studies.

Weinstein, F.B. 1976. *Indonesian Foreign Policy and Dilemma of Dependence*, Ithaca, NY: Cornell University Press.

Widodo, Joko. 2014a. 'Speech at the 9th East Asia Summit, Naypyidaw, 13 November, accessible at "Doktrin Jokowi: Indonesia poros maritim dunia"', *Rappler*, 13 November, http://www.rappler.com/world/regions/asia-pacific/indonesia/74928-pidato-jokowi-indonesia-poros-maritim-dunia (accessed 15 June 2015).

Widodo, Joko. 2014b. 'Remarks by Indonesian President Joko "Jokowi" Widodo at the APEC CEO Summit, Beijing, 10 November, accessible at "FULL SPEECH: Jokowi at APEC CEO Summit 2014"', *Rappler.com*, 10 November, http://www.rappler.com/world/regions/asia-pacific/indonesia/74620-full-speech-joko-widodo-apec-summit-beijing (accessed 15 June 2015).

Widyaningsih, Erlina, and Christopher B. Roberts. 2015. 'Indonesian Leadership in ASEAN: Mediation, Agency and Extra-Regional Diplomacy', in *Indonesia's Ascent: Power, Leadership and the Regional Order*, edited by Christopher B. Roberts, Ahmad D. Habir, and Leonard C. Sebastian, Basingstoke: Palgrave Macmillan, pp. 264–286.

Wu, Jiao, and Yunbi Zhang. 2013. 'Xi in Call for Building of New "Maritime Silk Road"', *China Daily*, 4 October, http://usa.chinadaily.com.cn/china/2013-10/04/content_17008940.htm (accessed 15 June 2015).

Yudhoyono, Susilo Bambang. 2005. 'An Independent and Active Foreign Policy for the 21st Century, Shangri-La Hotel, Jakarta, 19 May 2005', in *Transforming Indonesia: Selected International Speeches*, edited by D.P. Djalal, Jakarta: Office of Special Staff of the President for International Affairs & PT Buana Ilmu Populer, pp. 381–397.

Yudhoyono, Susilo Bambang. 2009. 'Inauguration Speech, Jakarta, 20 October, accessible at "Pidato Lengkap Presiden SBY 20 Oktober 2009"', *Kompas*, 20 October, http://sains.kompas.com/read/2009/10/20/1324076/pidato.lengkap.presiden.sby.20.oktober.2009 (accessed 15 June 2015).

Yudhoyono, Susilo Bambang. 2012. 'An Architecture for Durable Peace in the Asia-Pacific', Shangri-La Dialogue 2012 Keynote Address, The IISS Shangri-La Dialogue: 14th Asia Security Summit, Singapore, 1 June, https://www.iiss.org/en/events/shangri%20la%20dialogue/archive/sld12-43d9/opening-remarks-and-keynote-address-9e17/keynote-address-7244 (accessed 15 June 2015).

Part 2
Reflections on the rise of the Indo-Pacific

6 China anxieties in the geopolitical cartographies of the Indo-Pacific

Chengxin Pan

He who controls the Indo-Pacific controls the future.

Peter J. Munson (2013)

Concepts about space and time, such as the Asia-Pacific and the Asian Century, are not articulated lightly in international relations discourses. When a spatial or temporal term comes into vogue, it often comes with political connotations and policy implications. This is the context in which we ought to consider the making of the spatial term Indo-Pacific, which has recently made it into the lexicon of official speeches, think-tank reports, government white papers and scholarly works. While many pundits and practitioners are embracing this new formulation, others cast doubt on its usefulness or even question its actual existence. Yet, despite its sudden stardom in foreign policy circles and some debate around its policy implications, how the Indo-Pacific as a political spatial concept came about has not been well understood.

To address this gap, this chapter will first briefly survey the Indo-Pacific debate and examine how the debate has not paid adequate attention to the issue of the Indo-Pacific as a discursive construct. It then turns to how the United States, Australia, Japan, India and China together contribute to the formation of this concept amid ongoing geopolitical anxieties about the shape and trajectory of future Asian regional order. While acknowledging China's role in this constitutive process, I argue that as a discursive construct the Indo-Pacific has been motivated primarily by geopolitical anxieties about a perceived emerging regional order dominated by China. Driven by such anxieties, the concept is not an innocent description of a natural region out there; it has the potential of fuelling regional rivalries and exacerbating security dilemmas. Given its possible destabilising consequences, the chapter concludes with a call for a critical reimagination of this now increasingly accepted term.

The Indo-Pacific debate

For much of the twentieth century, the concept of the Indo-Pacific, coined by German geopolitician Karl Haushofer in the 1920s, had attracted little attention among international relations scholars or practitioners. It was not until the late 2000s that the term began to make an impressive comeback, and is now widely touted as reflecting new geopolitical realities. Indian strategic analyst C. Raja Mohan (2012, 212) argues that the seas of the western Pacific and the Indian Ocean constitute 'a single integrated geopolitical theater' that is the Indo-Pacific. In Australia, Rory Medcalf (2012, 3; see also this volume) believes that the new term is 'a valid and objective description of the greater regional system in which Australia now finds itself'. Australian Ambassador to the United States Kim Beazley (2012, 52) agrees, maintaining that the Indo-Pacific presents 'a practical, strategic reality that has to be addressed'. Crucially, the *Australian Defence White Paper 2013* (Commonwealth of Australia 2013, 7) for the first time identifies Australia's region as the 'Indo-Pacific strategic arc'.

In the United States, then Secretary of State Hillary Clinton (2011, 57) referred to the Indo-Pacific as the new Asia-Pacific. If this geographical fact was not clear enough before, we are told that it is because its importance had been 'obscured' by recent 'messy land wars' such as those in Iraq and Afghanistan. Now that the fog of war has largely lifted, the Indo-Pacific has presented itself with 'a vivid geographical face' (Kaplan 2010, xi–xii). Thus Robert Kaplan (2010, xiii, emphasis added) suggests that his book *Monsoon* merely tries to '*describe* the ceaseless currents of historical change [in the Greater Indian Ocean region] as they shape the contours of the new century'. His invocation of a 'monsoon' seems to remind us, among other things, of the region's timeless natural coherence.

Others remain sceptical of the Indo-Pacific idea, at least with regard to its strategic repercussions. Retired Rear Admiral Michael McDevitt (2013, 65) suggests that it 'would be premature to make too much' of this notion. Some Australian scholars argue that the emphasis on the Asian littoral (the Indo-Pacific) ignores Asia's vast territorial expanses, or 'horizontal Asia' (Bubalo and Cook 2010). Nick Bisley and Andrew Phillips (2012) question the strategic wisdom of promoting the Indo-Pacific, given the risk that it may intensify regional competition (see also Chacko 2012b; Gnanagurunathan 2012). Similarly, Rumley, Doyle and Chaturvedi (2012) point out that the concept is US-centric/China exclusive. Even India's former National Security Advisor Shivshankar Menon (2013) does not see the Indo-Pacific as 'one geopolitical unit'. He argues that by invoking this concept, we risk 'prescribing one medicine for the different security ailments' characteristic of its diverse places.

I agree that the Indo-Pacific is not a natural geographical space, but rather a discursive construct with strategic implications. Even former US Assistant Secretary of State for East Asia Kurt Campbell seemed to have unwittingly admitted it when he suggested that 'the next challenge' of US strategic thinking was the task of *operationally* making the linkage between the Indian and Pacific Oceans (see Manyin et al. 2012, 5). Yet, as Chacko points out in her introduction to this volume, until now, questions such as how the Indo-Pacific is discursively constructed, within what metageographical frameworks, against what types of regional backdrop, and for what purposes have yet to be more thoroughly examined. The main focus of this chapter is on how the Indo-Pacific has been enabled by a suite of

China anxieties in the 'Indo-Pacific' 99

geopolitically informed discourses and practices concerning the rise of China in the Asian regional order.

Imagining/doing the Indo-Pacific through geopolitical anxieties

National imaginations and geopolitical anxieties

The Indo-Pacific as a region does not exist prior to its 'discovery' by astute observers; rather, it has been imagined into being by them. I will return to this point in a moment, but one thing about imagination is worth noting here. According to David Brin (1989, 67, emphasis in original), imagination is a uniquely human talent that 'lets us "know" what has *never* happened, and even what might truly *never* happen!' Therefore by definition there is always a gap between what is imagined and what is putatively real, a gap which renders the imagined object both psychologically exciting and ontologically insecure. In this sense, anxiety, fear and fantasy tend to go hand in hand with such imaginative practices.

To illustrate, one need only look at the imagined community of the nation-state. Despite its seemingly organic status, the state from the beginning suffers chronic anxiety about its precarious ontological being, hence the incessant concern with national identity, survival, security, sovereignty, living space, territorial integrity, border control, 'access', foreign threats, regional order, and power balance. As Europe was the birthplace of the nation-state, it is not surprising that it was there that classical geopolitics, the dominant metageographical framework about the world, was first developed as a 'science' to help account for and manage nationalist anxieties about how to survive in an 'anarchical' inter-state system. In popular culture, copious invasion novels testify to the prevalence of such geopolitical anxieties in the public imagination.

Geopolitical anxieties are often associated with and managed through a raft of practices of spatial security: war, territorial annexation, expansion, alliance-formation, military build-up, arms race, missile defence, military exercises, forward defence, strategic talks and so forth. As a result of such practices and their international interactions, boundaries of a region may be invented, redrawn or reinterpreted with new meanings. To better understand how the Indo-Pacific has come about, I now turn to the specific geopolitical anxieties and imaginations in the United States, Australia, Japan, India and China, and examine how their imaginative geographies and associated security practices together help construct this new geopolitical space. My focus on these countries, I should add, does not imply that these countries are the only players in the imaginative and constitutive processes.

American geopolitical imaginations of China's rise

To understand the discursive production of the Indo-Pacific, we need to examine American geopolitical imaginations about the world in general and the rise of China in particular. As the 'imagined community par excellence' (Campbell

1998, 91, 132), geopolitics has been central to the US self-imagination. US security and survival, for instance, is often predicated on various spatial practices of geopolitics, with ever-expanding frontiers seen as crucial for its self-renewal as the exceptional and indispensable nation. Dean Acheson (1950) once asserted that Americans 'are children of freedom' and 'cannot be safe except in an environment of freedom'. Thus to create and maintain this living space for freedom, the American value of freedom has to be communicated to the four corners of the earth. This belief reflects what Hardt and Negri (2000, 165) call America's imperial sovereignty, with 'its tendency toward an open, expansive project operating on an unbounded terrain'. Thus, moving beyond the Monroe Doctrine, the new imperial imagination of the United States, combining both geopolitics and a certain New World idealism, urged Americans to seek new frontiers in the Pacific and Asia. In this context, it is easy to understand a long-standing strategic article of faith in US foreign policy that the United States ought to 'dominate the western hemisphere while not permitting another great power to dominate Europe or Northeast Asia' (Mearsheimer 2001a, 46). Only through such an expansive geopolitical strategy can the United States ensure its security.

While pursuing this strategy may help ease particular geopolitical anxieties facing the United States, the geopolitical mindset that underpins the strategy is in a constant state of anxiety. It often looks at the behaviour of other powers through the same strategic prism, fearful that what the United States has done is what its peer competitors will do. After the collapse of the Soviet Union, the United States increasingly sees its own mirror-images of imperial expansion in the rise of China (Pan 2004, 2012a). With its vast landmass and fast-growing economy, China is seen as a natural candidate to dominate Asia and uproot US primacy in the region. Drawing from the same logic that explains the US expansion and ascendancy in the past, many American observers perceive China's rise in Asia as following an essentially similar geopolitical trajectory. As John Mearsheimer (2001b, 401) argues, like the rise of the United States in the nineteenth century, a rising China 'would surely pursue regional hegemony' with its own Monroe Doctrine. It is predicted that this Chinese Monroe Doctrine would 'push U.S. forces out of the Asia-Pacific region' (Walt 2012) and lead to 'the loss of the Indian and Western Pacific oceans as veritable American military lakes' (Kaplan 2009, 45). As the imaginative catchphrase of 'Red Star over the Pacific' implies, the days of US control of the vast ocean seem to be numbered (Yoshihara and Holmes 2010). Washington's heightened concerns over its freedom of navigation in the South China Sea and China's 'anti-access, area denial' (A2/AD) capabilities epitomise this anxiety. Indeed, 'access denial has become the prism through which policymakers in Washington survey the rise of Chinese sea power' (Yoshihara and Holmes 2010, 6).

American anxieties about China's rise are not just about its economic and military power per se (Zhang 2013). Increasingly the 'China threat' is seen in the context of this so-called Middle Kingdom's growing regional ambition. In other words, underneath the traditional bilateral rivalry between Washington and Beijing is believed to be a larger struggle of competing regionalisms (Zhu 2013), a struggle in which China appears to be gaining an upper hand. After the Asian financial crisis, China emerged as a 'responsible economic actor' in the region (Breslin 2008). In contrast to George W. Bush's 'shock and awe' unilateralism and his administration's preoccupation with the War on Terror in the Middle East, Beijing's subsequent 'charm offensive' in Southeast Asia and elsewhere seemed to have won itself many friends – so much so that it was widely believed that a Sinocentric East Asian order was on the horizon (Beeson 2009).

Thus even at the height of the US War on Terror, the neoconservative Francis Fukuyama (2005, A18) urged the United States not to forget that 'the biggest geopolitical development of this generation' was the rise of China. Meanwhile, then US Deputy Secretary of State Robert Zoellick (2005) made it clear that China's rise had generated 'a cauldron of anxiety' in the United States and elsewhere. Although Barack Obama distanced himself from his predecessor on many policy fronts, he seemed to have adopted a Bush-style, neoconservative vision of friends and foes, and democracies and autocracies in dealing with China (Kagan 2010). Through this lens, the increasing regional clout of an assertive authoritarian China took on a doubly sinister quality, exacerbating America's fear of losing the 'contest over defining an Asian regional identity' (Buzan 2012, 2–3). It is in this context that we can better understand Obama's tour of Asian democracies in 2010, the US-led Trans-Pacific Partnership (TPP) framework (which excludes China) as well as the rising popularity of the Indo-Pacific concept.

The Indo-Pacific construct offers a rationale for the Pentagon's AirSea Battle plan as well as recent US strategic deployment and realignment in this vast region, sometimes known as its 'pivot to Asia' (Medcalf, Heinrichs and Jones 2011, 19–20; O'Hanlon 2012; White 2012, 76–77). It serves a dual purpose of both constraining the rise of a 'peer competitor' in Asia and preventing regional integration from being 'inward looking and exclusive' (Quoted in Ciorciari 2011, 146). The second purpose reflects another US geopolitical imperative, which has been brilliantly summed up by Zbigniew Brzezinski. Imperial geostrategy, as he puts it, needs 'to prevent collusion and maintain security dependence among the vassals, to keep tributaries pliant and protected, and to keep the barbarians from coming together' (Quoted in Beeson 2009, 507). In this sense, the US motive behind the Indo-Pacific becomes clearer. It seems that there is no better way of keeping the barbarians separate than designing a super-region like the Indo-Pacific to allow the United States to legitimately claim 'we are here to stay', all the while thwarting the emergence of indigenous regional groupings (Buzan 2012).

This is how the Indian Ocean was brought to the fore. Another 'American lake', the Indian Ocean region appears to have become more fluid with the rise of India and the spectre of India-China rivalry, or worse, cooperation. For example, during Chinese Premier Wen Jiabao's visit to India in 2005, his Indian counterpart Manmohan Singh posited that 'together, India and China could reshape the world order' (Quoted in Prestwitz 2005). But such a pledge to work together is hardly music to the ears of US strategists. Invoking the vicious imagery of monsoon, Kaplan, whose writings have done much to educate US officials about the Greater Indian Ocean (Green and Shearer 2012, 175), promptly warned that the dawn of the Indo-Pacific era could not have come at 'a more turbulent time'. Crowded with 'highly volatile and populous pivot states', the region is characterised by 'weak institutions, tottering infrastructures, and young and restive populations tempted by extremism. Yet they are the future' (Kaplan 2010, xii; see also Munson 2013).

To Kaplan (2010, xiv) and others, 'America's own destiny and that of the West as a whole' are on the line in these troubled waters. Yet by the same token, these menacing imageries also open up strategic opportunities for the United States to 'pivot' to this part of the world and enlist India as a 'desirable' partner (Blank 2007, 1). To US defence contractors, India's estimated $80 billion military modernisation program by 2015 no doubt adds another dimension to New Delhi's desirability (Berteau and Green 2012, 38). With more than sixty joint military exercises with the Pentagon in the past decade, India has conducted more exercises with the United States than with any other country (Berteau and Green 2012). Despite the US role in initiating those operations (Gilboy and Heginbotham 2013, 125–126), Clinton (2011, 58) insisted that it was the region that 'is eager for our leadership and our business'. In any case, as McDevitt (2013, 8) points out, it was India's emergence as a strategic partner and the strengthening of US-India security ties that 'led U.S. government policy officials to begin thinking about the interconnectedness of the Pacific and Indian oceans', not the other way around. Also, by insisting on 'old-fashioned alliance management' (i.e. the 'hub-and-spoke' system) instead of new regional multilateral initiatives (Green and Shearer 2012, 187), the elite conception of the Indo-Pacific 'fits with a longstanding and very clever antiregional diplomatic tactic of the US' (Buzan 2012).

Australia and Japan: Asia's 'odd men out' are in

If this new regional concept comes with a paradoxically anti-regional flavour, it begs the question of why regional powers like Australia and Japan are attracted to it. In fact, as the chapters in this volume by Medcalf and Jain and Harimoto show, both countries have been strong advocates for iterations of this concept. The reason, I suggest, also has to do with the geopolitical imaginations in which Australia and Japan position themselves vis-à-vis a rising China. Australia has a split identity between its history and its geography. As its economic prosperity is increasingly linked to Asia and particularly China, Australia has been anxious to become part of the action and capitalise on the Asian Century opportunity, and to that end it needs to cast off its 'odd man out' status in Asian regionalism (Beeson and Yoshimatsu 2007). This partly explains why Canberra wanted to join the East Asia Summit (EAS), to 'have a say in building any new regional architecture from the ground up' (Richardson 2005, 360). Another case in point is Australia's decision, although not before much dithering, to sign up to the China-led Asian Infrastructure Investment Bank (AIIB). But once getting inside, Australia was troubled by another type of anxiety: the danger of dominance by and dependence on China. Indeed, as former Australian Prime Minister Tony Abbott admitted to German Chancellor Angela Merkel, fear is one of the key drivers of Australia's policy on China (Garnaut 2015). Long imagining itself as a Western colonial outpost in the

East, Australia on its own has rarely felt naturally at home, much less safe, within Asia, despite Paul Keating's famous catchphrase that 'Australia should find its security in Asia', not 'from Asia'. As former Prime Minister Kevin Rudd reasoned, the overshadowing of US and British dominance by looming Chinese and Indian ascendancy would leave Australia vulnerable to a 'much more complex region'. To ease such anxiety Canberra predictably sought to strengthen its US alliance, hence Rudd's 'Asia-Pacific Community' proposal designed to bring in the United States to keep China in check (Pan 2012b, 249).

While the Asia-Pacific Community proposal never got off the ground, the seemingly unrelenting rise of China (and India) created the ever-aching longing for US strategic reassurance, a desire that has a great chance of fulfilment in the Indo-Pacific idea. Among other things, this regional design seems able to allay Australia's dual anxiety of being an odd man out and an odd man in, for this expanded region not only places Australia 'at the centre of the action' (Taylor 2013) but also allows the inclusion of two powerful democratic friends (the United States and India) to buttress its hedging strategy towards China. No wonder that many Australians now feel that the Indo-Pacific 'makes more sense' and '*want* to talk about' it (Varghese 2012, 2; quoted in Scott 2013b, 4, emphasis added). It sounds like a desire fulfilled, with anxiety kept under control.

Canberra's moment of being at the geopolitical centre of action well and truly arrived in November 2011 when Obama chose the venue of the Australian Parliament to declare the US pivot to Asia. During the same visit, the two allies announced the rotational deployment of 2,500 US Marines in Darwin. In 2012, a Pentagon-commissioned report expressed strong US interest in using Australian facilities at the Cocos Islands in the Indian Ocean and the Stirling naval base near Perth for US surveillance operations and increased US Navy access (Berteau and Green 2012, 33). The report made no secret that an added advantage of choosing Stirling is that it remains beyond 'the growing coverage of Chinese A2AD capabilities' (Berteau and Green 2012, 33). Perhaps not coincidentally, in the 2012 *Australian Defence Force Posture Review* and the 2013 Australian *Defence White Paper*, upgrading the Cocos Islands airfield facilities to support unrestricted P-8 and UAV operations and exploring opportunities for enhanced cooperation with the US Navy at Stirling are key recommendations and promises (Hawke and Smith 2012, iv; Commonwealth of Australia 2013, 10). With the Indo-Pacific now actively promoted as a single strategic arc central to Australia's defence, these enhanced military ties with the United States look natural and hardly need justification.

Japan's interest in creating an Indo-Pacific arc follows a similar geopolitical logic. Emphasising its dependence on the 'security of maritime navigation from Africa and the Middle East to East Asia', Japan finds it necessary to engage closely with India, which shares similar interests (Ministry of Defense 2010, 9; see Jain and Harimoto in this volume). In 2007, while visiting India, Prime Minister Shinzo Abe (2007) proposed 'a dynamic coupling' of the Pacific and the Indian Oceans 'as seas of freedom and of prosperity'. In 2008, Japan and India signed the Joint Declaration on Security Cooperation, and in 2010, the two countries held their first senior-level dialogue on foreign affairs and security.

A fear of China's rising clout in Asian regionalism can largely account for Japan's overture to India and its enthusiasm about the Indo-Pacific concept. Before Shinzo Abe was elected prime minister for the second time in December 2012, he penned an essay, titled 'Asia's Democratic Security Diamond', outlining his continued interest and investment in Japan's expanded strategic horizons 'starting from the Indian Ocean Region to the Western Pacific' (Abe 2012). In the short essay, he openly named the threat of China as the rationale for his strategic vision: 'Increasingly, the South China Sea seems set to become a "Lake Beijing". . . . Soon, the PLA Navy's newly built aircraft carrier will be a common sight – more than sufficient to scare China's neighbors.' Takashi Terada (2010) argues that it was this China factor that led Japan's Ministry of Foreign Affairs to advocate the EAS, an Asian regional concept that would allow Japan to redraw the geopolitical map of East Asia so as to include Australia, New Zealand and India as additional counterbalances against China. In this sense, the Indo-Pacific, or what Abe termed 'a broader Asia', is a continuation of Japan's expanded EAS (ASEAN+6) regional initiative. A reason behind Abe's new proposal, as Terada (2010, 78) notes, was that the United States, an essential country to Asia's new regional architecture, was absent in the EAS at the time.

India: looking and acting east

As the 'child of partition' with a deep sense of 'cartographic anxiety' (Krishna 1996, 196; see also Chacko 2012a, 144–151), India has also been uneasy about its geopolitical milieu. In the late 1990s, the US military presence at Diego Garcia in the Indian Ocean caused alarm among certain Indian scholars and officials, but more often than not it is China that is considered India's arch-rival. According to a 2013 Lowy Institute poll, 83% of Indians view China as a threat (Medcalf 2013a, 15). The US-based analyst Mohan Malik (2006) describes a Chinese strategy of containing India and squeezing its traditional strategic space in the region. Indian analysts such as Gurpreet Khurana and C. Raja Mohan see an Indo-Pacific 'rivalry arc' between India and China. With India's sea lines of communications apparently at the mercy of the Chinese, they call for projecting India's power into the Pacific to match China's growing presence in the Indian Ocean (Yoshihara and Holmes 2010, 15).

To be sure, India's official positions on the Indo-Pacific are not as assertive. Also, since the beginning of its Look East policy, India's interest in the Indo-Pacific formulation has much to do with geoeconomic considerations (see Chacko in this volume). Nonetheless, given the mistrust between India and China after their brief but bloody border conflict in 1962, a strategic logic is not far below the surface. For example, the 2007 *India's Maritime Military Strategy* defines the South China Sea as an area of strategic interest for India's deployment of future maritime forces (Scott 2013a, 53). Seizing on such common threads of apprehension about China within the American and Indian strategic communities, Secretary Clinton urged India, which still has a 'strategic autonomy' tradition, to 'not just look east, but continue to engage and act east as well' (Quoted in Gupta 2012). As Mohan (2012, 97–100) has documented, since the 1990s India has expanded its joint naval exercises with all Southeast Asian countries and extended its military presence in the western Pacific through multilateral exercises with US, Japanese, Australian and Singaporean navies. After the election of Narendra Modi, India has become more active in strengthening regional security arrangements, such as with Australia and Japan, with whom it shares concerns about 'access and security' (Modi 2014). Commentators wrote that 'burgeoning Indian-Japanese security cooperation is one reason to believe that the Look East policy is genuinely now the Act East policy' (Cronin and Baruah 2014).

Before I turn to China, a brief look at the four countries just discussed reveals that the Indo-Pacific is not just a purely realpolitik enterprise. It also has a distinctively neoconservative ring to it. These four democracies in the Indo-Pacific, perhaps more than by coincidence, were the old cast of an earlier Quadrilateral Strategic Dialogue (QSD) initiative pursued during the George W. Bush administration. The 'Quad', as it is known, was initiated by Abe, whose 2007 speech to the Indian Parliament appealed to the values of freedom and democracy as an organising principle of his broader Asia proposal. An experimental meeting of the Quad took place in May 2007, three months after Abe and US Vice President Dick Cheney discussed the idea of forming a quadrilateral grouping among likeminded democracies (Terada 2010, 85). Drawing on the neoconservative foreign policy ideas of both military strength and moral clarity, the defunct Quad idea never went away. After attending the Trilateral Strategic Dialogue with her American and Japanese counterparts in October 2013, Australian Foreign Minister Julie Bishop (2013) left the door open for resurrecting the quadrilateral dialogue, as she promised to keep it in mind when looking to 'more deeply network our strategic defence and security alliances and partnerships in the region'. Strategic observers from influential American and Australian think tanks recently made a similar call for the 'return to the U.S.-Japan-Australia-India "Quad" concept' (Green and Shearer 2012, 184). As the United States, Japan, Australia and India regroup as the core 'diamond' members of the freshly minted Indo-Pacific, it may be argued that it has already been revived under a different guise, namely, through the existing US-Japan-Australia and US-Japan-India trilateral dialogues, and the newly created Japan-Australia-India trilateral dialogue.

China: the new 'odd man out'?

As the Indo-Pacific takes on a value-based quality, China now seems to emerge effectively as the new odd man out of Asia. While the formation of the Indo-Pacific may have been premised on China as the geopolitical (and ideological) Other in the region, this does not mean that China's role in this process is innocent. It too has been part of the construction of the Indo-Pacific with its own version of cartographic anxiety and associated practices of security. But it is perhaps equally true that China's contribution has been largely defensive and reactive (Li and Chan 2011, 54).

Although Beijing has long been wary about US hegemony, its main concern continues to be about internal stability and regime legitimacy. To that end, Beijing's favourite mantra about its international strategic environment remains 'peace and development'. Its eagerness to join the World Trade Organization (WTO), its enthusiasm for a free trade agreement with the Association of Southeast Asian Nations (ASEAN), and more recently its Maritime Silk Road initiative (now part of the so-called One Belt, One Road strategy) demonstrated that its foreign policy has been driven more by agendas of domestic development and geoeconomics than by regional geopolitics. In any case, Beijing is well aware that regional geopolitical dynamism is fraught with obstacles of lingering sovereignty issues and popular nationalism (He 2004). Yet, by virtue of its rapid rise as an economic powerhouse, China has emerged as an indispensable force in regional economic and financial integration. In doing so, it seems to have begun 'knitting together the "spokes" of the US-centred hub-and-spoke security-alliance system' (Quoted in Terada 2010, 76), something directly at odds with the aforementioned US geopolitical imperative of keeping the 'barbarians' apart. Although China's regional strategy is not simply power balancing (Breslin 2008, 136), its regional economic engagement has nevertheless been widely seen as a bid for regional primacy.

Geopolitical reasoning is a contagious state of mind. As foreign observers see China's rise in stark geopolitical terms, their Chinese counterparts also increasingly look at China's security environment through a dark geopolitical lens. As Wang Jisi (2012a, 3) notes, although their country is now much stronger, 'some Chinese now feel a sense of greater insecurity, more anxiety, and deeper victim complex.' The 2013 Chinese defence white paper is not immune to this sense of insecurity (Information Office of the State Council 2013).

Indeed, facing the US's own well-established 'string of pearls'/'first island chain' strategies, China has found itself surrounded by what Yoshihara and Holmes (2010, 284) call a 'Great Wall in reverse'. With 80 percent of its oil flows passing through the Strait of Malacca, Chinese leaders are allegedly deeply disturbed by the 'Malacca Dilemma' (Li and Zhang 2010), made even more acute by their awareness that both ends of the Strait are controlled by US fleets. In response to these real or imagined geostrategic predicaments on China's Pacific coasts, some Chinese analysts turn their gaze to the Indian Ocean:

> With China's security in the Western Pacific region hamstrung by the US and Japan, the South China Sea issue has no short-term solution. The Indian Ocean thus is not only the main passage for China to break through the American military's Pacific island chain and tackle the 'Malacca Dilemma', but also the ideal option for China's seaward strategy as well as the testing ground for building a blue-water navy.
>
> (Lou and Zhang 2010, 43)

In a *Global Times* article, Wang Jisi (2012b) urges China to develop a westward strategy as China's own geostrategic rebalancing to counter the US rebalance to

Asia. Indeed, in recent years Beijing has sought to court Pakistan, Sri Lanka, Thailand and Myanmar and to build port facilities and listening posts in some of those countries. It has sent naval vessels on counter-piracy missions and port calls throughout the Indian Ocean region. Consequently, mirroring America's new two-ocean (Indo-Pacific) navy strategy and India's Look East policy, China has launched its own two-ocean navy strategy in the same waters (Wang 2005, 105; Kaplan 2010, 134; Li and Zhang 2010).

China's two-ocean strategy culminated in the announcement of the Maritime Silk Road by Chinese President Xi Jinping in October 2013 during his visit to Indonesia. Together with its land-based Silk Road Economic Belt and AIIB initiatives, China seeks to expand its trade routes, increase regional connectivity, and gain better access to natural resources as well as boosting its 'soft power' along those routes. In part, these initiatives, which are open to all interested countries in those regions, are also China's responses to anxieties among its neighbours about its growing influence. While some countries in the region welcome the initiatives, many remain sceptical of Beijing's strategic intentions (Chaturvedy 2014). The 2014 US-China Economic and Security Review Commission Report argues that these represent 'China's increasingly strident efforts to intimidate and coerce many of its neighbors' (USCC 2014, 14). More ambivalent attitudes are found in India. Geethanjali Nataraj (2015) at the Observer Research Foundation urges India to accept China's invitation to be part of its Maritime Silk Road, but former Indian Foreign Secretary Kanwal Sibal (2014) argues that this is China's 'string of pearls' strategy under a new guise, designed to unsettle India. Brahma Chellaney (2015), at the New Delhi–based Center for Policy Research, similarly contends that China is seeking to 'challenge America's sway and chip away at India's natural-geographic advantage'.

No doubt, geopolitical anxieties about China's rise will continue. Alongside the pivot to Asia strategy of the United States, India's Look East policy and China's Maritime Silk Road strategy have begun to 'stamp their authority on the same region'. As a result, their 'widening geopolitical horizons' (Scott 2008, 1, 19) increasingly overlap, thus giving some operational substance to the Indo-Pacific imaginary. Although China has not warmed to the Indo-Pacific concept, its Maritime Silk Road concept has been seen as 'analogous (or as a rival) to the Indo-Pacific' (Jakobson and Medcalf 2015, 4). China's interests in the Indian Ocean and its geopolitical anxieties and policy responses are thus contributing to its emergence as a strategic centre of gravity of sorts. As many Chinese strategic planners now begin to 'look at China's grand strategy across a wide Indo-Pacific swath' (Zhao 2013), the new region may become still more real.

Conclusion: what's in a name?

In this chapter, I have argued that the Indo-Pacific was primarily conceived as a collective geopolitical construct with a neoconservative bent, but it is worth stressing that its arrival is not entirely a matter of *geopolitical* imaginations. It also has something to do with geoeconomics, global supply chains and increasing economic interdependence. In fact, even the most enthusiastic geopolitical advocates such as Kaplan (2010, 291) acknowledge that regional relations are not always about geopolitical manoeuvring. On that basis, many proponents of the Indo-Pacific deny that the new regional concept is about containing China. Medcalf (2013b, 64), for example, insists that the Indo-Pacific is 'a geo-economic reality . . . not a strategic project to contain that rise'. Others point out that the US pivot to the Indo-Pacific is motivated by a range of issues such as energy supplies, failing states, climate change, piracy, terrorism, Iran, and drug trafficking, not just great power rivalry (Green and Shearer 2012, 176).

Yet, despite such exceptions and denials, the geopolitical mindset has been central to mainstream Indo-Pacific discourses. If anti-piracy, disaster relief and fighting terrorism were the main purposes of the new regional design, then the reported plan to deploy giant unmanned patrol planes to Cocos Islands and aircraft carriers and nuclear-powered attack submarines near Perth would not make much sense (Taylor 2012). Even when there was anti-piracy or disaster relief cooperation, geopolitics seemed still at play, as exemplified by China's exclusion from both the 2004 tsunami core group (from which the short-lived quadrilateral talks emerged) and the US-led Task Force 151, the main multilateral anti-piracy group (Green and Shearer 2012, 185). Such geopolitical practices of security seem to lend credence to a senior US official's admission that 'China is a central element in our effort to encourage India's emergence as a world power' and that 'we don't need to talk about the containment of China. It will take care of itself as India rises' (Twining 2007, 83; see also Gilboy and Heginbotham 2013, 139). Given that the criteria or principles for regional cooperation often entail 'democratic values' and 'a willingness to help shape and abide by rules and norms for a secure and stable region' (Medcalf 2013b, 66), it is not difficult to see which country is the main intended target for socialisation, and failing that, exclusion. The fact that such a geopolitical undertone is not always palpable may be due to 'the sensitive presentation of initiatives with an emphasis on broader benefits to the region' (Berteau and Green 2012, 33). But in her appeal to Congress to maintain State Department funding, Secretary Clinton felt obliged to talk straight: 'We are in a competition for influence with China; let's put aside the moral, humanitarian, do-good side of what we believe in, and let's just talk straight realpolitik' (Dombey 2011).

This geopolitical, and to some degree neoconservative, construction of the Indo-Pacific should raise concerns about its long-term political implications. As this concept gains traction, we need to look more closely at its conflicting regional agendas and ask whose interests it serves (Bisley and Phillips 2012). For all its apparent inclusion of such low-politics do-good issues as climate change and anti-piracy, this spatial imagination has been galvanised by the perceived rise of China and concurrent great power rivalries for regional hegemony. This geopolitical obsession not only obscures the extensive regional cooperation and transnational issues of human security such as poverty, hunger, public health, small arms and drug trafficking, environmental degradation, and natural disasters in the region (Bateman, Chan and Graham 2011, 8–9). It also plays on and exacerbates existing anxieties, mistrust and security dilemmas. When the United States turned down the request by the United Nations to include China in the joint tsunami disaster relief operations in December 2004, China allegedly hastened the 'rollout of its out-of-area "military missions other than war" activities' (Gupta 2012). And in response to China's military modernisation, alongside the pivot to Asia, a long article in the prestigious *Journal of Strategic Studies* (Mirski 2013), with a shorter version appearing in the influential *National Interest* magazine, now openly advocates a US naval blockade against China, specifically targeting its oil imports. The likely tit-for-tat cycles of such fanciful but potentially self-fulfilling game plays do not bode well for the future regional order.

It is in this context that it is imperative to critically examine the influential mindset of reading the regional dynamism from a purely geopolitical perspective, although this is not to deny that some degree of geopolitical rivalry is evident in the region. Insofar as all regions are 'social constructions created through politics' (Katzenstein 2002, 105) rather than predetermined by certain mysterious, irresistible geographical forces, the Indo-Pacific can and should be made for the better through less geopolitically driven imaginations. In this sense, the term per se is not the issue. What is problematic is the ways in which it has been defined almost exclusively in geopolitical terms.

References

Abe, Shinzo. 2007. 'Confluence of the Two Seas', Speech at the Parliament of the Republic of India, 22 August, http://www.mofa.go.jp/region/asia-paci/pmv0708/speech-2.html (accessed 8 June 2015).
Abe, Shinzo. 2012. 'Asia's Democratic Security Diamond', Project Syndicate, 27 December, http://www.project-syndicate.org/commentary/a-strategic-alliance-for-japan-and-india-by-shinzo-abe (accessed 8 June 2015).
Acheson, Dean. 1950. 'Speech in Washington', 22 April, http://teachingamericanhistory.org/library/document/speech-in-washington-2/ (accessed 8 June 2015).
Bateman, Sam, Jane Chan, and Euan Graham. Eds. 2011. *ASEAN and the Indian Ocean: The Key Maritime Links*, Singapore: S. Rajaratnam School of International Studies, Nanyang Technological University.
Beazley, Kim. 2012. 'Australia in the Indo-Pacific Century' (interview with Sergei DeSilva-Ranasinghe), *Policy* 28:3, 50–52.
Beeson, Mark. 2009. 'Geopolitics and the Making of Regions: The Fall and Rise of East Asia', *Political Studies* 57:3, 498–516.
Beeson, Mark, and Hidetaka Yoshimatsu. 2007. 'Asia's Odd Men Out: Australia, Japan, and the Politics of Regionalism', *International Relations of the Asia-Pacific* 7:2, 227–250.
Berteau, David J., and Michael J. Green. 2012. *US Force Posture Strategy in the Asia Pacific Region*, Washington, DC: Center for Strategic and International Studies.
Bishop, Julie. 2013. 'Questions at the National Press Club Tokyo', 16 October, http://foreignminister.gov.au/transcripts/2013/jb_tr_131016.html (accessed 8 June 2015).
Bisley, Nick, and Andrew Phillips. 2012. 'The Indo-Pacific: What Does It Actually Mean?', *East Asia Forum*, 6 October, http://www.eastasiaforum.org/2012/10/06/the-indo-pacific-what-does-it-actually-mean/ (accessed 8 June 2015).
Blank, Stephen. 2007. 'The Geostrategic Implications of the Indo-American Strategic Partnership', *India Review* 6:1, 1–24.

Breslin, Shaun. 2008. 'Towards a Sino-Centric Regional Order? Empowering China and Constructing Regional Order(s)', in *China, Japan and Regional Leadership in East Asia*, edited by Christopher M. Dent, Cheltenham: Edward Elgar, pp. 131–155.

Brin, David. 1989. 'Metaphorical Drive – Or Why We're Such Good Liars', in *Mindscapes: The Geographies of Imagined Worlds*, edited by George E. Slusser and Eric S. Rabkin, Carbondale: Southern Illinois University Press, pp. 60–77.

Bubalo, Anthony, and Malcolm Cook. 2010. 'Horizontal Asia', *American Interest* 5:5, 12–19.

Buzan, Barry. 2012. 'Asia: A Geopolitical Reconfiguration', http://www.ifri.org/downloads/barrybuzanengpe22012.pdf (accessed 8 June 2015).

Campbell, David. 1998. *Writing Security: United States Foreign Policy and the Politics of Identity* (rev. ed.), Minneapolis: University of Minnesota Press.

Chacko, Priya. 2012a. *Indian Foreign Policy: The Politics of Postcolonial Identity From 1947 to 2004*, London: Routledge.

Chacko, Priya. 2012b. 'India and the Indo-Pacific: An Emerging Regional Vision', Indo-Pacific Governance Research Centre Policy Brief, Issue 5, http://www.adelaide.edu.au/indo-pacific-governance/policy/Chacko_PB.pdf (accessed 8 June 2015).

Chaturvedy, Rajeev Ranjan. 2014. 'New Maritime Silk Road: Converging Interests and Regional Responses.' ISAS Working Paper, No. 197, National University of Singapore.

Chellaney, Brahma. 2015. 'What Are Chinese Submarines Doing in the Indian Ocean?' *Huffington Post*, 19 May, http://www.huffingtonpost.com/brahma-chellaney/chinese-subs-in-indian-ocean_b_7320500.html (accessed 8 June 2015).

Ciorciari, John D. 2011. 'The United States and Regionalism in the Asia-Pacific', in *East Asia Regionalism*, edited by Narayanan Ganesan and Colin Dürkop, Tokyo: Konrad Adenauer Foundation, pp. 135–161.

Clinton, Hillary. 2011. 'America's Pacific Century', *Foreign Policy* 189, 56–63.

Commonwealth of Australia. 2013. 'Defence White Paper 2013', Canberra: Commonwealth of Australia.

Cronin, Patrick M., and Darshana M. Baruah. 2014. 'The Modi Doctrine for the Indo-Pacific Maritime Region', *Diplomat*, 2 December, http://thediplomat.com/2014/12/the-modi-doctrine-for-the-indo-pacific-maritime-region/ (accessed 8 June 2015).

Dombey, Daniel. 2011. 'US Struggling to Hold Role as Global Leader, Clinton Says', *Financial Times*, 3 March, 5.

Fukuyama, Francis. 2005. 'All Quiet on the Eastern Front?' *Wall Street Journal*, 1 March, A18.

Garnaut, John. 2015. '"Fear and Greed" Drive Australia's China Policy, Tony Abbott Tells Angela Merkel', *Sydney Morning Herald*, 17 April, 5.

Gilboy, George J., and Eric Heginbotham. 2013. 'Double Trouble: A Realist View of Chinese and Indian Power', *Washington Quarterly* 36:3, 125–142.

Gnanagurunathan, D. 2012. 'India and the Idea of the "Indo-Pacific"', *East Asia Forum*, 20 October, http://www.eastasiaforum.org/2012/10/20/india-and-the-idea-of-the-indo-pacific/ (accessed 8 June 2015).

Green, Michael J., and Andrew Shearer. 2012. 'Defining U.S. Indian Ocean Strategy', *Washington Quarterly* 35:2, 175–189.

Gupta, Sourabh. 2012. 'The US Pivot and India's Look East', *East Asia Forum*, June 20, http://www.eastasiaforum.org/2012/06/20/the-us-pivot-and-india-s-look-east/ (accessed 8 June 2015).

Hardt, Michael, and Antonio Negri. 2000. *Empire*, Cambridge, MA: Harvard University Press.

Hawke, Allan, and Ric Smith. 2012. *Australian Defence Force Posture Review*, Canberra: Australian Government.

He, Baogang. 2004. 'East Asian Ideas of Regionalism: A Normative Critique', *Australian Journal of International Affairs* 58:1, 105–125.
Information Office of the State Council. 2013. 'The Diversified Employment of China's Armed Forces (White Paper)', 16 April, http://www.china.org.cn/government/white paper/2013-04/16/content_28556792.htm (accessed 8 June 2015).
Jakobson, Linda, and Rory Medcalf. 2015. 'The Perception Gap: Reading China's Maritime Strategic Objectives in Indo-Pacific Asia (Report)', Sydney: Lowy Institute for International Policy.
Kagan, Robert. 2010. 'America: Once Engaged, Now Ready to Lead', *Washington Post*, 1 October, http://www.washingtonpost.com/wp-dyn/content/article/2010/09/30/AR2010093005528.html (accessed 8 June 2015).
Kaplan, Robert D. 2009. 'China's Two Ocean Strategy', in *China's Arrival: A Strategic Framework for a Global Relationship*, edited by Abraham Denmark and Nirav Patel, Washington, DC: Center for a New American Security, pp. 43–58.
Kaplan, Robert D. 2010. *Monsoon: The Indian Ocean and the Battle for Supremacy in the 21st Century*, Collingwood: Black.
Katzenstein, Peter J. 2002. 'Regionalism and Asia', in *New Regionalisms in the Global Political Economy*, edited by Shaun Breslin, Christopher W. Hughes, Nicola Phillips, and Ben Rosamond, London: Routledge, pp. 104–118.
Krishna, Sankaran. 1996. 'Cartographic Anxiety: Mapping the Body Politic in India', in *Challenging Boundaries: Global Flows, Territorial Identities*, edited by Michael J. Shapiro and Hayward R. Alker, Minneapolis: University of Minnesota Press, pp. 193–214.
Li, Jingyu, and Zhang Zhuo. 2010. 'Guanyu Zhongguo mianxiang shijie kaituo liangyang chuhai datongdao de zhanlue gouxiang' ('A Strategic Concept on China's Opening Up of Two-Ocean Maritime Gateways to the World'), *Zhongguo ruan kexue* (Soft Science in China) 8, 46–60.
Li, Mingjiang, and Irene Chan. 2011. 'China's Pessoptimist Views on and Pragmatic Involvement in East Asian Regionalism', in *East Asia Regionalism*, edited by Narayanan Ganesan and Colin Dürkop, Tokyo: Konrad Adenauer Foundation, pp. 49–69.
Lou Chunhao, and Zhang Mingming. 2010. 'Nanya de zhanlue zhongyaoxing yu Zhongguo de Nanya zhanlue' ('The Strategic Importance of South Asia and China's South Asia Strategy'). *Xiandai guojiguanxi* (Contemporary International Relations) 2, 42–47.
Malik, Mohan. 2006. 'China's Strategy of Containing India', *Power and Interest News Report*, 6 February, http://www.pinr.com/report.php?ac=view_report&report_id=434&language_id=1 (accessed 8 June 2015).
Manyin, Mark E., Stephen Daggett, Ben Dolven, Susan V. Lawrence, Michael F. Martin, Ronald O'Rourke, and Bruce Vaughn. 2012. *Pivot to the Pacific? The Obama Administration's 'Rebalancing' Toward Asia*, Washington, DC: Congressional Research Services.
McDevitt, Michael A. 2013. *The Long Littoral Project: Summary Report: A Maritime Perspective on Indo-Pacific Security*, Alexandria, VA: CNA.
Mearsheimer, John J. 2001a. 'The Future of the American Pacifier', *Foreign Affairs* 80:5, 46–61.
Mearsheimer, John J. 2001b. *The Tragedy of Great Power Politics*. New York: W.W. Norton.
Medcalf, Rory. 2012. 'Pivoting the Map: Australia's Indo-Pacific System', The Centre of Gravity Series Paper No. 1. ANU Strategic and Defence Studies Centre, http://ips.cap.anu.edu.au/sdsc/cog/COG1_Medcalf_Indo-Pacific.pdf (accessed 8 June 2015).

Medcalf, Rory. 2013a. *Facing the Future: Indian Views of the World Ahead* (India Poll 2013), Sydney and Carlton: Lowy Institute for International Policy and Australia India Institute.

Medcalf, Rory. 2013b. 'The Indo-Pacific: What's in a Name?', *American Interest* 9:2, 58–66.

Medcalf, Rory, Raoul Heinrichs, and Justin Jones. 2011. *Crisis and Confidence: Major Powers and Maritime Security in Indo-Pacific Asia*, Sydney: Lowy Institute for International Policy.

Menon, Shivshankar. 2013. Speech at the Book Release of *Samudra Manthan: Sino-Indian Rivalry in the Indo-Pacific*, 4 March, http://www.orfonline.org/cms/export/orfonline/documents/Samudra-Manthan.pdf (accessed 8 June 2015).

Ministry of Defense (Japan). 2010. 'National Defense Program Guidelines (for FY2011 and Beyond)', http://www.mod.go.jp/e/d_act/d_policy/pdf/guidelinesFY2011.pdf (accessed 8 June 2015).

Mirski, Sean. 2013. 'Stranglehold: The Context, Conduct and Consequences of an American Naval Blockade of China', *Journal of Strategic Studies* 36:3, 385–421.

Modi, Narendra. 2014. 'Prime Minister's Address to the Joint Session of the Australian Parliament', Canberra, 18 November, http://www.mea.gov.in/Speeches-Statements.htm?dtl/24269/Prime+Ministers+Address+to+the+Joint+Session+of+the+Australian+Parliament+18+November+2014 (accessed 8 June 2015).

Mohan, C. Raja. 2012. *Samudra Manthan: Sino-Indian Rivalry in the Indo-Pacific*, Washington, DC: Carnegie Endowment for International Peace.

Munson, Peter J. 2013. 'Back to Our Roots: Marines' Future in the Indo-Pacific', *Marine Corps Gazette*, http://www.mca-marines.org/gazette/back-to-our-roots (accessed 8 June 2015).

Nataraj, Geethanjali. 2015. 'India Should Get on Board China's Maritime Silk Road', *East Asia Forum*, 27 June, http://www.eastasiaforum.org/2015/06/27/india-should-get-on-board-chinas-maritime-silk-road/ (accessed 8 June 2015).

O'Hanlon, Michael. 2012. 'The Case for a Politically Correct Pentagon', *Foreign Policy*, 18 September, http://www.foreignpolicy.com/articles/2012/09/18/the_case_for_a_politically_correct_pentagon (accessed 8 June 2015).

Pan, Chengxin. 2004. 'The "China Threat" in American Self-Imagination: The Discursive Construction of Other as Power Politics', *Alternatives* 29:3, 305–331.

Pan, Chengxin. 2012a. *Knowledge, Desire and Power in Global Politics: Western Representations of China's Rise*, Cheltenham: Edward Elgar.

Pan, Chengxin. 2012b. 'Getting Excited About China', in *Australia's Asia: From Yellow Peril to Asian Century*, edited by David Walker and Agnieszka Sobocinska, Crawley: UWA Publishing, pp. 245–266.

Prestwitz, Clyde. 2005. 'China-India Entente Shifts Global Balance', *YaleGlobal*, 15 April, http://yaleglobal.yale.edu/content/china-india-entente-shifts-global-balance (accessed 8 June 2015).

Richardson, Michael. 2005. 'Australia-Southeast Asia Relations and the East Asian Summit', *Australian Journal of International Affairs* 59:3, 351–365.

Rumley, Dennis, Timothy Doyle, and Sanjay Chaturvedi. 2012. ' "Securing" the Indian Ocean? Competing Regional Security Constructions', *Journal of the Indian Ocean Region* 8:1, 1–20.

Scott, David. 2008. 'The Great Power "Great Game" Between India and China: "The Logic of Geography" ', *Geopolitics* 13:1, 1–26.

Scott, David. 2013a. 'India's Role in the South China Sea: Geopolitics and Geoeconomics at Play', *India Review* 12:2, 51–69.

Scott, David. 2013b. 'Australia's Embrace of the Indo-Pacific: New Term, New Region, New Strategy?', *International Relations of the Asia-Pacific* 13:3, 425–448.
Sibal, Kanwal. 2014. 'China's Maritime "Silk Road" Proposals Are Not as Peaceful as They Seem', *Daily Mail Online*, 25 February, http://www.dailymail.co.uk/indiahome/indianews/article-2566881/Chinas-maritime-silk-road-proposals-not-peaceful-seem.html (accessed 8 June 2015).
Taylor, Brendan. 2013. 'The "Indo-Pacific" Places Australia at the Centre of the Action', *Strategist*, 7 May, http://www.aspistrategist.org.au/the-indo-pacific-places-australia-at-the-centre-of-the-action/ (accessed 8 June 2015).
Taylor, Paige. 2012. 'Drones Just Another Hazard for Islanders', *Australian*, 2 April, 1.
Terada, Takashi. 2010. 'The Origins of ASEAN+6 and Japan's Initiatives: China's Rise and the Agent-Structure Analysis', *Pacific Review* 23:1, 71–92.
Twining, Daniel. 2007. 'America's Grand Design in Asia', *Washington Quarterly* 30:3, 79–94.
USCC (US-China Economic and Security Review Commission). 2014. *USCC 2014 Annual Report*, Washington, DC: US Government Printing Office.
Varghese, Peter. 2012. 'Australia and India in the Asian Century.' *IPCS Special Report*, New Delhi: Institute of Peace and Conflict Studies, May, http://www.ipcs.org/pdf_file/issue/SR127-AustraliaandIndiaintheAsianCentury.pdf (accessed 8 June 2015).
Walt, Stephen M. 2012. 'Dealing with a Chinese Monroe Doctrine.' *New York Times*, 2 May, http://www.nytimes.com/roomfordebate/2012/05/02/are-we-headed-for-a-cold-war-with-china/dealing-with-a-chinese-monroe-doctrine (accessed 4 February 2013).
Wang Jisi. 2012a. 'Zhonggou de guoji huanjing weihe quyu yanjun' ('Why Is China's International Environment Becoming More Precarious?'), International and Strategic Studies Report, No. 70, Center for International and Strategic Studies, Peking University, 31 May.
Wang Jisi. 2012b. 'Xijin: Zhongguo diyuan zhanlue de zai pingheng' ('Marching Westwards: The Rebalancing of China's Geostrategy'), *Huanqiu shibao* (*Global Times*), 17 October, http://opinion.huanqiu.com/opinion_world/2012–10/3193760.html (accessed 8 June 2015).
Wang Lihua. 2005. 'Yinduyang haiquan zhi zheng: diyuan zhengzhi shijiao xia de Mei Zhong Yin sanjiao boyi' ('Sea Power Competition in the Indian Ocean: The U.S.-China-India Triangular Chess Game From a Geopolitical Perspective'), *Yunan xinzheng xueyuan xuebao* (*Journal of Yunan Administration College*) 6, 104–106.
White, Hugh. 2012. *The China Choice: Why America Should Share Power*, Collingwood: Black.
Yoshihara, Toshi, and James R. Holmes. 2010. *Red Star Over the Pacific: China's Rise and the Challenge to U.S. Maritime Strategy*, Annapolis, MD: Naval Institute Press.
Zhang, Yongjin. 2013. '"China Anxiety": Discourse and Intellectual Challenges', *Development and Change* 44:6, 1407–1425.
Zhao Minghao. 2013. 'The Emerging Strategic Triangle in Indo-Pacific Asia', *Diplomat*, 4 June, http://thediplomat.com/china-power/the-emerging-strategic-triangle-in-indo-pacific-asia/ (accessed 8 June 2015).
Zhu Feng. 2013. 'Zhong Mei zhanlue jingzheng yu Dongya anquan zhixu de weilai' ('Sino-US Strategic Competition and the Future of East Asian Security Order'), *Shijie jingji yu zhengzhi* (*World Economics and Politics*) 3, 4–26.
Zoellick, Robert. 2005. 'Whither China? From Membership to Responsibility (Remarks to the National Committee on US-China Relations)', *NBR Analysis* 16:4, 5–14.

7 Imagining the Indo-Pacific region

Marijn Nieuwenhuis

The economic rise of China and India has given birth to new temporal and spatial geopolitical vocabularies. The twenty-first century has popularly been labelled as the Asian Century, Pacific Century, Asia-Pacific Century and now the Indo-Pacific Century in a manner which is reminiscent of the preceding British and American Centuries. The fundamental difference between the former and the latter is, however, not one merely of scale but also representative of a different underlying political geography. The mapping of a region is in the post-Cold War context no longer solely determined by a small group of states as it arguably had been in the previous period. The contours of the region now seem instead shaped by the interests of multiple, interacting states. The diversity of states translates, in other words, into a range of both competing and overlapping geographical imaginations. This contribution will look at the development of such imaginations and, more specifically, how they have given rise to the idea of an Indo-Pacific region.[1]

The region is in this chapter, contra conventional geopolitical analyses, not accepted as a natural or fixed category. My discussion starts from the premise that the geography of the region is neither spatially static nor temporally permanent. The Indo-Pacific is instead shown to be a discursively imagined and politically constructed geographic entity. The Indo-Pacific region is argued not merely to transcend power, but to actively help preserve, contest and question existing relations of power. Imagining the region serves, in other words, a specific political purpose. A spatial sensitivity and vocabulary is required to understand how and why new regions come to be while old ones are forgotten. What or who determines where the lines in the sand are drawn, and how are these borders diffused to become part of a geographic imagination? The spatial approach employed in this chapter helps us to problematise the idea that the region functions as a static container in which politics merely happen, and allows us to appreciate the region as a political category in and for itself.

The chapter argues that contemporary macro regions are a political project of state imaginations. This is not to argue for a return to a crude realist geopolitics in which powerful states decide which regions come into existence and which ones do not. The geography of regions is a far more messy, open-ended and historically embedded process in which multiple states, small and large, participate in and compete over cartographic realities. The result is consequently an overlapping of

Imagining the Indo-Pacific region 115

different geographies that represent and help affirm or contest existing relations of power.

The category of region suffers in the geopolitical discipline from a tragic history, one which can be traced to the colonial period and to what Nazi geographers called *Großraumpolitik*. Indeed, it is no coincidence that the Nazi idea of a German region (*Deutsche Großraum*) drew inspiration from the American Monroe doctrine. Since the 'spatial turn', initiated by a more critical generation of geographers, the region is slowly again becoming a theme worthy of enquiry in the study of critical geopolitics (e.g. Jones and Paasi 2013). This reorientation will help me in deconstructing the region by placing it into a discourse of competing spatial imaginations and historical narratives.

The first section of this chapter will provide the conceptual preamble to the other sections to enable a deeper understanding of the meaning and function of the space that is the region. I will borrow from existing work on the concept of state territory to propose the idea of seeing the space of the region as territorial. The introduction of a territorial politics for conceptualising the region is, admittedly, not without its problems. Discussions on territory have historically been the domain of the sovereign state. I will argue, however, that we can substantially benefit by adopting a more territorial conceptual framework. It enables us to appreciate that the space of the region is, similarly as the space of the state, a political category with 'specific embedded logics of power and of claim-making' (Sassen 2013, 38). The second section is an attempt to historicise the gradual formation of the idea of an Asia-Pacific region in the Cold War context. The third section proceeds to explore the reasons how and why the emphasis on an Asia-Pacific region shifted to the idea of an Indo-Pacific region. The section pays special attention to the regional incorporation of Australia and India as a means to geographically cement the latter region. The fourth section explores the ways in which the Indo-Pacific region has been imagined into existence and how competing geographic imaginations challenge this new spatial classification. The conclusion provides a short summary of the main arguments.

The territory of the region

Political geographers have at least since Agnew's (1994) seminal 'Territorial Trap' started to argue against conventional international relations (IR) analyses that treat space as the static and permanent backdrop where and on which politics supposedly happens. Geographers put the space of IR on its head to argue that 'there is a politics of space because space is political' (Elden 2007, 107). Space is for geographers a historically contingent and relational category that is the product of politics but also in itself inherently political.

This should be familiar territory. The last two decades witnessed the birth of a body of literature which adopted a spatial sensitivity to the politics of territory. Territory does, in such accounts, no longer revolve around the physical terrain of land, but is analysed as a 'political technology' and a 'political category' in and of itself (Elden 2010). The space of territory governs and informs governance. The relationship between politics and the region is less obvious. How to conceptualise the political space of the region? How to account for the emergence, evolution and inevitable demise of regions? How do regions produce cartographic realities, and how do they come to be perceived and internalised as part of someone's (regional) identity? Asking such questions means treating the space of the region as unbounded, relational and 'central rather than merely derivative of nonspatial processes' (Agnew in Harrison 2012, 56). I will adopt the conceptual logic and relational traits of territory to argue for a politics of region.

The territory and territoriality of the region differ admittedly in fundamental ways from those of the sovereign state. Before elaborating further on this point, however, we first need to familiarise ourselves with the specifics of the region. The region is an admittedly much more ambiguous and theoretically much less explored spatial category than the territory of the state. The region is an abstract spatial-political category whose location cannot but roughly and discursively be located on maps. Its often non-jurisdictional borders are dependent on the creative geographic imagination of states that have a geostrategic stake in its discursive construction and maintenance (or destruction). The spatialisation of the region is therefore arguably much more fluid, dynamic, contested and arguably more complicated than the territorialisation of states. Yet, I think that the concept of territory as an open-ended and historically contingent relation between politics and space will help us to politicise the region.

Before I continue, I think it is important to distinguish between three relevant concepts: territory, territoriality and the act of territorialisation. I define *territory* as an imagined bordered space which, on the one hand, is the historical consequence of social and political action (*territorialisation*) and, on the other hand, contains and is composed of a specific social, cultural and historical meaning (*territoriality*). The space of territory is political for it draws an explicit line between an inside ('us') and an outside ('them'). This does not mean that territorialisation occurs only 'at the border'. I see territory instead as a performative relation in the formation of regional subjectivities that absorb the politics of the border. Green (in Balibar 2002, 75) talks about '*being* a border'.

That what the imagined border contains (territoriality) is therefore considered to be socially as well as ontologically meaningful, since it helps to spatially separate oneself from other regional territories and identities. We need to be careful in assigning territory a permanent quality since its relational characteristic implicitly refers to a mode of perpetual 'becoming' (Paasi 1996, 2009). The relational and open-ended aspect of territory exposes its historical underpinnings. New territories are imagined into existence while others are forgotten. The region is continuously and contingently territorialised, deterritorialised and reterritorialised, as geographic imaginations clash, compete and negotiate over the question where the lines in the sand ought to be drawn.

Competing geographic discourses over the whereabouts of the region rely on the way history presents, perceives and, indeed, imagines the region. The writing of history and the drawing of cartographic lines have historically been the preoccupation of the state. Indeed, states continue to play also the predominant role

Imagining the Indo-Pacific region 117

in the territorialisation of regions. This has not changed with the arrival of 'new regionalist' projects, even though these require alternative, broader geographical and historical imaginations. The absence of sovereignty within such new regionalisms limits the possibilities for a coherent and stable common regional identity. Even the borders of the strongly institutionalised European Union are in a perpetual mode of change, deliberation and disagreement. Competing ideas over the territorial extent of the region, its borders and history have inevitably led to unceasing processes of territorialisation, deterritorialisation and reterritorialisation. The successful dissemination of a regional imagination among those inside, but also outside the region is consequentially of crucial importance to both legitimise the existence of the region and prevent the risk of alternatives. This means that we have to understand the region historically, as its emergence, evolution, inevitable fading and possible return transcend the contemporary geostrategic interests of and relations between states. The role of the United States in the creation of Western Europe or, indeed, in the formation of an Asia-Pacific region are cases in point.

That is not to say that smaller states are insignificant in the spatial makeup of the region. Their inclusion helps, in fact, to legitimise the very geographic contours of the territory of region itself. This will be demonstrated later in the chapter, when we look at the significance of Australia and India in the construction of the Indo-Pacific region. The construction of the region is neither a one-dimensional affair nor a top-down process. Competing geostrategic interests cause other states, as discussed in the case of China, to challenge geographical constructs and create new ones. The result is a constant territorialisation and reterritorialisation of the world. The map transforms into an open-ended geostrategic discourse in which relations of power are responsible for continually and contingently reshaping cartographic boundaries and their underlying social realities. The following analysis of the region conventionally identified as East Asia starts with the Cold War divide, which played an instrumental role in the carving-up and remaking of older regional categories.

From East Asia to the Asia-Pacific

The disintegration of the Greater East Asia Co-Prosperity Sphere and the subsequent ideological spatial divisions in the region were of formative importance in the geographic reorganisation of what then was recognised as Asia. The new geographic imagination, based along Cold War ideological lines, led to the carving-up of the older regional order into smaller regional entities. Asia was partitioned into a distinctive set of subregions: Northern Asia, Central Asia, East Asia, Southeast Asia and South Asia. The rise of so-called area studies, a sub-discipline encouraged by American geostrategic security concerns, helped the construction of political-cultural identities that were linked to the new cartographic classification (see e.g. Wallerstein 1997). Van Schendel (2002, 648) argues that such 'geographies of knowing' led to 'conceptual empires that were thought of as somehow essentially homogeneous and self-contained' and paid no heed to 'pre-existing social realities'. The new subregions sometimes reinvented and at other times broke with older geographic imaginations, such as the old Confucian regional order or early twentieth-century anti-imperialist visions of a united, grassroots Asia.

The Cold War spatial reconfiguration had an immediate effect on the rise of regional anthropological studies (Lewis and Wigen 1997). Their taxonomic classifications directly and indirectly helped to socially embed the territorialisation of these new regions. Such trends were soon followed by functionalist accounts in the political sciences which, inspired by Europe's post-war reconstruction experience, attempted to make sense of the institutionalisation of these regionalisms. Such efforts started off by taking the abstraction of the region for granted which helped little to explain their emergence in the first place. They instead helped affirm the validity of the new regional system which, in turn, led to their further territorial embedding. The new spatial reorganisation had, in short, a strong ontological impact on the ways in which identities were located on maps and were placed in direct opposition to identities in regions with different ideological convictions.

The post-war process of geographic deterritorialisation and reterritorialisation emerged initially as a consequence of US attempts to contain the regional spreading of Chinese communism. The early geographic formation of a distinctive East Asian territory was therefore only partially successful in the form of a loose US-led hub-and-spokes model. Organisations such as the 1954 Southeast Asia Treaty Organization (SEATO) exposed US fears over the spreading of communism towards neighbouring Southeast Asian states. Glassman (2005) demonstrates how SEATO was dedicated to posit a separate Southeast Asian 'we-self' against an imaginary unified Chinese 'Other'. Area studies worked in tandem with geopolitical cartography to provide the necessary legitimacy for a cruder US geopolitics. The lack of engagement with the abstract and political nature of the regional borders led geographers, cartographers, anthropologists and social scientists to depoliticise the newly founded borders. Divisions between the US and European colonial powers soon obstructed the chances of cementing Southeast Asia's social, ethnic and historical heterogeneity into a coherent geographical whole (Ravenhill 2001). The fact that the region was exogenously imagined further prevented the possibilities for its territorialisation on the ground.

The projects of the Association of Southeast Asia (1961–1967) and the proposal for a Greater Malayan Confederation (1963) were, in contrast, locally initiated. Inter-state disputes over territory, border disputes and diverging geopolitical interest led these projects, however, to fare little better than their predecessors. It was only with the founding of the Association of Southeast Asian Nations (ASEAN) in 1967 that the new regional geography gradually started to materialise in a more enduring and institutionalised manner. Disputes among and between ASEAN members and regional non-members over power alliances meant, however, that the meaning and identity of the region remained largely ambivalent and ambiguous.

The fact that such institutions intentionally excluded and isolated communist China was much to the distress of the then Japanese foreign minister, and it severely handicapped the possibilities for firmer regional integration (see e.g. Terada 1998; Braddick 2006). Anti-communist initiatives, such as the first

Imagining the Indo-Pacific region 119

organisation that bore the word 'Pacific' in its title, the Asia-Pacific Council, were abandoned shortly after the onset of the Nixon Doctrine and the subsequent normalisation of diplomatic relations between the United States and communist China. The Soviet split and China's rapprochement with the United States heralded the end of an ideologically inspired regionalism and the onset of a more explicit economic geography. It provided opportunities for a project of regional reterritorialisation which favoured a more inclusive form of regionalisation.

Japan played a crucially constructive role in the regional expansion of the East Asia regional category. It formed both the economic and the geographic link between the undeveloped southeastern part of Asia and the industrialising northeast. Terada (1998) stresses the importance of Japan's role in the establishment of non-governmental institutions, such as the Pacific Trade and Development conference which later paved the way for the Asia-Pacific Economic Cooperation (APEC). Japan's geographic and geopolitical proximity to other Pacific Rim countries, a geostrategic category of US design (Connery 1994), allowed it also to actively support and encourage the United States and Australia to participate in the formation of a wider Asia-Pacific region (Ravenhill 2001).[2] Dirlik (1998) shows that the geographic shifting towards a Pacific category, the ocean which historically had been a dividing rather than a unifying medium, led to a project of regional reterritorialisation driven by a capitalist rationale. Indeed, as Connery (1994, 40) notes, 'water is capital's element . . . [The Pacific was imagined as a] *non*colonial space where a pure capital would be free to operate.' Dirlik (1998, 10) further states, 'The Pacific First World supplies the capital – the Pacific Third World supplies the labour.' The capitalist foundation of APEC in 1989 proved, however, to have been built on geographically shaky foundations that soon after its birth proved to be detrimental to the project (see e.g. Oga 2004 and Beeson 2009, among others).

Geographic imaginations are historical. Every episode is embedded in and constructs its own geography. The end of World War II and the onset of a so-called bipolar world resulted in a deterritorialisation and reterritorialisation of space in Asia. The region most important for understanding the later emergence of an Asia-Pacific category is that of East Asia, and specifically Southeast Asia. The containment of Chinese communism was in the new geographic system of 'world regions' given priority. This helped, in turn, to imagine and solidify a regional capitalist block. China's later rapprochement with the US and Japan's crucial geopolitical and geographic position were the catalysts for the geographic shifting of the region's core and its subsequent expansion to the north and later into the Pacific. The next section argues that the post-Cold War period did not so much signal 'a period of regional "extinction"' (Agnew 1999, 91), but that China's 'rise' rather compelled a new round of regional reterritorialisation.

The rise of China and the Indo-Pacific response

The gradual disintegration of the world regions model was the consequence of the end of the Cold War, the withdrawal of area studies and the reintegration of

China into a broader Asian order. The post-1976 economic reforms led to China's integration into a liberal East Asian order. This process was of a gradual nature, but accelerated after the 1989 Tiananmen Incident. The 1990s witnessed China's swift rapprochement with its eastern neighbours and later with the Asian continent at large. The country joined APEC's open regionalist architecture in 1991 as a stepping stone for World Trade Organization (WTO) negotiations and as a means to further increase its trade with other APEC members.

The rise of China and the country's success in the numerous free trade agreements[3] it signed with its regional ASEAN partners significantly weakened the aforementioned presence of the United States in its self-imagined APEC region. The lack of a common identity formed another challenge to the Pacific organisation. The territorial contours of the region subsequently allowed China to decentre and magnetically appropriate and reimagine the East Asian region as historically and culturally belonging to China. The contest over the definition of the region's identity subsequently moved from a US-centred to a China-centred sphere of influence. The 'Sinification of Asia' underlines, according to Beeson (2005, 978), 'China's capacity to shape political and strategic relations even when not directly participating in them'.

Much has already been written on how the resultant new Sinocentric Asian order led to the United States 'pivoting' to East Asia. Then State Secretary Hillary Clinton (2011) emphasised that a geographically widened Asia-Pacific 'stretching from the Indian sub-continent to the West shores of the Americas . . . has become a key driver of global politics'. Clinton's remark reveals how the historically dynamic and discursive nature of regional space allows it to become a malleable geostrategic instrument. She compared US dedication to the mapping of the region with its 'post-World War II commitment to building a comprehensive and lasting transatlantic network of institutions and relationship'. Such a sentiment finds expression in US support for a broad Trans-Pacific Partnership (TPP). Ravenhill and Capling (2011, 559) argue that the TPP has become 'the centrepiece of US trade policy towards the Pacific and a key element in Washington's determination to "return to Asia"'. The attempt to economically widen the region, as a means to geopolitically and geographically decentre the focus on China, led to calls for an Indo-Pacific region (e.g. deLeon and Yang 2014).

The new regional imagination entails a departure from the previous Asia-Pacific category and supplants the idea of a so-called Pacific Century. Some US defence policy makers (e.g. Pellerin 2013) have come to define it as a strategy of rebalancing. Others (Rumley et al. 2012) describe it 'in part as an attempt by the United States to engage India and Australia (and others) while simultaneously being a mechanism for facilitating its hegemonic transition'. There is little discernible evidence in official reports to suggest that the creation of the region is explicitly targeted *against* China, but there exists tacit agreement in the literature that the 'implicit issue remains the state-level challenge of China' (Scott 2012, 101).

More interesting, at least for my purposes, is the US attempt to instil the term Indo-Pacific into conventional geopolitical vocabularies. US policy documents (deLeon and Yang 2014, 99) have recently welcomed China (and India) to 'have dialogue on the term of Indo-Pacific, and more broadly, the strategic system that encompasses both the Pacific and Indian Oceans'. The last couple of years have seen numerous efforts by US policy makers to concretise the abstract geographic imagination inside and outside of the region (Kerry 2013a, 2013b).[4]

India and Australia, as a result of their geostrategic location and political proximity to the United States, play an important constructive role in this US-led reterritorialisation of space in Asia.[5] The geopolitical incorporation of India has institutionally been strengthened by the country's unofficial observer status in APEC (in 2011) and its inclusion in the East Asia Summit (EAS) in 2005. Breslin (2009, 818) writes that there 'is an increasing regional desire to see India play a greater role and perhaps change the basic understanding of what is meant by "region" in the Asian context'. Former Prime Minister Manmohan Singh's persistent referencing to the Indo-Pacific category in, for example, his 2012 inauguration speech to the India-ASEAN session, are suggestive of India's willingness to entertain the idea of an Indo-Pacific category. Current Prime Minister Narendra Modi has since his election not only deepened but also broadened that aspiration (Cronin and Baruah 2014). The political emphasis on and significance of the new geographic classification has led the category to become accepted as a household name in analyses and commentaries on India's role in Asia.

The geopolitical importance of India to enable a regional shifting towards the Indian Ocean is paralleled by the political weight given to Australia as 'the southern tier of the focus of the global political system' (Beazley in Rumley et al. 2012, 4). Clinton (2011) sees the new region as a means to transform 'the alliance with Australia from a Pacific partnership to an Indo-Pacific one'. The importance of Australia for the United States was repeated during President's Obama's historic state visit to Australia in 2011 and was in 2012 again confirmed by then Australian Defence Minister Stephen Smith.[6] Satake and Ishihara (2012, 7) logically conclude that the United States and Australia have consequentially not 'only deepened their existing cooperation, but also have expanded potential areas of cooperation toward a more "dynamic" partnership'. The discourse of the Indo-Pacific is also geostrategically deployed in the last Australian Defence White Paper (2013, 7) which argues that the Indo-Pacific 'is a logical extension' of 'the wider Asia-Pacific region'. The greater emphasis given to the former over the latter becomes apparent when counting the instances in which the two categories are mentioned. The report mentions Indo-Pacific no less than fifty-eight times whereas Asia-Pacific is mentioned only three times. The Australian Secretary of the Department of Foreign Affairs and Trade (Varghese 2014) recently noted in an apt-titled talk 'Mapping the Future' that the 'Indo-Pacific represents the centre of gravity of Australia's economic and strategic interests'. The notion of centredness also applies to Australia itself which finds itself repositioned from being located at the geographic periphery of world politics to 'the centre of the action' (Taylor 2013).

The (re)discovery of the Indo-Pacific region has led to an impressive rise of popular commentaries, academic contributions and policy reports which, more often than not, seem to take the space of the region as the décor for politics.

Relatively little has been written or said about the ways in which the space of the new region is itself political. The region serves a geostrategic purpose, provoking competing geographic imaginations while challenging identities that stem from older regional territorialities. The point is that regions are not the innocent podium on which politics happens but are themselves through and through political. The next section discusses how the arrival of the Indo-Pacific compels some states to renegotiate their own historical geographical locations while other states offer entirely new regional imaginations.

Competing regional imaginations

The ambiguity surrounding the geographic contours of the Indo-Pacific region is acknowledged by policy makers and commentators (see e.g. Rumley et al. 2012). There is, apart from the obvious relation to the Indian and Pacific Oceans, very little which unifies the countries within the region that according to some accounts stretches all the way to the eastern coast of Africa.

The region needs first to be geographically imagined and territorially cemented before it can successfully serve a geostrategic purpose. This section will, however, not dwell on the purpose of the region. I am rather more interested in the techniques used in, and the justifications given for, the territorialisation of the region. The cartographic configuration of the region is a process of negotiation and competition over where the new lines in the sand ought to be drawn. The act of mapping becomes as such a political project constitutive of the question of who is inside and who is outside.

The geostrategic discourse of the Indo-Pacific in India and Australia

The geographic location and geopolitical role of Australia and India (and the relationship between them) is, as mentioned earlier, of fundamental importance in the geostrategic discourse of the region. The attempt to integrate India into the Pacific category is not merely a plain imagining of a new regional entity, but a performative act in and for itself. The process of reterritorialisation requires, in other words, an effort on the part of both India and Australia to reimagine their place on the map. The territorialisation of the region is thus as much a geostrategic discourse as it is a historical and an ontological one. The project requires a reimagining and redrawing of cartographic lines to establish and legitimise new regional identities and alliances and/or reinvent older ones.

Recent maps and historical narratives have starting telling a story of India's historically and culturally central position in an expanding region (see e.g. Frost 2009; Muni 2011). They implicitly or explicitly challenge the influence of Chinese narratives that conventionally dominate the region. This Indian-oriented narrative finds currency in popular commentaries that, for example, emphasise the 'historical interconnectedness of the region' (Chaulia 2013) and India's longstanding relationship with Australia dating back to the time of the Dutch East

Imagining the Indo-Pacific region 123

India Company (Mohan and Medcalf 2013). Such historicised accounts are often unproblematically deployed to justify and serve contemporary policy objectives. Naidu (2004, 333), for example, begins his analysis on India's Look East policy by arguing that 'no other country has influenced the region [i.e. Southeast Asia] as much as India by way of religion, language, culture and civilisation.' Such efforts to historicise help legitimise and reify the abstraction of the region.

The construction of historical narratives that emphasise India's historical and cultural relationship with Southeast Asia helps the state, in short, to reimagine its geographical location. The geography of India becomes re*oriented* to cement the formation of what has officially been labelled the 'extended neighborhood' concept (Scott 2009).[7] One of most vocal proponents of India's entry into East Asia, Ellen Frost (2008, 22), shows how, by remapping Asia and India's place in it, it is possible to 'alter the perception of foreign policy interests, economic priorities, and national security strategy in a context of rapid change. The way people see and think about a place influences the way they act'.

India's Look East (and the more recent move to also Act East) policy should in this light be seen as a strategic attempt to geopolitically reposition the country closer to Southeast Asia.[8] Deputy Defence Secretary Ash Carter (Quoted in Pellerin 2013) recently stated that US 'security interests with India converge on maritime security and broader regional issues, including India's Look East Policy'. This more than hints at the importance attached to 'Southeast Asia, where India's "Look East Policy" and the US "rebalance" meet' (ICRIER 2013, ix). The vision of an Indo-Pacific region which sees the Indian and the (long-ignored geographic imagination of the) Pacific Ocean as a united continuum with Southeast Asia as its interlocking centre is also shared by the Australian Defence White Paper (2013). India's geography is, in other words, gradually transformed from being peripheral to being central for bridging the two waters in the formation of the new super region.

A recent report by the Indian Council for Research on International Economic Relations (2013, 4) emphasised India's distinctive 'geographic location [which] gives it a unique advantage in reaching out to the countries in the Indo-Pacific'. The report repetitively quotes Jawaharlal Nehru's (2013, 4) well-cited 1947 statement that 'India is so situated that she is the pivot of Western, Southern and Southeast Asia.' It is this rediscovered historical and geographic centrality, paralleled and inspired by its growing economic and political engagement with the region, that enables India to cartographically integrate itself into the Southeast Asian region 'that links East and South Asia' (ICRIER 2013, x).

Using cartography as a means to accentuate certain locations and enable particular perspectives for looking at the world is, of course, not unique to India. For example, the Indo-Pacific Asia web page of the Lowy Institute, which has played a pivotal role in the promotion of the Indo-Pacific category, hosts on its main page an old map of the Indo-Pacific region.[9] A former Lowy Institute member, Rory Medcalf (2012, 2), argued for Australia's 'distinct two-ocean geography' in the Indo-Pacific region in an aptly titled policy report, 'Pivoting the Map: Australia's

Indo-Pacific System'. The reconstruction and deployment of specific historical narratives also play an important role in the establishment of a cartographic reality.

The Indo-Pacific framework for Australia's interests is hardly new. Indeed, long before 1964, from 1788 right up until the Second World War, there was no question that the maritime Asian region that mattered to Australia economically and strategically was what we might now call the Indo-Pacific.

(Medcalf 2012, 2)

Interestingly enough, the year 1788, which in conventional historical accounts symbolises the mythical founding of an Australian nation, is elsewhere described as the moment 'the ocean was transformed from asylum to a barrier representing [what the historian Paul Carter has called] 'the tyranny of distance' [from Empire]' (Rangan and Kull 2010, 46). Attempts to politically historicise the region, as a political means to concretise its spatial abstraction, are not limited to the Indo-Pacific. Chinese geographic imaginings rely on similar historical interpretations to construct an alternative geographic discourse.

The Chinese response to the Indo-Pacific discourse

Chinese policy makers have expressed fears that the idea of an Indo-Pacific entity could hinder Chinese access to the Indian Ocean.[10] It is therefore not surprising that the subject of the Indo-Pacific (*Yinduyang-taipingyang* or *yin-tai*) has either been received with great scepticism or is completely ignored (e.g. Zhao 2013; Chen 2015). A recent commentary in the *Global Times* (Liu 2014) suggests ideas of integrating China's Silk Road project, stretching from East Asia to Western Europe in the north and to East Africa in the south, into a wider 'geoeconomic "Indo-Pacific" plan'. The idea of combining the water of the Pacific with the sand of the Central Asian plains has led to a formation of the so-called Belt and Road project.

The territorialisation project is accompanied by attempts to historicise and orientalise China's geographic identity through the publication of Silk Road atlases (Xinhua 2015a), exotic trade fairs (Xinhua 2014), ethnic dance performances (Xinhua 2015b) and other means towards a geographic reimagining of China's regional position. Most of China's geostrategic attention remains, however, fixed on the South China Sea, which forms the connection between the Pacific and the Indian Ocean.

The South China Sea forms an important component in the imaging of the country's geographic ordering in which it positions itself centrally in a region that extends southwards into Southeast Asia. China's alternative geographic imagining has led to a thriving historical and cartographic discourse which, not unlike elsewhere, is disseminated through popular media, universities and school curricula (see e.g. *Historical Atlas of China* 1996).

The publication of the new official state atlas shows the more than 130 islands in the South China Sea for the first time 'in equal scale to that of the Chinese mainland' (Xinhua 2013). The chief editor of the official publishing house argued that the atlas was 'very significant in enhancing the Chinese people's awareness of national territory, safeguarding China's marine rights and interests and manifesting China's political diplomatic stance' (Xinhua 2013). Instead of referring to the ambiguous and controversial 'nine dash' map, which in 2009 was submitted to the United Nations, this map actually has an extra tenth dash. More recently, we have seen attempts to take the space of representation into the actual changing of territorial reality itself. According to US officials (US Secretary of Defense 2015), Chinese land reclamation efforts in the South China Sea have since late 2014 totalled 500 hectares, challenging existing cartographic realities but also traditional understandings of territorial sovereignty. China seems eager to materially build its geographic imagination into existence.

The fact that the South China Sea constitutes a crucial piece in the Indo-Pacific jigsaw, however, also places it 'squarely at the centre of U.S. maritime interests' (Yoshihara and Holmes 2011, 55). Imaginations of an Indo-Pacific region would make little sense if China successfully territorialises the region which joins the Indian and the Pacific Oceans. As several high-ranking US officials (McCain et al. 2015) have already warned, the outcome of the South China Sea dispute will be crucial for the success of turning the imagined Indo-Pacific region into an accepted cartographic reality.

The ambiguous and abstract character of the Indo-Pacific region exposes the need for the region to be imagined before it can perform as a political reality. The discussion has attempted to show how the Indo-Pacific region constitutes a political representation of space which is territorialised as being historical, factual and truthful. The need for a geographical imagination takes place in the context of a political struggle over the question of whether the region should exist at all. The result is a dynamic discourse waged in the geographical imaginings of competing states.

Conclusion

Mapping enables a particular way of looking at the world. This so-called cartographic gaze has 'always had a political intent and/or consequences' (Pickles 2004, 80). This chapter provides a historical account of the evolution of different and competing cartographic representations of regions in the broader Asian context. I specifically looked at the (re)invention of the Indo-Pacific region to argue that the space of the region is not merely the theatre in which politics performs. The Indo-Pacific region is instead shown itself to be a performative spatial-political category. The territorialisation of its geography transcends but also gives form to geopolitics.

The Indo-Pacific region was described as a process which started with the redrawing of lines in the sand. Australia and India play a crucial role in the geographic imagining of the region. Both states have to cartographically reposition themselves to find their place in the new region. This dynamic process of deterritorialisation and reterritorialisation translates into a popular rewriting of regional histories from which new cartographies and new geographic identities arise.

The imagining of one region leads to the creation of another. China's interest in the South China Sea, which crucially interlocks the Indian and Pacific Oceans, has led it to contest the very idea of an Indo-Pacific category. It instead proposes an alternative geographic imagining with a distinctive cartographic history of its own. It is as of yet however unclear as to what such an imagination will look like. The recent decision to invest USD 900 billion in the Belt and Road project (He 2015) provides more than a glimpse into its counter-cartographic plan to revive the tales of Marco Polo in reverse.

The result of such diverging geostrategic interests leads to a dynamic discourse over the territorialisation, reterritorialisation and deterritorialisation of the history and identity of the region but also to a questioning of the location of states therein. Indeed, enquiries into whether or not Mongolia and Tanzania belong to the Indo-Pacific region are not geographical absurdities but rather show how the space of the region is political. Regions therefore not only compel the reconstruction of state identities but also challenge identities of and relations between the Self and the Other. Seeing the region as political therefore forces us to appreciate that the territory of the region is not merely the passive product of geopolitics but that its imagining in fact allows for the possibility of the geopolitical.

Notes

1 The Nazi geopolitical theorist Karl Haushofer (1924), was arguably among the first to use term as part of the Nazi's *Großraumpolitik*.
2 Members of APEC originally envisaged an ASEAN-centred region that would exclusively consist of members from Oceania and Asia (see e.g. Beeson 2009, 37). Australian support for US and Canadian membership soon led to a rift between the economic interests of the 'Anglo-Saxon bloc', which preferred 'economic liberalisation', and the 'Asian bloc', which focused more on 'economic and technical cooperation' (Oga 2004, 298). It was from the outset unclear what the organisation was about and who should (or not) be included.
3 China became 'increasingly being viewed as an engine of growth, a distinction which previously belonged to Japan' (Snitwongse 2003, 39). There was a qualitative transformation of the way China was perceived. The perception of the country as a 'threat' gradually translated into one of a 'challenge' to eventually become an 'opportunity'.
4 The term is now part of the name of the online magazine of Berkeley's School of Journalism (http://www.indopacificreview.com).
5 The third major contributor is Japan, whose earlier described historical interest in a broader Asia also paved the way for the inclusion of the US in the EAS.
6 'The Indo-Pacific has risen as a region of global strategic significance including the growth of military power projection capabilities of countries in the Indo-Pacific. The Indian Ocean and the Pacific Ocean spanned by the South East Asian archipelago is emerging as a single strategic system' (Scott 2012, 86).
7 India's former Foreign Minister (Sinha 2003) argued:

> The first phase of India's 'Look East' policy was ASEAN-centred and focussed primarily on trade and investment linkages. The new phase of this policy is characterised by an expanded definition of 'East', extending from Australia to East Asia, with ASEAN at its core.

8 Anindya Batabyal (in Scott 2008, 12) adds that from a critical review of India's Look East strategy as part of her overall foreign policy in Asia reveals that one of the important objectives behind this strategy is to play a new balancing game against China in the Southeast Asian and the Asia-Pacific region.

9 See http://lowyinstitute.org/regions/indo-pacific-asia (last accessed 15 October 2013).
10 A vast and growing Chinese body of especially realist IR literature urges Beijing to take on a more assertive stance in the Indian Ocean and to protect the country's 'core interests' (*hexin liyi*) in the Southeast Asian seas or, indeed, the South China Sea (Yoshihara 2012). Wu Xinbo (in Liu 2011) argues that as a South Asian country, India actively takes part in East Asian issues through the support of the US, which has been advocating for Asian countries to counter China. The US takes every opportunity to counter China, and its joint military manoeuvres with Japan and other regional countries have been more frequent in recent years.

References

Agnew, John. 1994. 'The Territorial Trap: The Geographical Assumptions of International Relations Theory', *Review of International Political Economy* 1, 53–80.
Agnew, John. 1999. 'Regions on the Mind Does Not Equal Regions of the Mind', *Progress in Human Geography* 23, 91–96.
Balibar, Etienne. 2002. *Politics and the Other Scene*, London: Verso.
Beeson, Mark. 2005. 'Rethinking Regionalism: Europe and East Asia in Comparative Historical Perspective', *Journal of European Public Policy* 12, 969–985.
Beeson, Mark. 2009. *Institutions of the Asia-Pacific ASEAN, APEC, and Beyond*, London: Routledge.
Braddick, C. W. 2006. 'Japan, Australia and ASPAC: The Rise and Fall of an Asia-Pacific Cooperative Security Framework', in *Japan, Australia and Asia-Pacific Security*, edited by Brad Williams and Andrew Newman, Abingdon, Taylor & Francis, pp. 30–46.
Breslin, Shaun. 2009. 'Understanding China's Regional Rise: Interpretations, Identities and Implications', *International Affairs* 85, 817–835.
Capling, Ann, and John Ravenhill. 2011. 'Multilateralising Regionalism: What Role for the Trans-Pacific Partnership Agreement?', *Pacific Review* 24, 553–575.
Chaulia, Sundar. 2013. 'Join the Asean Way', *Times of India*, 10 October, http://timesofindia.indiatimes.com/edit-page/Join-the-Asean-way/articleshow/23830850.cms (accessed 12 October 2013).
Chen, Weihua. 2015. 'Obama's Trip to India Smells Like a Conspiracy to Some', *China Daily*, http://usa.chinadaily.com.cn/opinion/2015-02/02/content_19471528.htm (accessed 1 May 2015).
China Note. 2009. 'Note From the Permanent Mission of the People's Republic of China to the Secretary General of the United Nations', *Note Verbale: CML/17/2009.*
Clinton, Hillary. 2011. 'America's Pacific Century', *Foreign Policy*, http://www.foreignpolicy.com/articles/2011/10/11/americas_pacific_century (accessed 19 April 2013).
Connery, Christopher L. 1994. 'Pacific Rim Discourse: The U.S. Global Imaginary in the Late Cold War Years', *Boundary* 2:21, 30–56.
Cronin, Patrick M. and Darshana M. Baruah. 2014. 'The Modi Doctrine for the Indo-Pacific Maritime Region', *Diplomat*, http://thediplomat.com/2014/12/the-modi-doctrine-for-the-indo-pacific-maritime-region/ (accessed 1 May 2015).
Deleon, Rudy and Jiemian Yang. 2014. *U.S.-China Relations: Toward a New Model of Major Power Relationship*, Washington, DC: Center for American Progress China-U.S. Exchange Foundation.
Department of Defence. 2013. 'Defence White Paper', Canberra: Australian Government.
Dirlik, Arif. 1998. 'Introduction: Pacific Contradictions', in *What Is in a Rim?: Critical Perspectives on the Pacific Region Idea*, edited by Arif Dirlik. Oxford: Rowman & Littlefield, pp. 3–13.

Elden, Stuart. 2007. 'There Is a Politics of Space Because Space Is Political: Henri Lefebvre and the Production of Space', *Radical Philosophy Review* 10, 101–116.
Elden, Stuart. 2010. 'Land, Terrain, Territory', *Progress in Human Geography* 34, 799–817.
Frost, Ellen. 2008. *Asia's New Regionalism*, Singapore: NUS Press.
Frost, Ellen. 2009. 'India's Role in East Asia: Lessons from Cultural and Historical Linkages', *RIS-DP*, New Delhi: Research and Information System for Developing Countries.
Glassman, Jim. 2005. 'On the Borders of Southeast Asia: Cold War Geography and the Construction of the Other', *Political Geography* 24, 784–807.
Harrison, John. 2012. 'Configuring the New "Regional World": On Being Caught Between Territory and Networks', *Regional Studies* 47, 55–74.
Haushofer, Karl. 1924. *Geopolitik des Pazifischen Ozeans (Geopolitics of the Pacific Ocean)*, Berlin Kurt: Vowinckel.
He, Yini. 2015. 'China to Invest $900b in Belt and Road Initiative', *China Daily*, http://www.chinadaily.com.cn/business/2015-05/28/content_20845654.htm (accessed 29 May 2015).
ICRIER. 2013. 'Asia's Arc of Advantage. India, ASEAN and the US: Shaping Asian Architecture', *A Report of the ICRIER Wadhwani Chair in India-U.S. Policy Studies*. New Delhi: Indian Council for Research on International Economic Relations.
Jones, Martin and Anssi Paasi. Eds. 2013. 'Special Issue: Regional World(s): Advancing the Geography of Regions', *Regional Studies* 47:1.
Kerry, John. 2013a. 'Remarks on a 21st Century Pacific Partnership', Tokyo: Tokyo Institute of Technology.
Kerry, John. 2013b. 'Remarks on the U.S.-India Strategic Partnership', New Delhi: U.S. Department of State. http://www.state.gov/secretary/remarks/2013/06/211013.htm (accessed 1 July 2014).
Lewis, Martin W., and Karen E. Wigen. 1997. *The Myth of Continents: A Critique of Metageography*, Berkeley: University of California Press.
Liu, S. 2011. 'India Makes Waves With South China Sea Oil and Gas Exploration', *Global Times*, http://www.globaltimes.cn/DesktopModules/DnnForge%20-%20NewsArticles/Print.aspx?tabid=99&tabmoduleid=94&articleId=675647&moduleId=405&PortalID=0 (accessed 1 June 2013).
Liu, Z. 2014. 'New Delhi-Beijing Cooperation Key to Building an "Indo-Pacific Era"', *Global Times*, http://www.globaltimes.cn/content/894334.shtml (accessed 20 May 2015).
McCain, John, Jack Reed, Bob Corker, and Bob Menendez. 2015. 'Letter to Secretary Carter and Secretary Kerry on Chinese Maritime Strategy', Washington, DC: United States Senate.
Medcalf, Rory. 2012. 'Pivoting the Map: Australia's Indo-Pacific System'. *Centre of Gravity*, Strategic & Defence Studies Centre ANU College of Asia & the Pacific, Australian National University.
Mohan, Raja, and Rory Medcalf. 2013. *Two Nations Take Lead in Securing Indo-Pacific Century*. Sydney: Lowy Institute for International Policy (originally published in *West Australian*), http://lowyinstitute.org/publications/two-nations-take-lead-securing-indo-pacific-century (accessed 15 July 2013).
Muni, S. D. 2011. *India's 'Look East' Policy: The Strategic Dimension*, Singapore: National University of Singapore.
Naidu, G.V.C. 2004. 'Whither the Look East Policy: India and Southeast Asia', *Strategic Analysis* 28, 331–346.
Oga, Toru. 2004. 'Rediscovering Asianness: The Role of Institutional Discourses in APEC, 1989–1997', *International Relations of the Asia-Pacific* 4, 287–317.

Paasi, Anssi. 1996. *Territories, Boundaries and Consciousness: The Changing Geographies of the Finnish-Russian Border*, Chichester: Wiley.
Paasi, Anssi. 2009. 'Bounded Spaces in a "Borderless World": Border Studies, Power and the Anatomy of Territory', *Journal of Power* 2, 213–234.
Pellerin, Cheryl. 2013. *Partnerships Highlight U.S. Rebalance Within Asia-Pacific Region*, Washington, DC: U.S. Department of Defense, American Forces Press Service, http://www.defense.gov/News/newsarticle.aspx?ID=119733 (accessed 29 April 2013).
Pickles, John. 2004. *A History of Spaces: Cartographic Reason, Mapping and the Geo-Coded World*, London: Routledge.
Rangan, Haripriya, and Christian Kull. 2010. 'The Indian Ocean and the Making of Outback Australia: An Ecocultural Odyssey', in *Indian Ocean Studies: Cultural, Social, and Political Perspectives*, edited by Shanti Moorthy and Jamal Ashraf. Abingdon: Routledge, pp. 45–72.
Ravenhill, John. 2001. *APEC and the Construction of Pacific Rim Regionalism*, Cambridge, Cambridge University Press.
Rumley, Dennis, Timothy Doyle, and Sanjay Chaturvedi. 2012. '"Securing" the Indian Ocean? Competing Regional Security Constructions', *Journal of the Indian Ocean Region* 8, 1–20.
Sassen, Saskia. 2013. 'When Territory Deborders Territoriality', *Territory, Politics, Governance* 1, 21–45.
Satake, T., and Y. Ishihara. 2012. 'America's Rebalance to Asia and Its Implications for Japan-US-Australia Security Cooperation', *Asia-Pacific Review* 19, 6–25.
Scott, David. 2008. 'The Great Power "Great Game" Between India and China: "The Logic of Geography"', *Geopolitics* 13, 1–26.
Scott, David. 2009. 'India's "Extended Neighborhood" Concept: Power Projection for a Rising Power', *India Review* 8, 107–143.
Scott, David. 2012. 'The "Indo-Pacific" – New Regional Formulations and New Maritime Frameworks for US-India Strategic Convergence', *Asia-Pacific Review* 19, 85–109.
Sinha, Yashwant. 2003. 'Resurgent India in Asia'. Excerpted from the Text of the Speech Made by Indian External Affairs Minister at Harvard University on 29 September 2003, http://the.kashmirtelegraph.com/1003/five.htm (accessed 1 July 2013).
Snitwongse, K. 2003. 'A New World Order in East Asia?', *Asia-Pacific Review* 10:2, 36–51.
Taylor, Brendan. 2013. 'The 'Indo-Pacific' Places Australia at the Centre of the Action', http://www.aspistrategist.org.au/the-indo-pacific-places-australia-at-the-centre-of-the-action/ (accessed 1 July 2015).
Terada, Takashi. 1998. 'The Origins of Japan's APEC Policy: Foreign Minister Takeo Miki's Asia-Pacific Policy and Current Implications', *Pacific Review* 11, 337–363.
US Secretary of Defense. 2015. *Military and Security Developments Involving the People's Republic of China 2015*, Washington, DC: Office of the Secretary of Defense.
Van Schendel, Willem. 2002. 'Geographies of Knowing, Geographies of Ignorance: Jumping Scale in Southeast Asia', *Environment and Planning D: Society and Space* 20, 647–668.
Varghese, Peter. 2014. 'Speech on "Mapping the Future"', http://dfat.gov.au/news/speeches/Pages/mapping-the-future.aspx (accessed 28 May 2015).
Wallerstein, Immanuel. 1997. 'The Unintended Consequences of Cold War Area Studies', in *The Cold War and the University: Toward an Intellectual History of the Postwar Years*, edited by Noam Chomsky,. New York: New Press, pp. 195–231.
Xinhua. 2013. 'New Maps Highlight South China Sea Islands', *Xinhua*, http://www.china.org.cn/china/2013-01/12/content_27665192.htm (accessed 1 July 2013).

Xinhua. 2014. 'China Focus: Maritime Silk Road Expo Inaugurated, Brings Businesses', *Xinhua*, http://news.xinhuanet.com/english/china/2014-11/02/c_133760808.htm (accessed 29 May 2015).

Xinhua. 2015a. 'China Publishes First Silk Road Atlas', *Xinhua*, http://news.xinhuanet.com/english/2015-03/09/c_134051138.htm (accessed 29 May 2015).

Xinhua. 2015b. 'Dance Drama "The Dream of the Maritime Silk Road" Performed in Fujian', *Xinhua*, http://news.xinhuanet.com/english/photo/2015-02/12/c_133987954.htm (accessed 29 May 2015).

Yoshihara, Toshi. 2012. 'Chinese Views of India in the Indian Ocean: A Geopolitical Perspective', *Strategic Analysis* 36, 489–500.

Yoshihara, Toshi, and James R. Holmes. 2011. 'Can China Defend a "Core Interest" in the South China Sea?', *Washington Quarterly* 34, 45–59.

Zhao, Q. 2013. *Cong 'yatai' dao 'yin tai' (From 'Asia-Pacific' to 'Indo-Pacific')*, Guoji wang, http://memo.cfisnet.com/2013/0821/1296727.html (accessed 1 October 2013).

Index

Abe, Shinzo: foreign policy 31–3; speeches and writings of 28, 31–2, 104
Africa: increasing trade with 1, 3, 6, 49; in Indo-Pacific conceptualisations 64, 103, 124
Antony, A.K. 20, 51
ARF *see* ASEAN Regional Forum
ASEAN *see* Association of South East Asian Nations
ASEAN Regional Forum 15
Asia-Pacific: Cold War origins of 2, 3, 15, 117–19; to Indo-Pacific 6, 11, 12, 17, 26–9; limitations 15
Association of South East Asian Nations 5, 6, 15; and Australia 21; and India 16, 17, 49, 51, 52, 55; and Indonesia 5, 74–88; and Japan 32–3
Australia: alliance with United States 20, 21, 103, 121; conceptualisation of Indo-Pacific 12–14; cooperation with India 20–1, 122–4; Defence White Papers 11, 12, 19–20; geographic imaginations 122–4; identity 4, 13; relations with Indonesia 20–1

Bishop, Julie 105
Buzan, Barry 12, 63

Chellaney, Brahma 50, 107
China: Air Defence Identification Zone 53; cooperation with India 102; as an Indo-Pacific power 12–13; maritime military expansion 12–13, 18, 30–1, 106–7; Maritime Silk Road project *see* One Belt, One Road initiative; responses to Indo-Pacific 18, 37, 105–8, 124–5; rise of 119–20; territorial disputes of 5, 13–14, 82

climate change: military responses to 61, 65–70; neoliberalism 60–1, 68
Clinton, Hillary: speeches and writings of 3, 43, 82, 102, 104–5, 108, 120

EAS *see* East Asia Summit
East Asia Summit 15, 21, 54–5, 78, 83, 103, 121
Elden, Stuart 7

geoeconomics: China 106; definition 43–6, 61–2; India 52–5; United States 61–6
geopolitical anxieties 2, 53, 75, 88, 99–102, 104, 106
geopolitical imagination 99–100, 102

Haushofer, Karl 14–15, 97–8, 126

India: Act East 16, 52, 55, 104–5, 123; conceptualisation of Indo-Pacific 49–52; cooperation with China 102; economic reforms 47–8; extended neighbourhood 49; geographic imaginations 122–4; Look East 48–9; nonalignment 46, 50; rivalry with China 53–5, 104–5; strategic autonomy 5, 50–5
Indian Ocean 12; Australia's interests in 18, 20, 103; China's interests in 12–13, 18, 31, 106–7, 124; India's interests 51–2, 55, 105; in Indonesia's strategic vision 82–4; Japan's interests in 31, 32; Kaplan, Robert 98, 101–2, 108; and the United States 63–4, 103
Indian Ocean Naval Symposium 5, 21, 52
Indian Ocean Rim Association 5, 21, 52, 83

Index

Indonesia: conceptualisation of the Indo-Pacific 81–6; nonalignment 79; regionalism 75–9; relations with China 82, 83, 84, 85, 86; strategic independence 75, 79, 86, 87; views of India 81, 82, 83, 84

Japan: alliance with United States 28; 'broader Asia' 1, 4, 27–8, 31, 35, 37, 39 104, 105; cooperation with Australia 30; cooperation with India 30, 103–4; Indo-Pacific terminology in 29; as a 'normal state' 4, 31, 39; relations with China 26, 27, 37; strategic activism 36–9
Jowkowi *see* Widodo, Joko

Khurana, Gurpreet 104

liquid continuum 60, 62, 70

Malabar naval exercises 6, 31, 32, 36, 51
mapping and maps: Australian 124; Chinese 125; Indian 123; 'nine dash' 125
maritime diplomacy 5–6, 21, 52, 83
maritime security cooperation 21, 30–1, 37, 52, 103–4, 105
maritime trade 12, 14, 43, 49, 64, 65, 107, 119
Menon, Shivshankar 51, 98
Modi, Narendra 16, 35, 53, 105, 121
Mohan, Raja 14, 50, 98, 104

Natalegawa, Marty 1, 15, 16, 75, 80
National Democratic Alliance government 50–5
neoconservativism 101, 107, 108

One Belt, One Road initiative 6–7, 106, 107; atlases 124; Indian reception 53, 55, 107; Indonesian reception 88; orientalism 124

Pacific and Indian Ocean Region 75, 88
Pacific Ocean: in India's strategic vision 50, 52–3; in Indonesian foreign policy 84
PACINDO *see* Pacific and Indian Ocean Region

Quadrilateral Security Dialogue 30–2, 105, 108

regional architecture 6; American preferences 3; Australian preferences 4, 102; Indian preferences 50, 51, 54, 55; Indonesian preferences 74, 83, 86–7; Japanese preferences 104
regional geographic imaginations: Asia-Pacific 119; competing regional imaginations 122; East Asia 117; Indo-Pacific 119–26; Southeast Asia 118
regional imaginary 44; India 46–9
regionalisation 1–2, 19, 62, 131
regionalism 62; and Australia 102–3; and China 100–1, 104; during the Cold War 118–19; and India; and Indonesia 75–9; and Japan 102; and United States 100–1
rise of China 2, 7, 12, 119–22; opportunities presented by 3, 4; threat perceptions of 4, 30, 63, 99–102
Russia: in Indo-Pacific conceptualisations 50

Saran, Shyam 50
SCS *see* South China Sea
Singh, Manmohan 16, 36, 51, 101, 121
Smith, Stephen 17–18, 20, 43, 121
South China Sea disputes 14; and Australia; and China 106, 124–5, 126; and India 5, 51, 52, 53, 54, 104; and Indonesia 5, 75, 82, 83, 84; and Japan 29, 32, 51, 52, 53, 54, 104; and United States 82, 100
Southeast Asia: and India 48–9, 123; in Indonesian foreign policy 80; and Indo-Pacific 1, 12, 15, 20, 50, 123; in One Belt, One Road initiative 53
Sukma, Rizal 74, 75, 78, 81, 82, 85, 87, 88

territory: deterritorialisation 116; reterritorialisation 116–17; territorialisation 116, 117, 119, territoriality 115–117; territory and region 115–17
think tanks 4, 14, 29, 35, 39, 49, 62, 105
Trans-Pacific Partnership 7, 29, 54, 101, 120

United States: and China 18, 65, 69, 99–102; Indo-Pacific terminology and conceptualisation 16–17; pivot to Asia 5, 28, 38, 82, 101, 103, 107

Widodo, Joko 16, 75, 81, 83–7